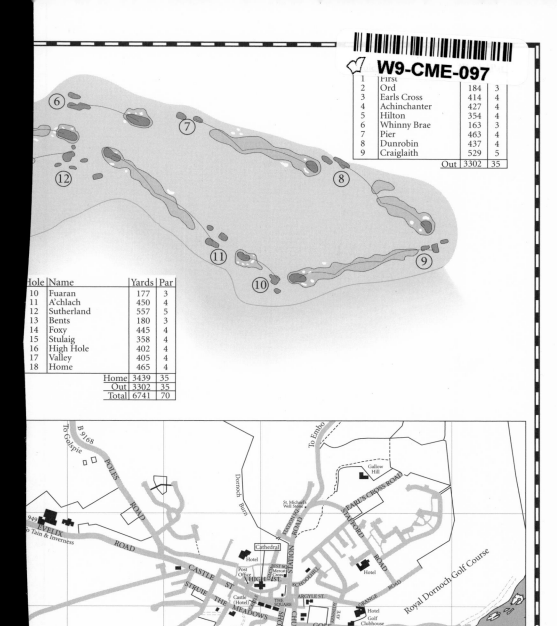

Hole	Name	Yards	Par
1	First		
2	Ord	184	3
3	Earls Cross	414	4
4	Achinchanter	427	4
5	Hilton	354	4
6	Whinny Brae	163	3
7	Pier	463	4
8	Dunrobin	437	4
9	Craiglaith	529	5
	Out	3302	35

Hole	Name	Yards	Par
10	Fuaran	177	3
11	A'chlach	450	4
12	Sutherland	557	5
13	Bents	180	3
14	Foxy	445	4
15	Stulaig	358	4
16	High Hole	402	4
17	Valley	405	4
18	Home	465	4
	Home	3439	35
	Out	3302	35
	Total	6741	70

Dornoch

Dornoch Links

Struie Golf Course

Royal Dornoch Golf Course

A Season in Dornoch

Also by Lorne Rubenstein

The Natural Golf Swing (with George Knudson) (1988)
Links (1989)
The Swing (with Nick Price) (1996)
The Fundamentals of Hogan (with David Leadbetter) (2000)

A Season in Dornoch

Golf and Life in the Scottish Highlands

LORNE RUBENSTEIN

National Library of Canada Cataloguing in Publication Data

Rubenstein, Lorne
A season in Dornoch : golf and life in the Scottish highlands

ISBN 0-7710-7570-7

1. Rubenstein, Lorne – Journeys – Scotland – Dornoch.
2. Dornoch (Scotland) – Description and travel.
3. Golf – Scotland – Dornoch. I. Title.

DA890.D67R8 2001   914.11'65   C2001-901250-0

We acknowledge the financial support of the Government of Canada through
the Book Publishing Industry Development Program for our
publishing activities. We further acknowledge the support of the
Canada Council for the Arts and the Ontario Arts Council
for our publishing program.

Designed by Terri Fong
Maps by Visutronx
Illustrations by Sarah L. Orr
Typesetting in Minion by M&S, Toronto

Printed and bound in Canada

McClelland & Stewart Ltd.
The Canadian Publishers
481 University Avenue
Toronto, Ontario
M5G 2E9
www.mcclelland.com

1   2   3   4   5   05   04   03   02   01

For, and with, Nell

Contents

Foreword by Sean Connery / *ix*

Chapter 1   Back to Dornoch / *1*

Chapter 2   The First Round / *15*

Chapter 3   Dornochers / *35*

Chapter 4   Rambles / *46*

Chapter 5   Nell and Me / *63*

Chapter 6   Palimpsest / *76*

Chapter 7   The Captain's Pink Balls / *95*

Chapter 8   The Bookshop / *110*

Chapter 9   New Friends / *123*

Chapter 10   The Clearances / *135*

Chapter 11   Highland Music / *142*

Chapter 12   Linksland / *153*

Chapter 13   The Golf World Comes to Dornoch / *165*

Chapter 14   Swing Thoughts / *177*

Chapter 15   The Scottish Amateur / *191*

Chapter 16   The Carnegie Shield / *210*

Chapter 17   My Heart's in the Highlands / *230*

Credits / *243*

Foreword

BY SEAN CONNERY

A few years ago I read *The Natural Golf Swing*, which Lorne Rubenstein had written with the Canadian professional George Knudson. I had a few questions, and called Lorne. We had the sort of intense discussion that only passionate golfers can have. Our conversations about the swing and other subjects – particularly golf on the Scottish links that I enjoy so much – continued later when we met during the 1997 Ryder Cup at the Valderrama Golf Club in Spain.

Three years later, I learned that Lorne was planning to spend a summer in Dornoch, which I had first visited when I was filming *Goldfinger*. In Dornoch I learned the essential challenge of links golf: that one must play a variety of shots under constantly changing conditions. As a Scot, I'm drawn to links golf and its enduring challenges. It's quite naked golf. There aren't many trees, or features to aid your alignment. Much is left to the imagination, and to picturing the shot. Then there's the wind, always a factor on a links. You're required to play run-up shots, and to work the ball this way and that.

Dornoch holds a special place in Scottish golf, and Lorne felt that from his initial visit, in 1977. *A Season in Dornoch*, the account of his return there in the summer of 2000, takes the reader on a fascinating and refreshing journey to a part of Scotland that many visitors miss when they travel there for golf. Lorne's writing offers a heady mixture of culture, geography, and landscape. He meets many people in the course of his three months in Dornoch, and illuminates these friendships in rare and insightful ways.

The brew that Lorne concocts soon cast its spell over me, as he weaves themes both historical and mythical into the narrative.

With all this, the golf in Dornoch – the game there, and Lorne's response to it – is the heart of the book around which he builds his story. The reader will learn a lot about links golf in Dornoch, and gain plenty of knowledge about the intoxicating Scottish Highlands and their haunting history. There are dashes and drams of good whisky here, and always you will sense the appeal of Dornoch, a place that feels timeless.

When I first visited Dornoch I simply put my money on a table to pay my green fee, which I think was £2. The entire work force on the course consisted of only five people, and all the greens were handcut. Sure, it's changed now that more people have visited Dornoch – although so many fewer than have made the pilgrimage to the Old Course in St. Andrews, or Carnoustie or Turnberry. Tom Watson and Ben Crenshaw visited Dornoch, and their feelings for the course made the world more aware of it. And yet the landscape and the course's features and the town's ambience – the peace one feels there – don't change no matter who comes and goes.

As for the people in Dornoch and the Highlands of whom Lorne writes so affectionately, everybody gets the initial impression that they are somewhat reserved. But the hospitality for which they are famous becomes apparent as you get to know them. It's all on their terms, as it were. Highlanders are very correct people. In the Highlands you find honesty.

You also find proper golf. What a marvelous course I found at the edge of the North Sea when I visited Dornoch. It was obvious that a par on any hole, or even a bogey, was rewarding.

A Season in Dornoch also rewarded me, with many pleasant memories and images of one of golf's distinctive places. It was good to spend the summer in Dornoch with Lorne through his writing, and I look forward now to a game with him there, the sooner the better.

– August 2001

"And when a man looks at a bird or feels the wind on his face, we should want him to tell us, if telling is his job, not only what he sees but how it affects him, in calm or in pleasantness or in ecstasy, so that we may nod in understanding and go about our business, however, grim, with greater heart."

– Neil Gunn, Highlands writer, *Memories of the Months*, 1941

Chapter 1

Back to Dornoch

There is a point, far out on the links of the Royal Dornoch Golf Club in the Scottish Highlands, on the edge of the North Sea, where the world opens up in all directions. If you stand on the seventh tee, on the high ridge overlooking much of the course, you will see the sweep of this ancient linksland. If you look just left, beyond the course, you will see on top of Ben Bhraggie a monument to the first Duke of Sutherland, an infamous personage in the "empty lands," as writer Tom Atkinson calls them in his book *The Northern Highlands*. The colossal statue of the duke – contemptuously called "the Mannie" by people hereabouts – commemorates a man who was at the forefront of the Highland Clearances in the early part of the nineteenth century. The Clearances emptied these high lands of some fifteen thousand people, most of them crofters, or tenant farmers, whose ancestors had lived here for generations. Sheep, it was argued by the duke and his minions, would prove far more profitable than people.

You avert your eyes from the Mannie and rotate farther left. You are still standing on the seventh tee at Royal Dornoch, on seaside turf where golf has been played since at least 1616, and you hear the North Sea surf and the songs of shorebirds, and you feel the warmth of the midsummer sun setting down your line of sight. You are now looking across fields of gorse bushes rendered a vivid yellow on this early-summer day and beyond to footpaths in the scrub where people are walking their dogs. You stand in place, your golf clubs in a bag strapped behind your back, your feet light on the firm, fast, running fairways where a golf ball bounces, as a golf ball should. The course is open and empty and nobody is in view ahead of you or behind you as you look westward. You are looking toward the hills where displaced crofters also traveled, and over those mountains, only ninety miles away, lies the western rim of Scotland. For here in the far north it is only that far from the North Sea on this east coast to the Sea of the Hebrides on the west coast, which flows into the Atlantic Ocean. And beyond, across the ocean, Newfoundland, in Canada. New Found Land to many of these refugees.

If you rotate to your left again, so that your back is to the Mannie and you are facing in a generally southerly direction, you will be looking toward the center of Dornoch, which Charles I designated a royal burgh in 1628. (Royal burghs, in theory, had a monopoly on foreign trade.) The club itself was granted its "Royal" designation by the monarchy in June 1906. Dornoch is dominated by the spire of a thirteenth-century cathedral, the links a five-minute walk from there, and the Dornoch Firth that empties into the North Sea. You are looking past a forest toward the clubhouse of the Royal Dornoch Golf Club, an unassuming edifice where no doubt golfers are gathering. They are drinking a club ale or a spicy rum or a whisky. They are considering their day's golf and their upcoming matches. Perhaps they are discussing the minutiae of the golf swing, or the merits of seaside versus inland golf. Is match play a more revealing test of ability than stroke play? They are doing what golfers have done for centuries – telling stories, reliving their rounds, revelling in the game. You look beyond the clubhouse and the end of the course and the practice putting green and over the club's lower course, the eighteen-hole Struie, toward Dornoch Point, and across the firth to a line of hills beyond.

You stand here and, mesmerized, spin yourself some ninety degrees left, so that you are facing generally east. You are looking across a few hundred yards of the links to the sea. Your eyes take in undulating fairways, bunkers small, large, and invariably deep, plateau greens, the dunes, the sea, and you look toward the fishing village of Portmahomack, and farther east, on a point, the Tarbat Ness lighthouse. The lighthouse is the second tallest in the United Kingdom, and flashes four times every thirty seconds; it has done so in peacetime every night since January 26, 1830. Silence. Peace. What feelings do you have in these empty lands? Here is a golf course renowned for the way its holes meander through sand dunes between the ridge and the North Sea, for the way its fairways bleed into the greens, and for the way its ground is a gift that nature bestowed for human recreation. Donald Ross was born in Dornoch, and before he became America's most famous golf-course architect in the first half of the twentieth century he walked its links regularly, worked and golfed there, and absorbed its spirit as if by osmosis. Transfixed by the views with which you are presented, you are not surprised. You sense that this place will absorb you, and you it.

• • • • • •

I have traveled to these Highlands and on to Dornoch from my home in Toronto, a sprawling city where four million people jostle for space. I flew to Glasgow, where I walked the streets and spent a few pleasant hours in the city's main library, then sat in a café until it was time to return to the airport. From Glasgow I took a small plane forty minutes northeast to Inverness, a city of forty thousand people that is the main population center in the Highlands. I rented a car at the airport, and drove an hour north in the long light of the first summer evening in June 2000. I immediately felt far from Toronto and from the south, the central belt of Scotland. There, in the south, are the big cities of Glasgow and Edinburgh, and the medieval town of St. Andrews, where lies the Old Course. Too busy for me.

I have spent twenty-five years chronicling golf around the world, roughly from Jack Nicklaus's successful mid-career through Tiger Woods's dazzling early career, and I have seen the game grow and find a home in countries all over the world. It has become a huge international business. Still, it remains a good game because a golfer can play for a lifetime, alone or in company, and in attractive settings that offer a peace that is not easily found elsewhere. It's now less easy to find courses that offer repose, that soothe the fevered brain, that provide clean oxygen to it, and exercise to the legs while one walks a course. Golf carts are ubiquitous, and even some Scottish courses now offer them (although mostly for people who need them for medical reasons). Carts are often compulsory in America. Sandy Tatum, a former president of the United States Golf Association, calls this not golf but cart-ball.

I have come to Dornoch for golf, not cart-ball. I have traveled to this seaside village of thirteen hundred permanent residents because Royal Dornoch is one of the most beautiful, and tranquil, courses in the world. I have come to explore empty lands, to fill myself with the virtues of golf as sport rather than commercial enterprise. Perhaps my season in Dornoch will help me understand whether people and land can exist in harmony, and if and how the former compromises the latter. I am searching for scale, for proportion, for perspective. I wonder what happens when too many people crowd a space, and believe that something essential is lost in the game when a course is clogged with golfers. Nobody enjoys it when players knock against one another. A golf course is not an elevator in an office building at closing time; it is a landscape meant to allow for breathing room and walking room and space to join with others, but not for golfers to overwhelm one another. Somewhere, somehow, I think, there is a way for people to live with consideration for a landscape, and for golfers to go gently on the course.

I have been here before, years ago, and something about this place stayed with me. What was it? What has changed? It's time to immerse myself in this course, these Highlands. I'm ready.

• • • • • •

In the spring of 1977 I found myself on a train north from Edinburgh, headed for the Highlands. My destination was Dornoch, specifically its golf course. Adrift in my life, I sought a place to anchor myself. I had read about Dornoch, and had decided I would visit there someday. At twenty-nine, I needed not so much a place to which I could escape but one in which I might find, or uncover, an authentic self. At the time I was working on a doctorate in psychology, and had written a minor paper on the psychology of golf.

While at university I had read widely in the literature of golf. Sir Charles Sherrington, an English neurophysiologist who shared the 1933 Nobel Prize in Physiology or Medicine, had written the foreword to a book called *The Brain and Golf*; the involvement of such an esteemed scientist intrigued me. I also read Dr. Louis Robinson's 1877 piece in the *North American Review* on the psychology of the game; he wrote of nerve endings, the way the game confounded us because it provides so much time to think. By 1977, I had acquired my master's degree but had stalled in my doctoral work. I wanted to study golf by living the game. How could something that was just a game capture us so? I was a low-handicap golfer, and that summer I would play in the British Amateur at the Ganton Golf Club in Scarborough, England. I looked forward to that event, but at the same time I knew I needed to sort some things out in my mind if I were going to play decently. Not all of these issues involved my golfing brain. For one thing, I'd been bouncing back and forth in a relationship for three years, unable to commit myself to it or to extricate myself from it. Ambivalence defined my way of living. I sought comfort on a golf course, far from home, where I felt I could discover myself anew.

Dornoch, at fifty-eight degrees north latitude, the same as Juneau, Alaska, would provide that place of pilgrimage for at least a few days. I wanted somewhere remote. Dornoch wasn't easy to get to, isolated as it was from Edinburgh by an expanse of moody hills and three great sea firths north of Inverness. The final one was the Dornoch Firth; there was no bridge across it then, and there wouldn't be one until 1991. To approach the Royal Dornoch Golf Club rolling above and along the firth was to do just that – approach it, slowly, with anticipation. I took a train north from Edinburgh's Waverley Station, stopping in Inverness. There, after a pint in a local pub, I boarded a bus bound for Dornoch that went inland at the Dornoch Firth. Traveling northwest for a while, the bus climbed into the hills above and crossed the firth inland at Bonar Bridge before turning east and making for the village with the rumpled, golden links awaiting me.

I had read and remembered the essay Herbert Warren Wind had written in 1964 in the *New Yorker* called "North to the Links of Dornoch." He wrote that the village's remoteness "explains the unique position that Dornoch has long held in golf; for over half a century it has been regarded as one of the outstanding courses in the world by men close to the heart of the game, yet very few of them have ever played it." Pete Dye, who was to become a celebrated American course architect, had told Wind, "No other links has quite the ageless aura Dornoch does. When you play it, you get the feeling you could be living just as easily in the eighteen hundreds, or even the seventeen hundreds. If an old Scot in a red jacket had popped out from behind a sand dune, beating a feather ball, I wouldn't have blinked an eye."

Dornoch called to some golfers. It was calling me.

I'd been to Scotland once before, in early 1972, when I spent a month there prior to visiting Israel. I had lived in a flat in Edinburgh, and played many courses. The first was Kingsknowes, in Edinburgh, and a rougher, more basic course you couldn't find — or so I thought then. I enjoyed the round with the proprietor of the bed-and-breakfast where I stayed. Later he invited me on an outing with other golfers to the plush Gleneagles course. We took a bus into the hills of Perthshire, and on the way everybody drank more beer in a couple of hours than I would normally drink in a month. We played our round, told tall golfing tales all the way back to Edinburgh, and planned our next games. I played the Old Course and Muirfield, and thirty-six holes one day at Dunbar in an all-day rain. I played North Berwick, where I was enchanted by the thirteenth hole that asks the player to hit his approach to the green over a low stone wall. On the Braid Hills overlooking Edinburgh I walked for miles over several days, gazing down at the ancient city. Well, it was ancient to North American me. I thought any city whose New Town is eighteenth century is a place where I would like to set down.

That trip proved what I had gathered from reading about Scottish golf: the game here was simply a part of life. It was part of the culture of the country. In a restaurant in Edinburgh I overheard two young women who had just graduated as teachers; they were discussing places where they might find work, and were basing their decisions in part on the golf courses in the area. I visited Archie and Sheila Baird at their home in Edinburgh; Archie was a member of the Gullane and Muirfield golf clubs, a veterinarian whose hobby was collecting golf memorabilia. His garage was a museum of the game. Sheila, meanwhile, was a physician in the Red Cross and a great-granddaughter of Mungo Park, the

1874 British Open champion. The Bairds and I became lifelong friends.

But I didn't play Dornoch that first trip to Scotland, and regretted my omission. It remained in my mind's eye a links in an empty, desolate region to the north, and came to appeal to me for those reasons. I'd enjoyed my golf the most when I played on a quiet course in the early morning or evening, and all the better when that course was a links. Golf as we know it began on links courses that connected the sea to, quite often, a village or town. The links was to a resident what a basketball court is to a kid growing up in New York or Los Angeles, or a natural ice rink was to me growing up in Toronto.

But what is a links, technically speaking? It's essentially a landscape of blown sand created by the action of the wind on the seashore. Sand blown onto the shore accumulated over the years and settled into various formations – mainly dunes, but also the plateaus and humps so characteristic of linksland. The rising and falling of sea levels over the eons combined to create at Royal Dornoch what is known as a raised beach. The ground over which one plays golf is thirty to fifty feet above sea level, and separated from the sea by dunes. The Scottish geologist and geographer Robert Price points out that linksland takes up only three hundred miles of Scotland's 7,500 miles of coastline. Royal Dornoch plays for the most part between a high bluff on its western edge and the dunes; only the seventh hole on top of the ridge and the upper portion of the eighth fairway feel as if they are more inland than seaside – and even here the sea makes its presence felt.

Links in Scotland have traditionally been places where people went for sport, for recreation and fun with friends, for communion with the self and the outdoors. In the Toronto winters of my childhood, that place was not a golf course, but a natural ice rink a couple of hundred yards down the street where I lived. I'd skate along the hard-packed snow on the road or in the frozen ditches before sewer systems were installed. Night after night my friends and I would shovel snow off the ice under a single lamppost and create banks that served as our boards. We would play and play, whacking the puck along increasingly rutted ice. But who cared about the condition? We were lost in the game.

In the warmer weather, golf replaced hockey, and I didn't care how rough the course was. The idea was to hit an object toward a defined target – not that different than hockey when I think about it. The simplicity of the game appealed to me. I'm afraid there was more to it, though. I became obsessed with why I could hit one good shot and then a terrible one. Rather too early in my golfing life I became overloaded with swing thoughts. That didn't happen with hockey. I've still never had a technical thought about my slapshot. Hockey was fast; you moved and didn't think. Golf was slow; you thought and didn't move.

On rugged golf courses and on crude ice rinks I found a feeling of freedom that usually escaped me in other parts of my life. Ken Dryden in his book *The Game* writes that the frozen ponds and ice pads of his youth were focal points for kids in communities across Canada; that was also true when I was growing up. A local golf links fulfilled the same purpose for Scots, and still does in many places. The less adulterated a course is by gatehouses, greeters, cart paths, halfway houses, and global positioning satellite systems, the firmer the attachment is for me. I believed Dornoch offered a pure golf experience, and in the spring of 1976, stagnating in my muddled relationship, I wrote my good friend Howard Ganz, who had gone to Scotland for a month. Howard was living in a flat in Troon, and golfing every day. We exchanged letters; mine were full of tortured prose that reflected my tortured mind. Howard was encouraging me to visit him in Troon, where he knew I would lighten up.

I have Howard's letters at my desk as I write. "Just get an open air ticket good for a year and surrender yourself," he wrote. "It'll do you a world of good. There's much life to live here and there ain't no time like now."

But I couldn't get moving. Then my father suddenly required bypass surgery, and so there was no question of my leaving Toronto. Still, I wrote Howard that I'd get to Scotland soon. I have that letter in front of me twenty-five years later. High on the list of things I wanted to do in Scotland was, I wrote, "playing the links of Dornoch." I added, "If I can work it out, I may even live in Scotland next year."

That next year, I did make it to Dornoch. I planned only a day there in the middle of a crammed schedule, but Dornoch wouldn't let go and I didn't want to let it let go. Instead I spent a week there. "Finally, Dornoch," I wrote in my journal of my first round, on a Sunday in May. The occasion was a one-day competition. "Shot 74 while in love," I wrote rhapsodically. I had high expectations, because I wasn't happy with my round. "Three-putted three of the first six holes, two from birdie range. Struck the ball tentatively. Think I was awed by the course, by just being here." But on the tee at the par-five ninth hole, I decided to stop being afraid, or so my notes tell me. "I aimed down the left centre and HIT the ball and didn't guide it. Made birdie after a 2-iron to 30 feet, birdied the 10th with a 25-footer and played well from there in. Found it was a good idea to try my best on each shot and not plan or hope. Lawrence Durrell wrote that we should live with no despair, but no hope either."

I played Dornoch every day for a week, just prior to the Scottish Ladies Amateur that was on that spring. I met Lesley Marsh, a low-handicap Scottish golfer who lived in Newcastle. We practiced on the ground that was used as an airstrip during the Second World War, and which still serves as a practice area for Dornoch golfers. Lesley and I remained friends; from time to time over the years we would designate a specific day when she would play a round at home and I would do the same in Toronto. We would then compare cards to see who won our transatlantic match. During one evening round in Dornoch, I played with a young woman named Fiona, a two-handicapper from

Perth who was up for the Amateur. "She hits the ball quite long, with a high draw, but she doesn't enjoy the game when she's under pressure," I wrote. "But she places a lot of pressure on herself by making golf so important. Sounds familiar."

In one round during that first visit to Dornoch I shot 73 while playing with Willie Skinner, the club professional, Dennis Bethune, a member who had played in a British Open during his time as a professional – "It's aye the pooter," Dennis told me about the importance of putting – and Sandy "Pipey" Matheson, a learned caddy who would later look after Nick Faldo and Bob Charles when they played the links. Dennis and I beat Willie and Sandy 3&1. Little did I know that I would spend time with these people twenty-three summers later. Sandy called himself an "unhappy" golfer that day we played, because once a round he hit a shank. "Och, there it is," he said when it happened.

My week in Dornoch introduced me to a place with which I felt a connection. Spending a week isn't the same as living there, but it was enough for Dornoch to imprint itself on my mind. I remembered the hours I spent tucked away in the clubhouse reading turn-of-the-century bound volumes of *Golf Illustrated* magazine – any club that kept these magazines was the kind of club I wanted to frequent. Dr. John Macleod introduced himself to me while I read; his history of the club would be published in 2000, when I next visited Dornoch. During my visit, I played the Brora Golf Club, a rugged links up the coast from Dornoch. There I played with John and Jenny Louden, who were living in Edinburgh. They were both low-handicap players, and while we had a superb day's golf we lost touch after I left Dornoch. John and Jenny told me about Jimmy Miller, a Brora golfer who was the best amateur in the Highlands. He'd won the Carnegie Shield, the biggest annual tournament at Royal Dornoch, a few times. But I didn't meet Jimmy then.

Between 1977 and 2000 I must have visited Scotland twenty times to cover events or play its courses. But I hadn't returned to Dornoch. That would wait, until there was time – time to give it time. I had moved on in my life, never finishing my doctoral work but taking up golf writing. In 1980, I married the woman with whom I had a troubled relationship when I went to Dornoch in 1977. I had deluded myself that marriage could make a difficult relationship better – commitment and all that. Things never did improve. The marriage lasted only a year. We divorced without rancor and put that chapter of our lives behind us. Years later, in 1992, I would get married again, to Nell Waldman. We share our lives in every way, even though she doesn't golf. But she knows golf and how it can consume a person's life. Together, in the summer of 2000, we would venture across the ocean to Scotland, and then north to the links of Dornoch.

• • • • • •

Our plan was simple. We would rent a flat in Dornoch for a summer. I would golf at Royal Dornoch, and presumably life would flow from there – emanations from the links, because of it, and through it. What would happen would happen. I wanted a village that had one of the world's outstanding links courses, and that Dornoch had. I wanted a place that was small enough that the golf course would be a focal point for many people. I also sought a remote village, or at least a place that most people who don't live there consider remote. Dornoch was far away, isolated to North Americans, although, as I learned, many Scottish, English, Irish, and Welsh people also considered it "out there." Not much had changed in attitudes since 1908 when one Thomas Murphy drove around the British Isles and ignored Dornoch. In his popular book *British Highways and Byways from a Motor Car, Being a Record of a Five-Thousand-Mile Tour in England, Wales, and Scotland*, Murphy included a chapter on the Highlands, but he got no farther than Inverness, forty miles south of Dornoch. In 1985, when the British

Amateur championship was held at Royal Dornoch, some Londoners complained that it was too far for them to travel. Even the esteemed English writer Bernard Darwin didn't include Royal Dornoch in his 1910 book, *The Golf Courses of the British Isles.*

Dornoch was an end-of-the-earth place to many people, and friends would get a faraway look when I told them that Nell and I planned to spend a summer there. The usual reaction was, "One day I'll go there. I've always wanted to. I've been to St. Andrews and Turnberry. But Dornoch is pretty far north. And I hear the weather is rough. But I'll get there."

Now was the time for me, and also for Nell. She teaches English at a college in Toronto, and can travel in the summer. Adventurous by nature, Nell had traveled with Jessamyn, her daughter and my step-daughter, to Ecuador and the Galapagos. Nell and I had been in the Atacama Desert in Chile, the highest and driest desert in the world, on her fiftieth birthday. Two years before our trip to Dornoch we had retraced the steps of writer Thomas Hardy in Dorset in southwest England for a magazine article; Nell's doctoral work had been on Hardy's novels and poetry, and he wrote of the vitality of Dorset's natural world. We walked in his footsteps and I golfed at courses in his landscape. To us golf and walking and the landscape were woven into the same quilt. In Dornoch, we confidently told ourselves, we would be living in a powerful setting, relatively untouched by the hand of man.

I left Toronto for Dornoch on June 19, 2000, the day after Tiger Woods won the U.S. Open at Pebble Beach Golf Links by a hard-to-comprehend record fifteen shots. I was venturing far from the professional tournament scene where I spent months every year. But professional golf is only part of the golf world, a small if intensely and intensively followed segment. There are also other types of golf. There's Dornoch golf, whatever that would prove to be in the year 2000. Nell had been to Scotland once, in 1992 when we went to the British Open at Muirfield, east of

Edinburgh. She too felt a kinship with the country and the countryside, and though not a golfer she established a tradition of hitting a shot on the last hole of famous courses. Her shot to the eighteenth green at the Old Course skipped through the Valley of Sin and up to the middle of the green.

I turned east from the A9 road north of the Dornoch Firth bridge to drive the two miles into Dornoch on the evening of June 20, during the summer solstice. The road meandered past woods and meadowland to my right and some homes on my left, then past the shops that framed either side of this main street for a couple of hundred yards. The sixteenth-century castle was on one side of the street, and the cathedral and graveyard were on the other. I turned right where the street ended, then took a quick left up Golf Road so that I could look at the links. I parked and walked out to the empty course.

It was getting on to ten o'clock when I took my first steps onto the links in twenty-three years, but there was plenty of light left. I stood quietly on the course where I would spend the next three months. Nell was scheduled to arrive a week later. Our visit to Dornoch was underway.

Chapter 2

The First Round

At midnight of the longest day of the year – summer solstice – even the centuries-old graveyard in Dornoch isn't dark. I walk in the square surrounding the graveyard and ancient cathedral, my only company a solitary seagull flying above, loosed from the shore a few hundred yards away. Alone, my footsteps are audible – clomp-clomp – as I meander this first night in Dornoch. The village sleeps at this hour. The only lights on are those in the flat above the Dornoch Bookshop at the east end of the High Street, across from the cemetery. These are the lights in Cheadle House, The Flat, High Street, Dornoch IV25 3SH, where Nell and I will spend the summer. I'd stopped into the flat for a few minutes before returning to the vacant street. Here I am in the far north of Scotland, in the night-morning. I'm sure I could still see my golf ball at Royal Dornoch, up a hill and only a few minutes by foot from here. But there will be time for night golf. For now I want to hear the silence.

After spending my first few minutes at the course, I had gone directly to Sinclair and Sandee Mackintosh's home on Bishopfield Road, set on higher ground above the village. Dornoch's central area sits as if in a dish. Sinclair, an estate agent, had rented me the bookshop flat. He owned the two floors above the bookshop that constituted the flat, and had informed me that I would need to furnish the rooms. A Scottish law compels landowners to pay a tax on furnished flats that are empty, he said, and so this flat comes unfurnished. "Am I expected to bring furniture from Canada?" I'd asked. He confirmed that I would have to make my own arrangements for furniture.

Not that I minded. There might be something salutary in living with a minimum of furnishings. No excess baggage and all that. I'd left behind my voluminous golf library and files that I had always believed I needed to do my work as a journalist. The bare flat certainly gave me the opportunity to furnish it with as little or as much as I wanted. I had brought only one putter along for the summer, though I felt a little anxious about that. It can be traumatic to leave home for a week's golf with only one putter, let alone for three months. But I figured that, as Lee Trevino had famously said, it's the archer and not the arrow that causes bad shots. Me and my one putter: we would travel lightly together for the season.

Traveling light had to be a good thing, but traveling hungry wasn't. I needed food upon my arrival in Dornoch, and Sandee came through as we sat in her home. Fish and chips, biscuits with Stilton and cheddar cheese, a single-malt whisky with a splash of water, and then tea provided a satisfying late dinner.

Sandee filled me in on a few necessary matters regarding golf at Dornoch. First, slow play was tolerated about as well as the Scots tolerated Westminster's decisions about their country; they lived with it but made it clear they didn't approve. That was true when locals as well as visitors played slowly. Ability, handicap, name, station, and rank didn't matter. What did matter was a golfer's pace of play, and it had better be snappy.

Sandee's credo was straightforward: play fast so that others can enjoy their golf. She believes that's the proper way to play the game. Sandee also said that golf is central to Dornoch life. "If you live in Dornoch, you must play golf. That's all there is to it."

* * * * * *

Dornoch wakes up early in the summer, perhaps because it's getting light by 4 a.m. I'm half-asleep at seven, still woozy from yesterday's travel. There's a knock on the door, and I plod down the stairs to find Don Greenberg. We had corresponded for a few weeks prior to my arrival here, because golf-writing pals had told me I had to meet Don. His name came up in most conversations I had with people familiar with Dornoch. Now here he was, my first visitor.

"I've booked a time for 6:30 tonight. You may join us if you wish," Don says at the door, feigning a formal tone. "My partner in our four-ball match will be Chippie Maillie. He's our finest young player, and I am sure you will find him a worthy opponent. Your partner will be Stuart Morrison, the assistant professional at the club. Now, Stuart is an excellent player who hits the ball a long way and has a superb sense of humor. I strongly suggest you accept this invitation. What did you say your handicap was?"

It was one just a few years ago. That was after I finished writing an instruction book with Nick Price, whose reputation as one of golf's best ball-strikers is undiminished, even in these Tiger Woods–dominated days. My swing got faster, tighter, more efficient. One evening, when we were hitting balls on the beach near Nick's home on Jupiter Island, Florida, he showed me that I tended to snatch the club back to the inside as soon as I started my backswing and also to stay on my left side. I swing right-handed, although I putt left-handed, so this was the classic reverse pivot. The club was moving back and I was leaning forward. No good. Nick helped me correct these flaws, and for once in my golfing life I stuck to only one or two simple swing thoughts. My handicap soon dropped from four to one. After one particularly enjoyable round in which I hit shot after shot just where I'd aimed, I told Nell that I played an entire eighteen holes without a swing thought. Nirvana.

But it didn't last. That summer of 1997 I was playing well in my club championship when, on the seventh hole in the third round, I faced a three-iron shot over a valley of no-man's land to the green. I felt anxious over the ball and that feeling expressed itself in my swing. I topped the shot into the valley and lost the ball. Always ready to concede defeat on a single shot's notice, I turned to my caddy, Shahzad, a smart young college student who was more confident in me than I was in myself, and told him, "That's it. There goes this tournament." I quickly dropped another ball and this time hit a roundhouse hook into the woods. Need I continue? Anything I'd learned from Price was gone. Rubenstein was back.

"I'm a five," I tell Don.

"Fine," he says. "So am I. Let's review then. Six-thirty. Me and Chippie. You and Morrison. I'm sorry for waking you, but you're here for golf, aren't you? And I should tell you what I've learned myself. The more golf you play at Dornoch, the happier you'll be."

There was no going back to bed. I invite Don up for a coffee. "Excellent. Let's talk," he replies.

He's a garrulous fellow, a stream-of-consciousness talker. A forty-seven-year-old former sportswriter, he was born in Port Chester, a town near New York City. He first visited Dornoch in late August 1985, a golfer in search of the good places in the game. Greenberg drove up from London, a 660-mile journey. He stopped as he crossed over Struie Hill, which rises above the village and the sea to the west. A heavy shower had passed through, and a shaft of light and a rainbow hit him, revealing the village to the east. "That must be Dornoch," Greenberg thought of what he calls "the most beautiful view I ever saw." He swooped down Struie Hill, revitalized after his long drive, and turned toward Dornoch. There, he went directly to the bar at the Royal Golf Hotel alongside the first fairway, talked with a fellow behind the bar, and arranged a game for seven the next morning. He shot 80 that sunny morning, and then met three doctors from New Orleans who were there for some golf therapy. They invited him to play in the afternoon. Why not? Greenberg shot 82 and won a few pounds. He rested a while before joining the doctors for a late-afternoon round, winning the money again.

Twelve hours. Three rounds at Dornoch. It was the first time Greenberg had walked fifty-four holes. Well, fifty-one and a half holes. Greenberg couldn't make it up the hill at the sixteenth, and tossed his golf bag to one of the caddies in the group. Finished, he was just starting. "Dornoch had its hooks in me," he remembers. "Deep."

He returned the next summer, and the next, and the next, finally joining the club in 1988. He was living in California, covering the NBA's Los Angeles Lakers for the *Orange County Register*. But when he was in Dornoch he wasn't thinking about California, and when he was in California he was thinking about Dornoch. In 1991, Greenberg had what he calls a "moment of clarity." "I looked into a mirror and asked myself, 'Why am I doing this? Why am I covering basketball? All I think about is Dornoch. I want to be in Dornoch. What's holding me back?' The answer was, 'Absolutely nothing.' I told my sports editor I was quitting. He said, 'Huh? Where are you going? What are they offering you?' I told him that wasn't it at all, that I was moving to the north of Scotland. I put my condo on the market, got rid of my leased car, and, by the way, I took a bath on that, but fine. And I came over to Dornoch."

That was in October 1991. In London, Greenberg had bought a small car at an auction, then drove it without insurance or proper registration north to Dornoch and rented a house two miles outside the village that had a view over the firth. It wasn't long after that the Lakers' Magic

Johnson revealed he was HIV positive. The Lakers' beat, Greenberg says, turned into "the assignment from hell. I was glad not to be part of that." He eventually bought a small row house that he calls the "ghetto" in the middle of Dornoch, where he lives like a college kid – golf stuff, dishes, books, and magazines everywhere. His life pattern was set: late spring, all of summer, and then a return visit in December for the holiday season in Dornoch, the rest of the year at his home in Tampa, where, I'm told, he's so tidy that he catches crumbs before they hit the floor. Nobody would say Greenberg is sentimental, but I detected a hitch in his voice when he told me about the piper who played from the top of the Dornoch Cathedral on the last night of the twentieth century. He joined in when locals who had gathered in the square sang "Auld Lang Syne" at midnight.

"But," Don says as we chat over coffee this first day of summer in Dornoch, "I needed to do something here besides play golf. And I wasn't all that interested in writing sports anymore, although I did some. I'd thought about caddying at the club, but I didn't think it was right for me to take jobs from locals. But I got that sorted out and I love it now. I don't want to be anywhere else but the course, and caddying gets me out there more."

As does playing. Greenberg had just competed in the club championship. On the short tenth he got his fourth hole-in-one at Dornoch, his second at that hole. However, he wasn't close to winning the event. John Lindberg, a Swedish member of the club, won by a Tigerish fifteen shots. "I'm a rising five," Don says of his handicap. "I was uncomprehensively involved in the club championship."

Was the problem his swing, which Greenberg himself acknowledges is unusual? He won't tell me because he'd rather I wait until we play to see what he means. Eddie Pearce, a former PGA Tour player for whom Greenberg had caddied, examined his swing. "You have a horseshit swing," Pearce told him. "I know you do and everybody knows you do.

The best advice I can give you is to love your swing, to trust your swing, and to learn to score from eighty yards in."

Greenberg also warns me that he has the yips. English golf writer Henry Longhurst once noted of the yips, "Once you've had 'em, you've got 'em." Another name for this involuntary twitch that can knock the ball on a one-foot putt off the green, or that can make a golfer freeze over the ball, is "whisky fingers." Or the "staggers." Brain researchers call the problem a "focal dystonia," which affects not only golfers but also surgeons, musicians, teachers. It's an occupational hazard that can wreak havoc in a person's life. Greenberg, who says he's developed a "middle-aged yip," calls it an eel, as in electric eel. It can show up anytime on short putts. The yips rarely appear for anybody on long putts, because golfers don't think they should make these. They're relaxed over putts that they aren't expected to make.

"I fight the eel and I'll always fight it," Don says, and he's not smiling now. But he does have a sense of humor about the eel, and includes the word in his e-mail address. That's either tempting fate or his way of looking it straight on and saying, "I'm not afraid of you." But he knows better. He's afraid of the eel. It can work its way into his game in the most insidious ways. "I've had rounds where I hit the ball great but could not hold the putter. I won't say it spoils my golf, but it doesn't enhance it."

Enough eel talk. Don offers some advice to me on playing Dornoch. He's reverting to caddy mode. For one thing, he declares, "Nobody plays to his handicap in Dornoch. And direction is much more important than distance. Two hundred yards straight is far better than three-ten and three feet in the rough. If you're thinking six-iron from the rough, take eight. If you're thinking you can get to the green with eight from the rough, take wedge, get out of the stuff, pitch on, and one-putt for par. Pros are pros because they don't follow one bad shot with another.

"Always take more club than you think you need, too. After you've played ten rounds, think of the number of times you were past the pin in regulation. You'll underclub eight of ten times. Amateurs underclub. The way I play Dornoch is if I think it's a full seven-iron I'll go down the shaft on a six-iron. Most of the trouble at Dornoch is short of the green. Very few times will you airmail a green. Remember also that 95 percent of three-putts happen because the first putt is short. I tell the golfers I caddy for to fall in love with the pace and to hell with the line."

Don's voice has taken on a more confident tone. He knows he can caddy. Caddies everywhere know more about golf than they demonstrate as golfers, when their vulnerabilities are exposed. We're all experts without a club in our hands. Greenberg is a decent enough golfer to play with anybody, but he's not that sure of himself as a player.

But this evening he'll be playing, not caddying. An evening round at Dornoch for my first game this visit, and with the eelmeister himself, the American who discovered that he felt at home in Dornoch.

As for now, Greenberg is off to work. He's wanted on the first tee to caddy in half an hour.

• • • • • •

It's easy to see why golf took hold along Dornoch's coastline once the game was introduced here in the early seventeenth century. The essential ingredients for a hit-the-ball-to-a-target game are present: open ground with natural obstacles such as mounds and sandy pits to traverse; larger, gently rolling areas to aim toward; sandy soil that dries quickly after storms that blow in off the sea or over the hills to the west; firm ground to walk on and bounce a ball along; wind to provide zest and challenge to an outing. In his *Personal Memories of Royal Dornoch Golf Club, 1900–1925*, Donald Grant, a member of the club who lived into his nineties, wrote that, as a boy, he saw hundreds of tons of sand blown onto the links as a result of a three-day easterly gale. "Translate that into periods lasting thousands of years and you get Dornoch Links," he wrote. "Unrivalled stretches of fine seaside turf; hillocks, banks, promontories, hollows and humps. Everything in terms of terrain for modern golf had been provided by the age-long forces of nature." The name of the village itself probably derives from *dor–n–ach*, which means "field between two waters." That's a concise description of the links, too.

The features to which Grant referred provide the basics of links golf, and when I first visited Dornoch I thought I had never seen a more exquisite setting for the game. I walked up Golf Road from the lower, central area of the village and looked forward to setting out on an adventure, where I would find golfing ground that had been there for centuries. John Macleod told me when I met him on that early visit that people had used these links for golf for some four hundred years. I wasn't surprised.

Hitting something along the seaside ground toward a target must have been as instinctive in the sixteenth century as it is now. What youngster hasn't picked up an object and thrown or hit it toward a target? That's the foundation of many sports, and it's always been the basis of golf. If people are drawn to the sea – and it's apparent on any fine day by the beaches of the world that they are – then they will also seek recreation there. Provide a generous expanse of ground and soon there is room for people to express themselves via a cross-country form of recreation.

Nobody could help but be taken with the setting – the village shouldering up to the edge of the links, the hills to the north and south, the half-moon curve of the beach, the grassed area between the dunes and the woods to the west that provided room for golf or other sporting activities, all framed farther west by hills rising to moorland to mountains, and to the east by the sea with its surf – known to some as "white horses" – and the peninsula where the lighthouse at Tarbat Ness now stands. Who wouldn't want to walk here, play here? All that was needed for golf to take hold was a person or people who knew the game. It's often said that golf is to many people a religion, and in the case of Dornoch, there is evidence that the first golfers were associated with the clergy. Maybe it's reasonable to suggest, then, that the game achieved an immediate sanctification here. When the five-time British Open champion Tom Watson played Dornoch in 1981 on a Sunday morning, he looked around at the crowd that had assembled and asked, tongue in cheek, "Doesn't anybody go to church here?" The local minister, James Simpson, is said to have turned red and then to have left the course. Reverend Simpson collected stories and jokes into a 1990 book *More Holy Wit*. Its longest chapter was on golf. Decision rendered: Golf does have religious overtones.

There's more evidence, too. Donald Grant wrote that, in 1540, one Bishop Robert Stewart of Catt – the county of Caithness, the next one north of the district of Sutherland – played golf on Dornoch Links. He did so with what was called a "play club," which is what the first drivers were called. One "played" with a club. Hence the term "play club."

Bishop Stewart was from Dornoch, and lived in St. Andrews starting in 1570. St. Andrews was the head bishopric of Scotland and its ecclesiastical center. Golf was already popular in St. Andrews, so it can be assumed that he was familiar with the game there and also played. Certainly many clergy made their way to Dornoch; bishops were the mucky-mucks of society, often connected to aristocratic families with substantial land holdings. We now think of clergy as having spiritual power only, but in those days they had political power as well. John Macleod writes of "a strong ecclesiastical connection between St. Andrews and Dornoch from the time of the construction of the Cathedral [in the thirteenth century] to the Reformation in the sixteenth century, and there seems to be evidence that visiting clergy, trained at St. Andrews, played golf on the links."

It appears that Bishop Stewart had a sporting spirit. He was also known as the Earl of March – this being a hereditary designation. One of the earl's roles was as commendator of the priory of St. Andrews, and as commendator he received an ecclesiastical grant when a priory became vacant. In 1582, a St. Andrews minister had left his position – "went on the loose," to use the proper term – which led to Bishop Stewart receiving some funds. He used them well, at least from a Dornoch golfer's point of view, in that he "colluded with the rewallars of the town to hold the ministerie vacand, and in the meantime took up the stipend, and spendit the same, with the rest of the kirk's rents of the Pryorie, at the goff, archerie, guid cheir, etc." This revelry occurred on the links in St. Andrews, but it was Bishop Stewart, a Dornoch man, who led the golfers.

The first actual reference to golf in Dornoch was in 1616, when Sir Robert Gordon made a note regarding his nephew, the thirteenth Earl of Sutherland – Earl John. Sir Robert, a Dornoch man who had studied at St. Andrews University, was the family historian. He also tutored his nephew, wrote widely, and knew everything that was going on in and around Dornoch. In 1616, he reported expenses for "My Lord's Golf Clubs and Golf Balls – 10 pounds and 12 pounds." Golf clubs in 1616 were rare items, hence these high prices. It's possible that the thirteenth Earl of Sutherland hoarded golf clubs and balls, but we have no records of whether the thirteenth earl was a low- or high-handicap player, or of the extent of his club collection.

The earl's uncle must have continued to golf at Dornoch Links, for in 1630 Gordon made this declaration: "About this toun along the sea coast, are the fairest and lairgest links of green fieldes of any pairt of Scotland. Fitt for archery, golfing, ryding, and all other exercises, they doe surpass the fieldes of Montrose or St. Andrews." This was quite a claim to make for the Dornoch Links, given that St. Andrews was already considered the home of golf and that Montrose was also home to links that made for excellent golf. The first mention of golf in

St. Andrews was in 1552 and in Montrose, 1628. Was Gordon being extravagant in his praise? After all, he was a Dornoch golfer who was no doubt predisposed to looking favorably upon the links. Judging by assessments that golfers such as Tom Watson and Ernie Els would make centuries later, Gordon was simply telling the truth.

But something strange happened, or didn't happen, after Sir Robert left the scene. There's no mention of golf in Dornoch for another two hundred years, which seems a long time without anybody playing over the links. It could be that nobody wrote anything about their golf on the links; besides, the links was just a place to whack the ball around, not a formal, designed course. The links were also used for other sports.

There was shinty, for one, a form of field hockey, played at least every "old" New Year's Day – not January 1, but close to it. Everybody from the "graybearded grandfather to the lightest heeled stripling" showed up on the links with their hockey sticks. They played from late morning until dark, "with keenness, accompanied by shouts."

Following Sir Robert Gordon's 1630 advertisement for Dornoch's golfing ground, the next indication of play there, according to John Macleod, occurs in the middle of the nineteenth century. George Dempster, from St. Andrews, had taken up residence in Skibo, a vast property just southwest of Dornoch. A sporting man, he brought friends over to Dornoch Links for golf in 1852. His great-uncle, George Dempster of Dunnichen, had purchased the Skibo estate in 1786, and, as Jimmy Bell, a Dornoch resident and amateur historian, told me later, had "stood out against the general attitude by helping people rather than putting them off the land." He, the great-uncle, was responsible for setting up a mill at Spinningdale, a hamlet near Skibo. The mill didn't succeed, but Dempster's hope had been that it would provide employment for people in the area at a time when the crofters were being evicted from their land. I like to think that his great-nephew was also concerned about the welfare of people in the area, and that he believed golf was a game for everybody. Whether that's true or not, I was glad to learn that a Dempster played on Dornoch Links.

Months after my season in Dornoch ended, I would come across nineteen volumes of correspondence from the first George Dempster. They had ended up in the Thomas Fisher Rare Book Library at the University of Toronto. His great-nephew, the Dempster who golfed on Dornoch Links in 1852, had collected and donated the letters to the university. Presumably, then, he felt a kinship with his great-uncle. He also inherited Skibo from him, which was a rather attractive inheritance.

In 1877, twenty-five years after Dempster played at Dornoch, the Sutherland Golfing Society was formed. Golf had arrived in a formal way at Dornoch, on a rudimentary nine-hole course. Alexander Machardy, the chief constable of Sutherland, was probably the primary influence on this early golf. He became secretary to the Dornoch Golf Club, which evolved from the Sutherland Golfing Society. Machardy worked as club secretary until 1883, when John Sutherland took over. Sutherland lived in a gracious home on the higher level of the village, and later worked as town clerk. He ruled the golf club for fifty-eight years, until he died in 1941, and wrote for golf publications and also for the *Northern Times*, the paper of record in the northern Highlands. Sutherland's word was law at the golf club. He was also a first-class player who won tournaments. Like secretaries who followed him, Sutherland played in club competitions. He also won his share.

By the end of the nineteenth century, Dornoch had a full eighteen-hole course, after commissioning Old Tom Morris, the professional in St. Andrews, to lay out the holes, assisted by Tom Simpson, the professional at the Carnoustie Golf Club in the county of Angus to the south. Old Tom had received a complete golfing education at the Old Course in St. Andrews, and brought his knowledge to Dornoch, where he found ideal golfing ground. It was on this ground, if not on the same holes because the course changed over the years, that Donald Ross spent so much time before he left for the United States.

Donald Ross was born in Dornoch in 1872, in a modest, ivy-covered row house at 3 St. Gilbert Street, a minute's walk from our flat, though a plaque on the front of the house is the only evidence he lived there. He had no aspirations to become a golf-course architect, or even a golfer. But how could anybody who grew up in Dornoch not take to golf? Ross was no different. The course was a ten-minute walk from his family home, through the center of the village and up Golf Road. He left school when he was fourteen, taking up carpentry as a profession, and, as Bradley Klein points out in his biography of Ross, Peter Murray, the master carpenter for whom he worked, made the wooden boxes that held the sand golfers collected into a pile to create a tee. Ross liked playing the game, too, and was quite proficient at it. He developed a classic Dornoch swing, one in which the golfer puts the ball far forward in the stance, takes a wide stance for better balance in the wind, and puts the right foot back to encourage a right-to-left flight. I'd heard of the "lazy" wind at Dornoch – the easterly wind that is so lazy it doesn't go around the golfer, it goes through him. Ross must have known this wind, and contrived a swing to cope with it. Stuart Shaw, a long-time Dornoch member who has won tournaments in the north, has a similar swing a century later. I felt as if I were looking at Ross when I encountered Shaw on the links. He hadn't been affected by modern instruction, which emphasizes a tighter, less hands-oriented swing.

Just about the time that young Ross was leaving school and taking his apprenticeship as a carpenter, Old Tom Morris showed up to create a formal course on the links. Ross was intrigued by what he saw, and in 1893, a year after Old Tom had returned to St. Andrews from a repeat visit to Dornoch, John Sutherland sent Ross to work with him at the Old Course. Ross, who had left carpentry, had already learned something of greenkeeping and clubmaking because he'd been soaking up the game in all its aspects, and he stayed in St. Andrews for a short while, then came back to Dornoch in November 1893. Sutherland hired him as club professional, greenkeeper, and clubmaker a year later. Five years after that, Ross met Professor Robert Willson, who was visiting Dornoch. Willson, a professor of astronomy at Harvard, was a golf aficionado who wanted to play a part in the development of the game in the United States, where it was beginning to make some inroads. Ross had walked the links at Dornoch daily; its landscape provided him with a sense of what a proper course should look like. He spent time with Willson in Dornoch, surely discussing all things golf. Willson was a charter member of the Oakley Country Club in Watertown, Massachusetts, ten miles from Boston. Willson invited Ross to come across to the United States, and to call on him there.

Ross left Dornoch in March 1899. His first position was as the green-keeper and professional at the Oakley Country Club. His interest in course architecture flourished, and he eventually designed nearly four hundred courses in the United States. Most every one had echoes of Dornoch: invitations to drive the ball into wide, sloping, and bouncy fairways, to hit a variety of shots into the greens, some at ground level or in low areas, others raised onto plateaus and falling off to hollows. Growing up in Toronto, I heard about various Ross courses and hoped one day I would play them, and I had: Pinehurst #2; Seminole in Juno Beach, Florida; Essex in Windsor, Ontario; The Orchards in South Hadley, Massachusetts. Now I had come to the village where he was raised, and the course whose very ground had nurtured his golfing soul.

Of Dornoch, Ross wrote, as quoted in *Golf Has Never Failed Me*, a collection of his commentaries on course design: "Modesty forbids me saying more than it is the most beautifully situated links in the world, and that no American golfer should omit to go there, where he will find the best golf, a royal welcome and no rabble."

John Sutherland made a speech at the club during a ceremony in 1933 on the occasion of his fiftieth anniversary as club secretary. "The whole wide world today worships at [golf's] shrine as it worships at no other," he said in a village where worship was a central part of life. "Other outdoor games belong to a common caste, the essential principles being attack and defense. The ball is common to both sides, and is negotiated mostly when in motion. Golf on the other hand is wholly, absolutely unique. From the time the first ape began to shy stones and knock down apples which he could not reach, the mind of man has devised no other game similar in structure or design and none so simple – the knocking of a stationary ball into a hole in the ground proportionately large. There is no one to oppose or interfere with you; no one to make a counter move against you; no human being to thwart your intention or stay your hand. In other games you have to reckon with a mortal foe. In golf it is your solitary self against the world."

My solitary self was ready to take on the world in the person of Don Greenberg and friends. The moment had arrived: my first round in Dornoch in nearly twenty-five years.

• • • • • •

Our game begins at 6:30 in the evening, leaving hours of light ahead. The first hole at Royal Dornoch is a short par-four, straightaway to a green that falls away right, left, and to the rear. A road to the beach crosses just in front of the tee. It's been a source of controversy for seventy years. Many golfers see it as an eyesore, a hazard that could cause accidents, and an intrusion into the beginning of their rounds. Local non-golfers, on the other hand, covet access to the beach by foot, bicycle, or car. Any land-use issue here is a "minefield," according to Jimmy Miller, the fine Brora golfer I'd heard about during my first visit to Dornoch. The Brora course is a weathered links fifteen miles north of Dornoch, where sheep and cattle graze the fairways and rough; crofters want to retain their ancient rights to the land, while golfers would prefer they take their animals elsewhere. These matters haven't lent themselves to easy solutions in the past. They're unlikely to yield easy solutions in the future.

Most golfers hit a long iron off the first tee at Dornoch for position and then a wedge in. Longer hitters might choose a driver, and when the wind is at one's back from the south it's possible to drive the green. Steve Smyers, a course architect based in Lakeland, Florida, drove the green here during a practice round for the 1985 British Amateur. Two or three people were standing around the first tee when he hit his drive, and a few others were watching through the wide picture windows in the clubhouse bar. A hundred or so people soon caught up to Smyers. Word had gone out that a long-hitting American golfer was on the course. Nobody in our group hit the green, but we did get away nicely and made our pars.

Our group moved at a good clip down the front nine. The first six holes weave their way north, framed by a western wall of gorse and other types of nasty rough a few hundred yards across the links from the sea. The seventh hole is on higher ground, still moving north, while the eighth continues in that direction, the fairway plunging to sea level from a high ridge. The ninth turns back to the south, running along-side the sea. The holes continue south until the seventeenth, which reverses direction into the middle of the links. The eighteenth turns south again, finishing at a massive green near the clubhouse. Unlike the Old Course at St. Andrews and most links, at Royal Dornoch the sea is visible from nearly everywhere.

On that seventh hole, a long par-four on the upper part of the course, I hit a six-iron within a couple of feet for a birdie. I'm playing some nice golf, and Don favors me with a compliment. At least, I think it's a compliment.

"You have a sound swing," he tells me. "It's repeating, the same shape every time. It's unorthodox, but it works." Unorthodox? What does he mean? I don't like the word. I'm nothing if not susceptible. Yet, why should the look of my swing matter to me?

Stuart and I halve the front nine against Don and Chippie. "All square, then," Don says as we stand on the tee of the par-three tenth hole. The hole is cut just beyond three small, hellishly deep pot bunkers that defend the front of the green, and winds off the North Sea only a few yards to the left create havoc in the golfer's mind and with his ball. The shot requires height to clear the bunkers, but also penetration, so that the wind won't affect it. I hit a solid shot that finishes thirty feet past the hole, then make my birdie putt. One-up for the good guys. "Outstanding maneuver," says Stuart, a powerful golfer in his late twenties.

Don snap-hooks his tee shot into the cabbage at the par-five twelfth, and then tries a shot that a tour pro wouldn't attempt. He chooses a fairway wood, though his ball is only half-visible, slashes at it, and watches as it comes out low and ugly and slams into a protruding hill. What was he thinking? There was no way he was going to carry all the rough on his line from that lie.

"I am the worst caddy for myself," the virtuoso caddy for others says. Agreed.

The twelfth hole runs nearly parallel to and in the opposite direction from the fifth, where I spot a father walking with his son and daughter. They're enjoying an evening stroll on the course. As we played the front nine another fellow out for a walk asked us, "Which is the best way to Dornoch?" He wasn't a golfer, nor was he local. His question startled me for a moment, because I realized that it would never come up at a course back home. Golf courses where I live are open to players only. It doesn't matter whether a course is private or public; walkers aren't allowed. Here things are different. Golf courses, even private ones, are public spaces. What is the proper use of land? That was a pivotal question in the Highlands, and it was becoming a pivotal question for me.

One of the proper and most enjoyable uses is just walking. A footpath called Granny Clark's Wynd crosses the first and eighteenth

fairways at the Old Course, and people walk the links every night after
rounds have been completed at Open championships there. It's public
land, as is most of the land at Dornoch. Royal Dornoch owns some of
its course property, while the rest is on Common Good Land, as it's
called. Dornoch is not a private club as we use the term in North
America, though it does have members, seventeen hundred of them
drawn from the Highlands, other parts of Scotland, the rest of the
United Kingdom, and from around the world. The joining fee at Royal
Dornoch is U.S.$600, the annual fee less than half that. Scots shake their
heads when they learn of clubs that charge tens – or even hundreds –
of thousands of dollars to join.

Visitors can play Dornoch, unaccompanied by members. The club
sets aside members' times and visitors' times every day. Visitors this
summer pay £57 per round during the week, £67 on the weekend; a discount applies for visitors staying in local establishments. A golfer who
plays with a member is charged a £10 guest fee. (The club has made me
a temporary member for the season, and I will later apply for membership.) Royal Dornoch brings in a million dollars or so a year from
visitors, which allows it to keep its joining and annual fees down. But
fees have traditionally been low at most Scottish clubs, even before some
became lures to visitors. This affordability goes back to the idea that
golf should provide elementary recreation for people. The local golfers
in Dornoch didn't know their course was famous until visitors started
telling them it was. To them it was the course at the end of the village
by the sea, where they took their exercise and air and in the process
played some matches with friends – as I'm doing, with new friends.

Our match is nearing the end. The sixteenth, the High Hole, runs
along the shoreline and climbs up rippling ground to a massive green
raised well above the fairway. It's helpful to check the pin position on
this green before setting out on one's round, because it's impossible to
see the green from the fairway. I don't do this, forgetting just about all
the time. Still, I find the fairway with my drive and hit the green with

my second shot. I walk up the hill and settle near the green to watch Stuart's approach. An elderly couple is sitting on the bench left of the green, and looking out to sea. When the woman spots me, a golfer, at the top of the hill, she swivels to watch the next shot. Stuart's ball lands on the green and she turns round some more to see where it finished. The man sitting with her turns round as well, and both follow our group's progress. Stuart and I halve the hole in par with Don and Chippie, then do the same on the seventeenth. We win the match 2&1, shake hands with our opponents, and make our way upstairs to the bar. But first Don hands me the pound I've won. I roll it around in the palm of my hand. Feels good. I've won my first match at Dornoch.

Chapter 3

Dornochers

After deciding to spend the summer in Dornoch, I didn't think it would be difficult to find a place to live. But it turned out to be harder than settling on one way to swing a golf club. A hotel room wasn't an option for three months, nor was a room in a bed-and-breakfast. Nell and I looked into renting a home, and faxed and e-mailed back and forth to people in Dornoch for a couple of months before we realized this option wasn't going to be feasible either. Homes for rent went for short periods to golfers willing to pay just about anything. Three-month leases were impossible to find, because the big money was in rapid-turnover rentals. Out-of-towners who owned homes in Dornoch also liked to visit during the months when we would be there. We did locate a cottage in Clashmore, a pleasant hamlet three miles from Dornoch, but preferred to hold out for a place in the village itself. A flat would be perfect, but we weren't coming up with any possibilities as our departure time neared.

One interesting possibility in the center of town did present itself. I'd corresponded by e-mail with Bill Gifford, an international tax lawyer and man about the golf world – is there a course he hasn't played? – and Dornoch member. Bill also belongs to Machrihanish, an isolated, romantic links on the southern tip of the Mull of Kintyre in Scotland, Lahinch in Ireland, and St. Cloud in Paris, where his membership status is that of a "societere étrangere," for the club is required to maintain an "appropriate" number of outsiders, or strangers, as members. Bill was a Dornoch man above all, though, as demonstrated by the fact that he owned a home beside the second fairway and also a flat in town, where Dornoch's young professional Andrew Skinner – son of Willie, the pro when I had visited the club in 1977 – had lived for a while. Bill and his wife, Adda, had first come to Dornoch in 1990, when he felt an immediate attachment to the links and she to Dornoch and the Highlands. It was for both of them, Bill said, quoting Claude Rains in the film *Casablanca*, the beginning of a beautiful friendship.

Bill told me that his flat in town was for sale, and, after he decided that we were kindred spirits, that I could have it at no charge, unless it sold before I came to Dornoch. His flat, inevitably, found a purchaser, so I couldn't take up his generous offer. Still, he did invite me to use the golf library in his bungalow. "There are hundreds of golf books there," he wrote, "and lots more on photography and other subjects. So maybe that will spare you lugging your whole library over. Let me know if you want to check the availability of any titles – I don't exactly have a card catalogue."

Nell and I now had a place to read but not to live. Then we learned about the bookshop flat that was directly across from Graham and Lorna Sawyer's newsagent's shop, near one end of a short block that had a pharmacy, a bank, a bakery, and a small store that stocked provisions. It was a bookshop, for heaven's sake, and it was adjacent to the local library and right in the village. In a perfect world I'd have asked for a flat near the bookshop, which I'd been told was very good. Now I'd learned such a flat was available.

This is when I first contacted Sinclair Mackintosh, the owner, and he provided the details. He told me that the flat was on two floors and that it was huge. By then I was in regular contact with Tom Mackenzie, a course architect who works with the accomplished designer Donald Steel in Chichester, England, and who is a member at Dornoch. I'd met Tom a few times and asked if his parents, Bridget and Alex, who lived just outside Dornoch, might inspect it for us. They pronounced it livable, so I told Sinclair we wanted to go ahead with the rental. Sinclair said he would mail the lease and that I'd get it within a couple of weeks, but when it didn't arrive then, I told Nell something had happened and that we wouldn't be getting the flat.

"Oh, you're just being Hopewellian," said Nell, a more optimistic person than I. The term "Hopewellian" referred to my tendency to expect bad things to happen, and derived from the time we were on a small bus in Jamaica that tore around curves on a road not twenty feet from the Caribbean Sea. I kept my eyes shut, convinced we were about to topple into the water. We were near the town of Hopewell, but I wasn't hoping well. I was hoping only to survive the journey. Since then we dub my feeling of imagining the worst that can happen as Hopewellian. Call it a survival mechanism.

But, happily, the lease came through. I signed it, wrote a cheque for the rental, and returned it to Sinclair. Nell and I had found a flat to live in Dornoch, a bookshop flat.

• • • • • •

"Hello. Dornoch Bookshop," Lesley Bell, who, with her husband, James, owns the bookshop, answers a caller on the phone. It's high summer, afternoon, and the bookstore is full of people. I'm here for what has become a daily ritual. "Would you like a cup of coffee or tea?" Lesley asks me when she is finished with the caller.

"Tea," I say, and continue to browse.

Bookshops are central to my idea of the good life. I could live without television, radio, the Internet, and perhaps even without news-papers. But I'd be unhappy without books. The novel *Fahrenheit 451* frightened me, because Ray Bradbury, the author, imagined a world where books are burned. It's difficult to think of a world without books, or a home without books. To lose oneself in a book can be to find oneself: lost and found.

The Dornoch Bookshop looks inviting even from the outside. Lesley, who purchased the store in October 1999, always makes sure that its wide, arched windows, separated by double doors, are filled with books. One section usually has books of local interest – history, nature, and, sometimes, golf. John Macleod's history of the Royal Dornoch Golf Club is in the window today. Malcolm Campbell's coffee-table contri-bution called *The Scottish Golf Book* is also here. And inside there are shelves and shelves devoted to history, nature, golf, politics, loads of fiction, and children's books. The golf books are shelved next to books on the Clearances.

A fellow pops his head in and asks if Lesley has a book about seaweed he has ordered. He purchases the book, then inquires, "Can I buy your books online?" Lesley responds as if she's offended, putting the fellow on. "We're *not* on the Internet. What do you think we are?"

"A bookshop," he answers.

"Exactly," Lesley says. "We're a bookshop. Now you just go out in the sunshine and enjoy your seaweed book."

I finish my tea, and walk to the course. There I follow the ridge that skirts the left side of the course, jog up the path to the seventh hole and then down to the eighth green, where I turn around and make my way back toward the clubhouse. I clamber over the dunes at the fifteenth and onto the beach, where I find a friendly boulder and do what I call "rock-ups" – push-ups on a rock. I do some Zokercises, after Richard Zokol, a Canadian golf professional who is about the most positive person I know. Zokol has told me for years that I need to be more flexible, and that I should stretch to a full backswing position, hold that for a minute, and do the same with my full finish position. Three sets of rock-ups and three sets of Zokercises, a run on the beach, up to the clubhouse, and home.

When I reach the flat I poke my head into the bookshop again. It's a magnet for me. Things have quieted down in the late afternoon, and Lesley and I have a brief chat. She invites Nell and me for dinner when we can make it. Lesley tells me she was an "average" reader, and that her husband, James, a retired school chaplain, born in Glasgow, is the avid reader in the family. Lesley, who is from Royal Tunbridge Wells, a spa town in Kent, England, was a nurse, then a social worker. "I'm only just learning to be a bookseller," she tells me. Nice place to learn.

• • • • • •

The bookshop has closed for the day, but that only means the long, light evening is beginning. Alan Grant, a fellow with whom I corresponded prior to coming over to Dornoch, has invited me to the home he shares with his partner, Dot, an artist/sculptor, and their infant daughter, Ruby Moon. Her name was first Ruby and Ruby only. But Alan was driving home soon after her birth, under a full moon, and decided her name had to be Ruby Moon. A friend of Alan said he and Dot were lucky it wasn't pouring rain.

Alan is an eighth-generation Dornocher who belongs to the golf club. He works at The Carnegie Club at Skibo Castle as the resident Highlands host and general wildman, always ready with a story or a joke or a quip or an insult or a compliment. His job as the host, meant to make visitors feel at home, suits him well. He usually wears an assortment of odd clothes that suggest he's grabbed what's in the vicinity with his eyes closed: a madras shirt with yellow slacks, perhaps, along with red socks. The combination is blinding. Alan's surname is Grant, but it could also be "Gregarious." I learned that when I met him in front of the bookshop after calling to say that I'd arrived in Dornoch.

"Oh, you're Rubenstein," Alan said. "I wasn't quite sure what to expect after our e-mails in terms of your age. But I did feel we would get along. Another golfer who had to come to Dornoch, are you? And you plan to stay three months. You're worse than most. But I warn you. This place will get to you. It will do something to you."

Alan, Dot, and Ruby Moon live a mile or so from our flat, on a 220-acre farm in the country. The property has been in Alan's family since his father, Malcolm McDonald Grant, bought it in 1958. I make my way onto the property and toward the house, past a pile of potatoes so high and wide that, if mashed, it would resemble a huge sand dune. There's also a pungent odor in the air – pigs. The tubers are food for the hogs at the center of the farming enterprise. The house itself defines ramshackle. I squeeze through a small rusty gate to the front door and knock. Alan opens it a smidgeon and tells me to close it quickly. The rat exterminator has been on the property, and Alan doesn't want the cats to eat the rats or the poison. Best they stay indoors. I enter gingerly and follow Alan into the kitchen, where he sits me down at a wooden table. We're surrounded by papers, CDs, a computer in the corner, cans of food, herbs, books. This is a house that's lived in. Wonderful.

Alan likes his work at Skibo Castle, where he's a showman. "The idea is to give the appearance of a hick from the country, and still be able to talk to people about stocks and shares," he explains. "The trick is to be lucid. I love the idea of a wild old Highlander with scruffy boots, a kilt, and socks giving the appearance I'm from *Braveheart*, but being lucid. It fazes people."

Just now Alan is looking for a book he'd like me to examine, but his search is hopeless. "Finding anything in this house is tough," he says. "But, as you can see, we don't do 'neat.' That isn't something that concerns us. Life is too short to worry about neat. That's out of the way, so I'd like to know if you want some coffee. Oh yes, I forgot to tell you that we don't do coffee, not the coffee you probably like. We do instant coffee. If you consider that coffee you're welcome to it." I tell Alan to bring it on, and we chat while the water boils. I can't see a clock anywhere in the kitchen, and not wanting to appear like the clichéd American with no time to spare, I don't ask if one is nearby. I've already slipped into a gentler way of being anyway, and realize I've left my watch at the flat. Good. Let it stay there.

"You're in the Highlands now, Lorne," Alan says. "If something affects us, we care. If not, we pay no attention. There's no sense of urgency here. You'll see."

• • • • • •

Alan knows golf and enjoys talking about it. We're having that cup of instant coffee. Within a few minutes we've established our common ground – a feeling for the game and a feeling for how it, inevitably, wins over the long run.

"People come to Dornoch to golf," Alan says. "They think that here they'll find a better game, or become better golfers. Somebody who is a really good surgeon, musician, cook, or artist might think he can be good at golf, and that Dornoch will bring it out because that's all they'll be concentrating on here. They figure there's something in the air here that helps golfers. But golf's not like that. You can't just be a better golfer, even in Dornoch. Golf's about too many things. You have to accommodate imperfections in yourself that the game shows you."

Alan was warming up. Now he was telling me about his Great-Uncle Donald, his grandfather's brother. Alan, who was approaching fifty, had attended art school in London, where he lived in the flat that belonged to Donald's daughter, Wendy. Donald was born just outside Dornoch in 1888, and became an ordained minister. He eventually moved to London, but that was only a stopover for his wayfaring soul. Donald was a free spirit who traveled around the United States on Greyhound buses, lecturing on philosophy, politics, religion, and the social sciences. By the mid-1970s, he had done sixteen such lecture tours, traveling sixteen thousand miles during some of his journeys. He wrote two monographs related to his golf in Dornoch, the one about his experiences, called *Personal Memories of Royal Dornoch Golf Club, 1900–1925*, and another about Donald Ross, with whom he played some golf. Most of the time, though, Donald liked to play on his own, so that he could study golf courses. As much as he traveled the world, he felt himself a Dornoch man:

> Often the query arose as to my origin, where did I belong and what was my background? Always I was the Highland Scot and I took my audience with me to Sutherland, to Cathedral Dornoch and to Dornoch Links. Usually I mentioned Donald Ross, that distinguished Dornoch man, so much more widely known in North America than in Scotland.

Donald and his wife, Irene, were responsible for spiriting thousands of Austrian Jews to safety during the Second World War. Alan's affection for him comes through as he speaks of him. "Uncle Donald kept in touch with many of the Scots who emigrated to America. He traveled around visiting ill people there. And every three or four years he would show up at our house to rest, or at his sister Auntie Maggie Murray's. He spent time with American Indians and would bring back these beautiful blankets. He was also a conscientious objector in the First World War, and was sent to Dartmoor Prison for his beliefs. Irene was also a huge intellect. His end of the family was way out there, for sure."

Uncle Donald was also an accomplished golfer. When I first visited Dornoch in 1977, I'd purchased his memoir. I'd later read it, but had lost the booklet and hoped to find a copy when I returned to Dornoch. Alan had a few copies and offered me an edition published in 1985. Tom Watson had written the foreword, Herbert Warren Wind the preface. Watson had met Donald for an hour in the club secretary's office in 1981, when he first played the course.

"Don Grant's knowledge of the history and the philosophy of golf seem to me unrivalled," Watson wrote in his foreword. "His championing of Royal Dornoch as the course of courses – coming as it did from a man who has known and played as many courses in his long life's span as it is given to any of us to do – must rate a serious appraisal. For myself, I can only agree with his thesis that Royal Dornoch is at least one of the great courses of the five continents. I have played none finer, a natural masterpiece."

"He introduced us to golf," Alan says of his uncle. "I remember him just swishing the club back and forth on the back lawn. The game meant a great deal to him, and I suppose he introduced it to us as a grand game, a historical game. But that can also be too much, because golf really isn't a science and it shouldn't be made into much more than a game and a game only. Maybe I feel this way because I didn't take it up until I was thirty, having played soccer before."

Alan and I spoke about living on a golf course, which neither of us did. I was pleased to be in the bookshop flat rather than overlooking the course. I had never wanted to live on a course, and can't see myself ever wanting to. "I like to live away from the course so that I can see it in my mind's eye rather than being right there," Alan says. "If you live on it you can't travel to it."

That's right, isn't it? Sitting here, with the course a five-minute drive away, we picture it and look forward to a round there together. "I've played Dornoch five times this year," Alan says. "And every time I get on the first tee I get a tingle, something like, 'Ohmigod, what will Dornoch do to me today?' Dornoch is a woman in golf-course form. It will fuck you in every way and you'll come back for more. How do you pick a club to hit the sixteenth green, way up there on top of the hill? I've played it all my life and I still don't know what club to hit in. It's a four-club green. Or the eighteenth. How do you get the ball on the green with that dip and those humps in front? Land it short and run it on, but don't cut it or it will run off. I like to think of these shots as I sit here."

"That's the game, though," I chime in. "When the game is at its highest level it creates confusion in our minds. It's not just hit the ball in the air and land it on a dime on the green knowing it will stay there. The sharpest course designers put some wickedness into the holes. They want you to stand over the ball and wonder what will happen if it hits that hump and deflects to the right. Hmmm, so maybe that's not the shot. So I'd better aim left more. But if I aim left more and hit the ball a yard or two too far it will carry to the back part of the green and roll down a hill there into the gorse. Now your mind is going. Now the architect's got you. You're in sensory overload."

The course at Dornoch has already put me into sensory overload a few times, but I don't mind. I enjoy having the opportunity to picture different shots; the game is more engaging in this way. Too much think-ing and imagination can also make a smooth swing choppy. But maybe Dornoch's elegant links will engage my smooth swing as opposed to my jerky one. I'll need to trust my instincts on the course, so that, as Alan points out, whatever golfing senses I have will be activated. His idea of good golf is when it becomes automatic golf – golf that oozes out of the player.

It's late evening now, and we're moving into that golf-as-mysticism zone. I'm wary of this approach, but happy to slide along for the moment with Alan as we talk about Dornoch. He tells me that the village faces south, toward the heavily populated regions of Scotland, and that this is a favorable setting.

"Dornoch is just a good place," Alan says. "Forces converge in Dornoch. An amazing number of people who have spent some time here are out in the world generating good vibes toward Dornoch. The place is the essence of golf. There's a rightness about it. It's why an MGB is more attractive than a Lexus. You can touch it, but you can't surround it. We have two hundred words for it, but we still miss it."

I leave the farmhouse and make my way to my car. But I've left my jacket and return to get it. Outside in the sharp night air I start the car but realize I've also left my notebook on the kitchen table. What's happening? I'm not usually forgetful.

"This is all for the good," Alan assures me. "You're letting go."

Slipping along the country road into Dornoch, I think that's not such a bad thing. My life is like those of so many other people I know – full of detail, daily lists as long as a three-iron, in touch all the time via cellphone, fax, e-mail. Here I've happily slipped into a daydream state. For the moment I was absentminded. And maybe I should absent myself from my mind more often, or at least from the details that fill it. Eastern philosophers refer to the state of having an "empty" mind. It's always sounded clichéd to me, and don't we need minds crammed with information to get along in the world? Do I really want an empty mind? Maybe an "emptied" mind, to appropriate Tom Atkinson's term for the Highlands. The lands were emptied of people, a tragedy. A mind could be emptied of the detail that obscures perception. That wouldn't qualify as a tragedy. That could be useful.

Chapter 4

Rambles

There are two opposing ways to look at the 150 acres or so that a golf course consumes. One is to agree that a key attraction of the game is that a course roams over a vast expanse of land. Golfers who feel this way enjoy the open space and consider a course a way to preserve land. Many non-golfers, though, consider a course a wasteful and inefficient use of space. Here in the Highlands it's impossible not to be conscious of the way the land is used and not used. Ian Crichton-Smith, a Scottish poet born in 1928, writes in his poem "The Clearances" that in the future the empty lands will be full of golf courses: "We will be the hunters of golf balls," he declares. I have come to a region where history, and not only golf history, resides in the holes where I walk. Does it enhance one's appreciation of the game to appreciate historical matters, and not only those in golf? And how is one to respond to land issues? Land is a precious resource. How to use it best?

I was twenty-four – a long-haired, bearded backpacker – when I arrived in Tel Aviv in 1972, hoping to work on a kibbutz. Communal land. Like-minded people growing their own food, creating a community, living on the land. The kibbutz office in Tel Aviv assigned me to Sdot Yam on the shores of the Mediterranean. I took the bus to within a few miles of the kibbutz, and then hitched a ride to Sdot Yam, in Caesarea. German Jews had founded the kibbutz after the Holocaust and Second World War. I worked in the orange groves from dawn until the heat of the day sent us inside. A war veteran who collected antiquuities showed me what he had found in this ancient area and took me out on the beach as the day's heat slipped away. We hunted for Roman coins and then returned to his flat to drink lemon tea. I put a few coins on the windowsill in my digs and read about the history of the settlement and the area. Golf was far away, I thought. I hadn't brought my clubs to Israel, although I had come directly from Scotland where I'd stowed them.

To my astonishment, I found the Caesarea Golf and Country Club over a fence, bordering the kibbutz. It was the only course in Israel. Somehow I always ended up at a golf course, even here. Golfers could immerse themselves in Jewish history and play golf at the same time – a history lesson sandwiched between rounds of golf. Drink Maccabi beer and learn about the Maccabee soldiers. Hit a ball out of bounds and it could end up near a Roman aqueduct. One day in winter, when the course wasn't open, I jumped a fence to walk the holes. An attack dog tore after me. I sped back to the fence, climbed it, and nearly shredded my legs. Bleeding, I returned to my room and soon washed away my heightened sense of peril by dipping into the sea.

Golf rubbed up against history even in Israel, where land issues are fraught with millennia of anguish. I hadn't bothered to ask if there were courses in Israel, because I had assumed they would represent a profligate use of land. Water was scarce there. Golf courses needed water. *Ergo*, a course had no place in the country. The land was tiny, and courses took up a lot of space. People needed places to live, and a course took away land where housing might be built. *Ergo*, a course was unthinkable in Israel. But here it was, and I felt the pull of the game and from time to time borrowed clubs and played. I didn't know if I felt free there or tangled in a mess of history and modernity. The kibbutz was a social experiment. A golf course was a social experiment only to the extent that you believed people should be divided – those who could afford the game and those who couldn't. Socialism and capitalism existed side by side here, separated only by an out-of-bounds fence. I straddled the fence, a 1960s kid who rationalized away some of his ideals when golfing. And when I didn't golf? I was proud to participate in a noble social experiment – the kibbutz. "Smug" is the word that comes to mind when I think about that young man. That young man is middle-aged now. Smug still? As the Mannie looms over Sutherland I wonder.

"We will be the hunters of golf balls." Indeed.

• • • • • •

Nell has arrived. I picked her up at Inverness Airport and we drove north on a sunny, mild afternoon. Tired from the overnight flight to Glasgow, Nell was soon energized. Scotland's central belt is crowded, but soon recedes as one flies or drives north to Inverness. Room, finally. Traffic? What's that? The A9 goes past Dornoch all the way north to Wick and Thurso, beyond which there's nothing but ocean. It's a pathway to a place where we can see wide and far and where there's sky and not buildings. Tonight we will see the stars in the northern sky. By happenstance we now see the Red Arrows, a top-notch team of pilots who put on riveting air shows, and stop by the side of the road a few miles south of Dornoch, near the town of Tain.

It's Tain Gala Week. It seems that every town or village in the Highlands holds a gala week, when kids and adults come out to play. Carnivals fill fields, and consumption of candy floss, ice cream, and other assorted sweets soars beyond the usual high level. So does mine; I've had a fondness for wine gums for as long as I can remember and find them in abundance here. There's a festive air. Town councils place fresh flowers on the sides of the roads. The Red Arrows put on one of the most highly regarded air shows anywhere. We're lucky to have come upon them. What a welcome for Nell!

The shore road is crowded with Highlanders who have paused in their day to watch the show. Airplanes zoom in formation from the west, between and behind mountains, then swerve over the sea, bank, and do more maneuvers. Plumes of red smoke pour out of the planes' exhausts – hence the name Red Arrows. The exhaust systems have been filled with red dye to create the dazzling effect. Scots love ceremony and celebration, as we're learning. The notice board in front of the newsagent's shop in Dornoch informs passersby of concerts, agricultural fairs, Highland Games. Where's the supposedly grim Scottish personality? Where's the reputedly dour Scot? – a caricature if ever there were one.

On our way again, we soon turn east from the A9 to Dornoch. I'm excited to show Dornoch to Nell, and drive slowly toward the village. We cut behind the cathedral to the High Street, where Nell gets her first glimpse of the bookshop and Cheadle House. "There it is," I tell her. "Our home for the summer."

Nell's pleased with the flat. She likes its roominess, the views across to the village square. We get a peek of the North Sea out of a third-floor dormer window, and the kitchen really is large – a big room with a big view through the three high, wide windows. We lack only furniture, and the next day we drive south to a charity shop. There we buy tables, chairs, a dresser, a teapot. I brought an inflatable bed with me and have purchased a few dishes at the local ironmonger's. I've already piled books throughout the flat and hung a few prints of local scenes that were on sale at a café on the High Street. We also score three cool wrought-iron kitchen stools that we set down at the counter. Very retro. Ten pounds for the three. We had stopped at a combination butcher, poulterer, and fishmonger on our way back to Dornoch. There we picked up some "New Season Wild Salmon, So Very Tasty," as the notice in the window indicated. The fellow who takes our payment expresses surprise that wild salmon is still available, because it was scarce last year. But not now. There's a feeling of abundance in the air.

• • • • • •

Back roads can be viewed as analogues to back tees in golf. We drive them to see the way things really are. Most course architects, meanwhile, design holes from the back tees forward: the real hole plays from the back tees, while those ahead provide easier, faster routes for most players. A hole is not only longer from the back tees, but looks and plays differently. The back tee at the par-three second hole at Royal Dornoch adds only five yards to the shot, but it's higher than the forward tees and introduces an angle into the otherwise straight shot. Now the deep pot bunker at the front right of the green comes directly into play. Golfers aren't allowed to play the back markers here unless they get special permission from the club secretary or unless those tees are in play for a competition. I like to look at a hole from the back tees even if I can't play there. A golf course isn't static. Who would want to play a course from the same tees every round, or to holes that are cut in the same positions, or in the same wind? I prefer golf as an adventure, the B roads as opposed to the A roads or the M roads. The letter M in the United Kingdom indicates a motorway – the congested M25 ring road out of Heathrow Airport in London, the M90 to points north out of Edinburgh. I drive these roads and the A roads to get somewhere quickly. But the B roads – these invite journeys. I drive them not to get somewhere, but to stop wherever the urge hits me.

There's no stopping in the middle of M or A roads, not if you value your life.

Nell and I wander freely on these back roads. One afternoon we head for the hills to the south and west of Dornoch. After crossing the Dornoch Firth bridge, we turn west and make our way to the B9176, as it pitches and swerves in the hills overlooking the sea. There's a viewpoint at Struie Hill, a perfect spot to stop. It was from here that Don Greenberg first saw Dornoch, its cathedral spire, the shore. He keeps this view in mind when he's in Tampa during the winter. It's a talisman for him when he's stuck in traffic on Interstate-4 out of the city, heading east to Daytona or Jacksonville on the Atlantic Ocean. But the only east he wants is Dornoch east.

Music. Bagpipes. A lone piper stands on Struie Hill, in a plaid skirt and red jacket, her hair tied in a bow. How did she get here? We don't see a car or a bicycle. The young woman is looking out past a stone wall, facing the firth, piping and tapping her right foot. We're 660 feet above sea level, halfway to the top of Struie Hill. Moments. The air show yesterday. A lone piper today. The hills are carpeted in yellow whins. Later, reading Bridget Mackenzie's book *Piping Traditions of the North of Scotland*, I learned that the ghost of a fifteenth-century piper haunts Struie Hill. Now we're transfixed, listening as the piper picks up the pace, tapping with her left foot, then her right. She ends with a long skirl. Her name is Morag, and she speaks to us in the language of pipers when we ask her what she's played.

"I did a march to Spey on a reel, then a jig up, then a slow air, and two hornpipes. I played off that, then I played four jigs," she explains. I have no idea what she means, but I like the pipes and always have. I hate to admit it, but I liked Andy Stewart's schlocky song "The Scottish Soldier." It was music to me, Scottish music. I don't need to understand the pipes for its music to hit me hard. Most golfers don't know about fescue grasses or annual bluegrasses or kick points or asymmetrical spin patterns or launch angles. But they enjoy smacking the pill around anyway.

Still, I'm also here to learn. Morag tells us that she lives up the road in Bonar Bridge, and that in addition to the bagpipes she also plays the fiddle. "The pipes get the heave sometimes," she laughs. Morag is busking here on Struie Hill after getting a lift to her place of business. Nell and I move on and stop in Bonar for lunch. A shifty, inebriated old guy at the bar in a pub hears me order some food and bleats, "Canada." Most people here find my Canadian accent indistinguishable from its broader-vowelled American counterpart. "How did you know that?" He tells me there's "more than shite" in his head. I jaw with the guy for a few moments before Nell and I sit down on a couple of tatty pink-velvet chairs and have our lunch of potato-and-leek soup and toasted cheese-and-pickle sandwiches. Nell's appalled by the cloyingly sweet dark relish that's been slathered on the cheese. Scots sweeten everything. I scarf down her toastie. We look in the adjoining shop and consider the Ribblesdale Goat Cheese and a bottle of red wine from France called The Dog's Bollock's, but make no further purchases.

Two hours later it's early evening and I'm playing some golf as Nell walks along the sea with me. I hadn't noticed it before, but there's a far back tee on the twelfth hole, set in the dunes. From the usual tee in the middle of the greensward the hole plays straightaway before bending slightly to the green, which is protected by a huge, confounding hairball of a mound ten yards short. The hidden tee is way back in the dunes and to the left, so that the drive from here must carry two football fields of mean, snaggle-toothed rough. If the ground is hard as a desktop, as it often is, well, the ball off a drive can bounce through the fairway and into the rough on the other side. Two sets of tees, two different roads. A roads. B roads. The one way straight, the other crooked, and more revealing.

• • • • • •

Why do some people treat caddies as if they're distasteful creatures? Don Greenberg has said some of the visitors to Dornoch treat them like pond scum. Up at Brora one day I'm in a game with John, a fortyish fellow from Chicago who worked with the developmentally handicapped for eighteen years before transforming himself into a management consultant. He's come over to Scotland with Dave Pelz's *Putting Bible*, a gigantic book that the former NASA research scientist has written. He has a rangefinder that provides the exact distance from one point to another on the golf course. The Scots scoff at these tactics. They prefer golf that's more art than science, especially rocket science. A golfer should see the distance and choose the club for the shot. Ben Hogan was once given a precise distance for a shot and snarled, "I play the shot. I don't play the yardage." Anyway, a caddy is there to help a player figure out a shot. There's nothing better than playing a course with a companionable caddy, walking along, getting to know him, hearing stories – some of which are no doubt true. Most of the caddies at Highlands courses are also members of the clubs.

John's caddy is a member at Brora. Mine is Roy Wood, the cheerful club captain. On one hole John berates his caddy for not telling him he could reach a ridge with his drive. I cringe. John needs to show some respect. He's not a bad guy, but has been infected with some of the viruses that have worked their way into North American golf. To him a caddy is a servant. John is also a numbingly slow player. He takes thirty-one seconds from the time he puts the tee in the ground on the twelfth hole until he takes the club back. He checks every yardage, compulsively. Alan Grant should have a chat with John. Maybe Alan could convince John to start letting go of the habits that are preventing him from getting into the spirit of the game here. At least he's not using his rangefinder. Maybe he would feel embarrassed if he did. There's hope for him here.

The obsession to calculate and figure out every aspect of the game and the course is troubling. A course resists absolute knowledge – notwithstanding rangefinders, yardage books, and even experience.

Peter Thomson, the five-time British Open champion, who visits Brora regularly, was fortunate enough to have Roy as his caddy one day here. "All I ask is that you're sober and you do not give me a yardage," Thomson told Roy on the first tee. Thomson played the entire course that way, eyeballing every shot.

Too much calculation can take away from the pleasure of playing a course. Isn't the fun of the game to get away from golf by rote, particularly for amateurs? Sure, tour professionals who know exactly how far they hit the ball with each club can benefit by knowing precise yardages. Their game is all about numbers anyway, more than enjoyment. But do amateurs require this level of detail? They don't hit the ball solidly in the middle of the clubface more than a few times a round, so their distances vary even with the same club. Better to get a general sense of the yardage, feel the shot you want to play, and then swing away.

The members of the Shivas Irons Society, a group of golf enthusiasts fascinated by Michael Murphy's book *Golf in the Kingdom*, are into this sort of golf, although I'm beginning to think they make too much of the golf-as-a-metaphor-for-life idea. Murphy, who founded the Esalen Institute on the Monterey Peninsula in California – a center for self-improvement – invented Shivas Irons, a mystical golf pro who made pronouncements such as, "Let the nothingness into your shot," and, "Gowf is a place to practice fascination. 'Tis slow enough to concentrate the mind and complex enough to require our many parts."

I once played the last hole at the Pebble Beach Golf Links on the Monterey Peninsula in the dark with Murphy. We used glow balls that hissed as they flew. It was a lovely moment, although I'm not quite sure what the experience meant. The good folks in the Shivas Irons Society might be able to tell me. They're here just now, playing Brora. I'm participating in some of the fun with them, and am told that the members sometimes play quiet or silent holes where nobody is allowed to talk. They did that the other day at Dornoch on the eighth and seventeenth holes. Each is a perfect hole for silence because the fairways plunge into areas insulated from the wind and other golfers. "You can hear your shoe-leather creak, and the ball hitting the clubface," the Shivas Irons Society founder Steve Cohen, a jovial man from Monterey, tells me. "It's like being on the Miramichi River and listening as the salmon jump." The Miramichi is in New Brunswick. I've never been there but would like to visit. Fish jumping. Shoe-leather squeaking. Brora greens so hard that if I drop a ball down it bounces as if it's Indian rubber. The feel of the club in my hands and the ground under my feet and wind in my face.

A rangefinder? Yardages? I'm looking for ways to intensify my involvement in the game, not diminish it. I want a good walk enhanced, not a good walk spoiled.

• • • • • •

Adrian Bagott, a Dornoch member – "One gin and two tonics," he says when I ask how he spells his surname – knows about a good walk unspoiled. We're having a game at Dornoch along with his friend and fellow member Roly Bluck. Adrian and Roly walk along the fairways quickly, heads down, pushing their trolleys forward with vigor. Golf to them is as much exercise as it is sport. They're outdoorsmen. Roly, a former greens convener at the club, first visited Dornoch in 1975 and was immediately enamored of the flora and fauna. He picked every wildflower he could see, put them inside a folded scorecard, and took them back to his hotel. He'd picked twenty-five varieties. Adrian, meanwhile, challenged himself recently. He and his fellow cyclists rode from Bilbao in Spain to Waterloo in Belgium, 975 miles in fifteen days as they followed the route of the Napoleonic Wars.

Before Adrian set out on his marathon journey he practiced by cycling to the end of Loch Shin, a lake northwest of Dornoch. He had never cycled more than fifty miles, so he needed the work. Adrian was in good shape, but not ready to cycle nearly one thousand miles. With practice, though, he completed the journey. "It was a millennium project that one guy cooked up," Adrian said as we sped along the ninth fairway. "It's a one-off for me, in that I won't take cycling seriously. But I was fifty-seven when I did it, so it was a great feeling of achievement."

Adrian was looking for that feeling now on the course. Like most every Dornoch golfer, he had a strong sense of the game. I turned a two-iron right to left toward the twelfth green, following the arc of the hole near the green. Adrian, bless him, admired the shot and knew it had provided me a feeling of achievement.

"You had the shape of the shot, didn't you?" he noted. "I think the secret of playing these courses is you have to see the shot. You have to see it in the air and landing on the ground and rolling, and then translate that into your swing."

"This is meant to be old-fashioned golf," added Roly. "You run the ball in. You don't take your trampoline-effect driver and bash it as far as you can and hit your next up in the air to the green."

Note to myself about competing in the Carnegie Shield, the big Dornoch tournament a few weeks away: "Trust the game you have inside you. You've won tournaments. You know the game. You can feel the shots. Stop thinking. Start playing."

Argument with myself: "You like thinking about the swing. You've done books with some of the best players and teachers – George Knudson, Nick Price, David Leadbetter. You like to know why this swing worked and that one didn't. Only then can you let yourself play well. Knowledge first, then freedom."

In February 1925, Bernard Darwin, a scratch golfer, wrote a piece called "To Think or Not to Think: Speculation on Just How Much Mental Activity is Good for a Golf Shot." Good question. Darwin didn't answer it. He was only speculating. How much is good anyway?

Lots to think about, or not to think about. Time for a drive. Enough golf for now. Enough speculating.

• • • • • •

Nell and I go for a Sunday drive. We take the back road from Dornoch past Embo and turn along Loch Fleet, which pours into the North Sea. The single-track road that runs alongside has become our preferred route from Dornoch up to the A9, and today the sun is out for the first time in a few days. James Watson, who discovered DNA, was quoted in today's *Observer*, my favorite Sunday paper. "We like food, sun, sex." He claims these desires are the basis for evolution. Nell and I agree with the esteemed scientist.

Loch Fleet is a haven for birds that flock to its tidal basin and mudflats. James McCarthy in *Wild Scotland* mentions the impressive variety of birdlife here, "shelduck, oyster catcher and redshank in summer, and later in the year, there are large numbers of curlew, golden plover and knot." By mid-July some two hundred pairs of shelduck nest at Loch Fleet. Winter birds include the mallard and long-tailed duck, and seals are often visible from the sandbanks. The environment, with its surface layer of sphagnum under which lie thick deposits of peat, is so conducive to birdlife that Loch Fleet and the Dornoch Firth account for most of the more than five thousand birds that winter in the county of Sutherland. As I become sensitized to their birdsong, their presence adds to my enjoyment when playing golf in Dornoch.

One afternoon I run into Alan Grant in Luigi's, the popular café on Castle Street, where in the course of a couple of hours it's possible to see just about everybody in the village; they either stop in or walk by on their daily rounds. Alan stops by nearly every day, and sometimes he and Dot take orders and work the cash register. Alan can usually be found at the counter, having a coffee while reading the paper. Nell and

I have also taken to dropping in regularly for coffee and conversation. Alan's told me about Donnie Macdonald, known affectionately as "the Birdman." Donnie and his wife, Nannie, live just across the road in a house called Embank. Donnie was born in this house in 1915 and has lived here nearly all his life. He's never driven a car, but has explored all around Dornoch on his bicycle, and, sometimes, enjoyed excursions farther out with his friend, the local history buff, Jimmy Bell. I've wanted to meet Donnie and Nannie, so Alan takes me across and introduces me. The couple invite me right in.

Nannie pours Donnie a sherry and me a wee dram of whisky as we chat in their book-lined front room. He's a consummate birdwatcher, and has kept records in bound books of what he's seen. The first entry, in a volume called "Nature Notes," is from 1933; he recorded the arrival of summer migrant birds, noting that a pied wagtail had arrived on March 19 in an area called Sandycroft. On May 28, Donnie wrote that he "found a delightful slope covered with bluebells beside the River Evelix," and that "pink campions and the greenery of the tender young bracken sprinkled amidst the bells gave a charming effect."

"The more I scutted about on my bike," says Donnie, a tall, slim man wearing a glen-check jacket, brown V-neck sweater, green tie, and green-, red-, and blue-checked shirt, "the more I would get to know certain places thoroughly. Oh, we have a very mixed environment here, the links, the shore, small woods, hill country, moorlands, and lochans. I rambled all over the place."

Donnie loved the links, and is fond of remembering that he pretty well started golf as a twelve-handicapper and finished as a twelve-handicapper. To him the course is a nature preserve, and the species isn't only that of "golfer." The shore from Dornoch Point north has been a vast repository of bird and plant life to him. At eighty-five, he still goes out on his bike. The only equipment he takes along is his trusty binoculars. Later he records what he's seen, filling in lists and raising questions he will try to answer later. I don't imagine there's a more comprehensive record of natural history in the Highlands. He tells me that a person is lost without a hobby. Mine is golf, but while talking with Donnie I remind myself that I like the game for reasons that go beyond hitting the ball. I was attracted to Dornoch long ago because of its natural landscape. Like Donnie, I will walk the links from time to time without clubs. Walking without clubs; looking at birds while playing golf: people would think I'm batty for doing these things back home. They're accepted here. It's no wonder that I feel comfortable.

• • • • • •

I feel small in the Highlands landscape, but it's an agreeable sensation that has something to do with being in a place where man and landscape seem in proper relative perspective. At the same time this feeling reminds me of a disagreeable past here – the Clearances. From the top of Ben Bhraggie, at the base of the Mannie, the infamous monument to the first Duke of Sutherland, you can see the villages of Brora, Golspie, and Dornoch, where some families forced from the hills of the Highlands were sent to live. Life for the displaced was even harder than it had been in the hills, where they were able to provide for their families. The duke and others tried to turn the crofters into fishermen, but the fishing industry deteriorated. Untold thousands of Highlands Scots chose or were coerced to leave their homeland. They went to Canada, the United States, Australia, and New Zealand, and while their immigration was a huge windfall for the New World, the Highlanders themselves felt the burden of exile. Sea journeys were perilous, often deadly. Far from their homes in the straths between hills, they would long for this land now emptied.

These hills are empty of people and they are desolate and they are wild and they are awe-inspiring because of what happened here. When

I walk here I feel the ghosts, and if my foot brushes against a boulder, I may wonder as to whether it once reinforced a croft and whether a soon-to-be-banished family once farmed the land and lived here.

• • • • • •

In Toronto, Nell and I walk often. Earl Bales Park is just around the corner from where we live. It was once a golf course where I caddied as a boy. I still see the raised areas that were tees, the mounds and hollows that framed greens. But I'm glad the property was turned into a public park. Singer Loudon Wainwright referred to a golf course as Mother Nature with a manicure. This park has gone natural again; it's not manicured. Large Filipino families hold barbecues and birthday parties there. People chatting in Russian walk their dogs. Older Yiddish-speaking folks play cards inside a park clubhouse and kibitz at tables outside. Kids ride their bikes and ski down a modest hill during the winter. We called it Killer Hill, probably because it's exactly the opposite. I remember the hill as the part of the course that sent golfers down to the ravine valley and near the Don River that carves through the center of Toronto.

Away from the park, Nell and I also walk city blocks. Blocks and blocks. I'm inspired by a couple I knew years ago who most every summer weekend picked a few blocks in the city and walked them intensively, stopping in shops and cafés. Walking is a good way to know the city. But these walks aren't hikes, nor are our walks in the park. To hike is to get out into the countryside, and, preferably, countryside with which one isn't familiar. We're not familiar with the Highlands, and enjoy losing ourselves in the environment. Not lost, literally, but lost in the sense that we leave our city selves behind and tramp along – as we ramble, like Donnie the Birdman.

Nell thinks of these hikes and the way we're spending our time in Dornoch as unconstructed time. We don't know where we'll be in an hour when we hike or set off for a drive. I'm starting to play golf like this also. I rarely make a starting time, showing up when I feel like playing. That's often in the early evening, and many times I play only a few holes before walking back to the clubhouse as twilight settles across the course and the moon fills the northern sky. I'm letting go, not keeping score, not playing the holes in their usual order, not playing a set number of holes. Golf as unplanned minutes and hours.

I think about these matters often in Dornoch, maybe because I'm outdoors so much. I feel free. After playing the course for a while I've come to think of it as a place for exercise and thought, as much as for the game itself. The horizons are so wide that, while looking around, I keep seeing places I'd like to explore. Tarbat Ness is one such place, nine miles away as the crow flies, and a fifteen-mile drive across the Dornoch Firth bridge, along a B road through the fishing village of Portmahomack – Port Tomahawk to most people after a few times of trying to pronounce it properly. It's the only Scottish town on the east coast that faces west, because of its location on the hammerhead of the peninsula. Portmahomack catches the evening light, and Dornoch the morning light.

Nell and I have planned a hike around the Tarbat Ness lighthouse. It's a long coastal walk of some nine miles, so we figure on a full day. The lighthouse is our eventual goal, but to start we move in the opposite direction, making for the shore. The hike takes up eight hours, some of which puts us on rocks strewn at the water's edge and across boggy land where sheep graze, their hooves leaving craters in the ground – and that's not the only trace they leave. Maybe the guidebook around which we're framing our hike should read, "Turn left at the kissing-gate stile near the end of the path, and take care to dodge the sheep turds as you make your way uphill." Along a shelf we walk above the water line, looking back at Dornoch and out to sea. This was the opposite view, of course, from the seafarers who used the Tarbat Ness lighthouse. They sought landfall. We sought the wide views and the feeling of being "out there" that an edge-of-the-world coastal area can provide.

Nell and I reach Tarbat Ness in late afternoon, at high tide. The only sounds are those of shorebirds. We feel the "agreeable sense of fatigue" that my friend Archie Baird feels after a round of golf at his beloved Gullane #1 course in East Lothian. That agreeable sense deepens while we drive back to Dornoch, along back roads. The ride takes us forty minutes. Why drive quickly?

Back at the flat we warm up with a wee dram. The propane tank out back hasn't been filled yet, so the flat is cool. It's no simple matter to get the tank filled, because the path from the High Street between the bookshop and the library next door is so narrow that the power company has to send a special truck to get to the tank. It doesn't come up this way regularly. No problem. Wee drams are always available. And Nell and I have each other.

Chapter 5

Nell and Me

Nell. Nell and me. Who would have thought? We had known each other for some twenty years before we were married in 1992, but had led lives that intersected only occasionally. Nell had been married in 1969 to Dennis Waldman, a Torontonian. They were two children of the 1960s who met at the University of Detroit, demonstrated against the war in Vietnam, and had even been tossed into jail briefly in Chicago – live at the Cook County Jail – because of their anti-war protests. They moved around for a while in Canada. Nell is American-born, from Grand Rapids, Michigan, but like others of her generation, she left the United States in something akin to despair in the late 1960s. Nell and Dennis finished their BAs and a couple of graduate degrees. Nell went on to teach college English, while Dennis, bright, funny, committed, intense, was a much-loved teacher in Toronto's Jewish community. They also had two kids, Jaron in 1973 and Jessamyn in 1976. In 1980 they moved back to Toronto, into pretty much the same neighborhood where I had grown up.

I'd completed a master's degree in psychology, but hadn't settled on what I was going to do from there. I was lucky in that I didn't focus on a career until one – golf writing – snagged me. By the mid-1970s, I had found a part-time job as the curator of the Royal Canadian Golf Association's museum and library at its new Glen Abbey Golf Club in Oakville, twenty miles southwest of Toronto. There I started to write for the Canadian Open program. In 1980, while caddying in the Canadian Open at the Royal Montreal Golf Club, I began to write a column for the *Globe and Mail* in Toronto.

Nell and I shared a large crowd of friends. As these things go, smaller groups of friends formed within the larger collection. Every so often we would all meet at a party or a family occasion, but for the most part we lived our lives as young adults within the smaller, tighter groups of closer friends. In the late 1980s, I started attending dinners that some of the guys organized periodically. Jerome Lyons, one of my best friends and one of Dennis's closest pals, had invited me to the dinners, but I'd been unable to attend because of my travel schedule. I finally got to one.

The conversation at that dinner flowed easily. Oddly enough, I'd known Dennis when we were boys, because his cousin Brian, a friend of mine, lived five houses down the road from me. Dennis and I saw each other when we visited Brian at the same time. I liked him and I think he liked me.

A few weeks after that dinner, in May of 1989, my father died of a heart attack. During the week of mourning known in Judaism as shiva, Dennis visited the house where my parents had lived since 1965. There were stories about my dad from his days as a professional football player with the Winnipeg Blue Bombers in the Canadian Football League. Dennis and I, along with other friends, parked ourselves on the deck and traded stories of our fathers.

The shiva ended, and family and friends returned to their lives. Three weeks after my father's death, on June 2, I got a call from Jan, Jerome's wife. She told me that Dennis had died of a heart attack that morning as he was teaching. He was forty-one years old.

Family and friends rallied around Nell and the children, who were somehow finding the strength to cope with their unthinkable loss. Day and night their home was filled with people who came to comfort them. I was one of those people, part of the larger group whose attention and care was focused on this family that had lost a father, a husband, a son. The home radiated a deeply affecting warmth, and within its cocoon everybody drew closer. In the next year, as one of the group of people who surrounded Nell and the kids, I became attached to them. Nell and I became close friends; we shared interests in books, music, and film. She had read some of my work over the years, and she willingly acceded to my request to read the manuscript of a book I was working on then.

"So, are we dating or are we still just friends?" I asked Nell after eighteen months of hanging around her house. Or maybe she asked me. Or maybe our mutual friends were starting to hope? Participating in one another's lives without the pressures of "dating" had generated a force field between us.

Nell and I were married in January 1992. We came together in the aftermath of a tragedy, which would always be the background to our story. But this was a beginning for both of us. Something very good had come in the wake of something very bad. There weren't any particular lessons to be learned in this, except for the old adage that it's important to keep on keeping on.

We kept on all right. Nell – acquainted with neither the game nor the world of golf – has come to know it on, shall we say, intimate terms. Once, in a column about her experiences as golf consort, she wrote about the sheer weirdness of some of the folks she met in (she would always acknowledge) some of the best places in the world: "There was Nick Faldo, pressing the flesh at a cocktail party in Jamaica, with a full glass of beer tucked into his breast pocket. Who could forget the batty British golf collectors at Gullane's course number three, gesticulating wildly as they impressed me with their prints, knick-knacks, and hickory shafts – truly Pythonesque in their strangeness?"

• • • • • •

Was anything odder to Nell, though, than the labyrinthine ways in which golfers inspected their swings? I've never heard Nell discuss how she might make her crawl stroke more efficient, or attain more speed while cycling if she develops more aerobic capacity or leans forward more on her bike. She knows golfers are different. It's analyze this, analyze that, and while I came to Dornoch with hopes of freeing myself from the tangle of swing thoughts in which I'd become ensnared, still, I am who I am. I don't think I'll ever be free of thinking about my swing. That being the case, I was pleased to meet David Thomson, the professional at Skibo's Carnegie Club. Nell dropped me off there and went for a swim at the colossal, spooky antique swim pavilion at Skibo Castle. I wondered whether I would sink or swim, because it wasn't long before David said the magic words to me.

"There are a few things we could do with your swing," he suggested while we played the course. "It's mostly a matter of your posture, your takeaway, and then your move through the ball. [Ah, that's all, I thought.] We'll get you into a more athletic position and a more physical swing. You obviously have a lot of talent, because you're a low-handicap player even with all the things you do wrong."

David hits the ball miles, and I've lost distance, especially with my driver. "I can get you thirty more yards with your driver," David told me. I was hooked. Anybody who promises me thirty more yards is sure to get my attention.

"Great, when can we start?" I asked him. He suggested we wait, because he would be traveling. Besides, the British Open was coming up soon at the Old Course, and we would both be attending. The two-time

U.S. Open champion Ernie Els was also coming up to The Carnegie Club, which might provide an opportunity for David to work with Els. He said he would have more time after the Open. Meanwhile, I salivated at the thought of getting those thirty more yards.

• • • • • •

The Carnegie Club at Skibo Castle opened in 1995. Peter de Savary, a British businessman, had purchased Skibo Castle and its 7,500 acres in 1990; little did de Savary, P.D.S. to his friends and family, know that, on December 22, 2000, pop star Madonna would choose the castle as the site of her marriage to film director Guy Ritchie. Nor could Dornoch itself – which the *Sunday Herald*, a national Scottish paper, described as "a sleepy shortbread tin of a town in Caithness," never mind that it's in Sutherland – imagine that it would be besieged by more media than it has residents. Madonna would also have her four-month-old son with Ritchie, Rocco, christened at Dornoch Cathedral. The week would bring Dornoch to the attention of the world – welcome CNN, welcome BBC – and cause a predictable tension between local people who weren't all that impressed and those who felt the publicity would enrich the village.

Andrew Carnegie, perhaps Scotland's most famous son – with a nod to Sean Connery – made his fortune in the steel business in the United States and became the world's most generous philanthropist; there are Carnegie Free Libraries all over Scotland, the rest of the United Kingdom, the United States, and Canada, including the one beside our flat. Having emigrated to the United States in 1848, he eventually wanted a home in Scotland, and so chose Skibo Castle. Carnegie bought Skibo in 1898 and took up golf ten years later, when he was sixty-three. There are a couple of ways to read his late interest in the game. One is that he simply liked the game once he discovered it. The other is that he wanted to become a member of Royal Dornoch, but didn't want to admit he hadn't played golf, and so decided to build his own course where he could learn the game. Carnegie enlisted John Sutherland, Dornoch's club secretary, to help design a nine-hole course for him on the property, between Loch Evelix and Dornoch Firth. He also took lessons from English golfer J. H. Taylor, who eventually won five British Opens.

The property at Skibo and the castle itself deteriorated after Carnegie died in 1919, but remained in the family until 1982. After de Savary bought it he hired Donald Steel to design a new course, the original nine holes having long reverted to nature. Tom Mackenzie was on-site for much of the construction of the course, whose views extend over the firth and Loch Evelix, and west to the mountains. The course traverses part of Carnegie's original nine-hole layout; it's a centerpiece of the property.

Steel, a golf writer and an accomplished player who had competed in the 1970 British Open at the Old Course, prefers to move as little earth as possible when designing a course, and to provide as many shot options to players as possible. Tom Mackenzie and Martin Ebert, Donald's other design associate, feel the same way. They believe golf should offer the player a feeling of freedom.

Tom elaborated on his design ideas one afternoon when we made our way around The Carnegie Club. It had poured the night before, the rain billowing over the hills immediately to the west of the course. The next afternoon, as we walked the course, all was clear. Tom had brought along the original plans. Things change on a course. Trees and bushes grow, which can mean that a course doesn't look the same after a while. The nature of a course can change over time – so much so that it's impossible to present it in the form the designer had in mind.

This has happened at The Carnegie Club in small but noticeable ways. As we walk the holes, Tom mentions that this course is all about the views – of the firth, Loch Evelix, Struie Hill. From the corner of the second hole, where the fairway turns to the right, Tom looks up the tenth fairway and notices that his view is blocked by bushes that have grown and that require trimming. "That worries me," Tom tells me and the course manager, Jock, a ruddy-faced man from the Black Isle in the Highlands whose full name is John Macgregor McDonald Mackay. "It's all cloaked now by the growth. We need to break it up."

There's a perfect example of what Tom means when we stand on the second green and look through a gap in the bushes. We can see Struie Hill from here, but, Tom explains, "We'll need to control these bushes, because if we don't it won't be possible to see the Struie."

Jock is a Dornoch enthusiast, and knows what Tom means. He enjoys walking the first couple of holes, then rounding the corner past a hedge to the third tee. "You can see very nearly the whole course from there," Jock says. "That's where Dornoch has an advantage over us. You can see the course from nearly everywhere. It's laid out in front of you, without trees and bushes to interfere with the views." Dornoch, a links, offers nearly 360-degree views at some points; a links, situated as it is beside the sea, is treeless.

At The Carnegie Club, Big Jock, as he's known, would like to present views that take advantage of the surrounding unbroken landscape. There's a delicate balance between controlling the landscape and allowing it to express itself. The entire site for the course was fenced off during construction to keep rabbits away. Yet rabbits also eat the tops of bushes and keep them under control. The rabbits haven't returned to the course, which indicates that artificial means have been used to control the growth of the bushes. Tom and his associates at Donald Steel's company aren't the controlling or imposing types, but they also don't want this course to turn into one where the golfer has to play down corridors between high bushes that obstruct views.

Less is more in the Steel camp. You won't see many bunkers on a Steel course, and what bunkers there are will be small, although deep and penalizing. I'd often played the first Steel course in North America, peaceful Redtail, near London, Ontario. The course is named for the red-tailed hawk found in the area, has but twenty-eight bunkers and only one forced carry over water, an eight- or nine-iron shot to a par-three. Steel likes golfers to enjoy themselves and their surroundings, but at the same time he challenges them by making them think. There's no such thing as an automatic shot at a Steel course, because the golfer often has the choice of running a shot into the green or flying it in, bouncing a chip shot off a knob or pitching it past the knob. It's artless design in the sense that Steel imposes so little on the landscape, or no more than necessary. But maybe that's not artless at all. His art is to leave just enough alone, which means adding just enough.

It's Jock's job to maintain the balance, along with input from Tom and Donald. He's attached to this landscape, a man at home on the course. Jock looks as if he lives outdoors; his face is a product of the wind and the sun. His hair is white and his thick sideburns are the color of whisky. Today he's wearing a long-sleeved green sweatshirt, olive corduroy jeans, and walking boots with rubber soles. He hasn't missed many meals, but doesn't look overweight either. I'm told the story of when he and his four sons consumed seven roast chickens at a meal in Inverness. A man who spends so much time outdoors walking a course will develop a hearty appetite. He lives in Embo, near the North Sea.

Jock helped build the Chunnel, that underwater link between England and France across the English Channel. He and the other workers received medals after breaking through to France in the under-ground shaft, four hundred feet deep. "What a tremendous job to work on," Jock tells me, with obvious pride.

I'm a little envious of a man so at home in his environment. He knows this place intimately. Jock points out a twelfth-century track on the course; it was once an old coach road in Dornoch. "The old A9," Tom says. We continue our walk to the end of the course. Struie Hill is carpeted in purple heather, an image that will become fixed in my mind as the backdrop to this course. We head in for lunch – cream of tomato soup, fish and chips, and sticky toffee pudding. Alan Grant eats with us, and soon we're talking about the Carnegie Shield. He asks somebody who played last year what he thought of the event.

"I wasn't around long enough to have any thoughts," the fellow says.

• • • • • •

The Clearances are in the news again, because de Savary has aspirations to hold a tournament at The Carnegie Club and wants to build a second course on the property. Today's *Northern Times* has published a story on the matter. The course that de Savary wants to build is earmarked for the Pulrossie estate, or farm, on the property, and the current tenant farmer, Graham Burnett, would have to move to make room for the course. He's been offered compensation and told he could move to another area of the estate, where he could continue to farm. But Burnett says he hasn't agreed to these terms. The paper is reporting that the National Farmers Union has taken up his cause because it's concerned about the implications for all tenant farmers.

To many people this idea – of the rich moving a tenant off land – recalls the Clearances; others in the Highlands consider this a knee-jerk reaction. John MacAdam, a candidate for the Scottish National Party in the Highlands, has written a letter to the *Northern Times* in which he refers to the situation at Skibo as the Pulrossie Clearance. "It is hard to believe at a time when feudal structures are finally being demolished," he writes, "that a hard-working family should be faced with the threat of an abrupt end to the diligent efforts of the last forty years."

This delicate matter goes to the core of land usage here. As Brora's Jimmy Miller said, the issue is a landmine of controversy.

• • • • • •

"Bennie 474," the man on the other end of the phone answers. It's Macarthur Bennie, the captain of the Royal Dornoch Golf Club. He answers the phone by stating his surname and the last three digits of his phone number. It wasn't that long ago when Dornoch numbers were only three digits, and that's how Macarthur remembers his. Things have changed as the population has swelled to over one thousand – one thousand three hundred, to be exact. Now one has to call 810474, and if you order a new number, you're an 811. That's us, 811742, as handed down by British Telecom. It's easy to tell who has been in Dornoch for a while, then. An 810, that is, not an 811.

Macarthur and his wife, Anna, are grandparents to the lovely Ruby Moon Grant. They're the parents of Dot Bennie, Alan's partner, and they live along the Cuthill Road – pronounced Kettle – that runs south and west of Dornoch for a few miles until it turns up against the A9, just to the north of the Dornoch Firth bridge. It's a single-track road, with room enough for one and a half cars, but not two. As on all single-track roads in the Highlands, passing places are provided – half-moon-shaped areas scooped out of the side to allow a driver to slip in and allow an oncoming car to continue. The Cuthill Road tracks past a few substantial homes just off Castle Street before heading through countryside. Now we're out in the open, with the firth to our south and east, past the Cuthill and Dornoch Sands – the beach. The Bennies' modern 1970s home is raised above the sands. The prospect from the living room, graced with three walls of windows, is toward the firth. There's a greenhouse, gardens, and, in the house, books everywhere. One of Dot's complex wire sculptures, this one of a bird, is sitting on the piano just inside the entrance. Ruby Moon and her mom are often at the house in the mornings. I could spend many mornings here, looking out at this corner of the Highlands while reading.

Macarthur is a sixty-seven-year-old retired dentist. He's serving the last couple of months of his two-year tenure as club captain, the most important position in a Scottish golf club. Bennie is wearing a lime sweater with the Royal Dornoch crest, and a club tie. He's a Dornoch man. Alan Grant says that a Dornoch man is one who would go straight from a late-afternoon wedding in full Highlands dress – kilt and all – for an evening round. Macarthur wasn't born in Dornoch; the Bennies are from Glasgow. But that was a long time ago.

Macarthur started practicing dentistry in 1959. In those days he worked morning and afternoon seeing his patients, and then returned to the office to see what he called the "casuals," people who needed dental work but weren't his own patients. The job of chief dental officer for the county of Sutherland came up in 1965, but the position didn't appeal to Macarthur. He had never been that far north in the Highlands, although he had heard of Royal Dornoch. Still, he was invited up for an interview and decided to come north to examine the terrain. The A9 was blocked by snow, and so the young Bennies drove up by the Glencoe Road, leaving Glasgow at five in the morning one late November day. They skirted Loch Ness as the sun came up and the sky turned pink, navigated around the Dornoch Firth along Struie Hill, and reached Dornoch in the early afternoon. There the Bennies learned that the meeting had been canceled because of the weather. A message had been sent to them at the Inverness rail station, because nobody thought the Bennies would chance a drive in the snow. Macarthur was invited back the following week for the meeting, but said he had but one plan, and that was to never return.

Right. The job wasn't settled by March and in the meantime Bennie had been offered another interview at his convenience. He came up with a friend in February, took the position, and started in May. The postmaster in Dornoch was the golf club's secretary. Macarthur handed him five pounds and became a member of the club. He practiced dentistry in the Highlands for nearly thirty more years, assisted by Anna, and took particular interest in the prevention from birth of dental problems. His work was the essence of practicality, as he worked toward introducing fluoridation into the water systems in the Highlands. That wasn't easily done, because there was resistance then that persists even now; fluoridation hasn't become standard in Scotland. Lesley in the Dornoch Bookshop told us of a middle-aged woman from the western Highlands who came into the store and said, proudly, "Look at my teeth. When I was twenty-one my mother decided she would give me a really nice birthday present. Every one of my teeth was pulled out and I got a full set of dentures." That was preventive dentistry then. Some prevention is practiced now, but there are disconcerting numbers of walking dental disasters all over Scotland. During my summer in Dornoch I also noticed more than a few announcements of meetings whose purpose was to protest further fluoridation. Macarthur boycotted the local grocery stores until these notices came down.

Oddly enough, Macarthur and Nell found a mutual dental connection, in Grand Rapids of all places. Nell's birthplace is one of the few cities where fluoridation was introduced into the United States in the late 1940s on an experimental basis. Macarthur was so happy to hear that Nell was from Grand Rapids that he leaned over and said, "I've spent my life using Grand Rapids as a model, but yours are the first teeth I've seen from there." He looked at her mouth, where sits a reasonably straight and white set of middle-class American choppers. All her own, Nell avers.

Nell and Macarthur talked about the Grand Rapids dental connection for a while. I sat back on a leather couch, enjoying the wine, smoked salmon, cream cheese, and shortbread that Anna had set on a coffee table. I looked out across the gardens at the firth. In a moment I was awakened from my reverie. Anna had brought out a hand-painted platter that schoolchildren in the west Highlands village of Kinlochbervie had presented her and Dr. Bennie. The platter showed a view over the village, and reminded Macarthur of the work he had done with the kids.

"To you this plate we do bequeath, for looking after all our teeth." We read the inscription, finished our wine, and left Macarthur and Anna. I felt so at ease that I was reminded of a saying a golfing pal of mine, a man in his seventies, likes to use. "I'm so relaxed I need a pill to tighten up." Alan Grant was having his way and proving he knew whereof he spoke. I was letting go. I was slipping into Dornoch ways, where people spent time with one another, and where time was more than something you had lost, or didn't have enough of. Even Madonna's wedding, I subsequently figured, wouldn't change that. Dornoch was too old to be flung forward into the new and changed by a super-celebrity affair. At least I hoped that would hold true.

Chapter 6

Palimpsest

There's an eerie legend attached to a farm with the fetching name of Cyderhall a mile or so to the west of Dornoch along the Cuthill Road. Cyderhall was originally called Sigurd's Howe, or Sigurd's burial mound, and marks the resting place of one of the Viking pillagers who wreaked havoc all over Scotland. Sigurd the Powerful was a Norse leader, the Earl of Orkney, who with his men in their longboats had succeeded in occupying the north of Scotland by AD 887.

Sigurd arranged a parley near the Dornoch Firth with a local chief, a Pict, named Maelbrigte. Maelbrigte was a brave man, renowned not only for feats in battle, but also for his oddly deformed front tooth that stuck out horizontally, or so the story goes. Sigurd double-crossed the Picts by bringing twice his allotted number of fighters. He slew Maelbrigte, and lopped off the chief's head.

Sigurd galloped back to his stronghold north of the firth with Maelbrigte's head bouncing alongside his leg, attached to his saddle-horn

76

by means of Maelbrigte's long hair. However, the Norse saga writers, who have bequeathed us this tale, portray Sigurd as a villainous cheat who violated the rules of civilized parley. Maelbrigte wreaked his revenge when his tusk, as it were, penetrated Sigurd's skin and inflicted a fatal case of blood poisoning. The Viking chieftain is said to be buried at Cyderhall (though nothing of him has been found). His story is a grim analogue to the nature of Scottish history, a tale of often grotesque violence and treachery that lies just millimeters below the country's seemingly placid surface. No doubt about it – it's got teeth.

As we approach Dornoch off the A9 via the Cuthill Road, Cyderhall soon comes into view. The road takes us past the Bennies' home and the Dornoch Lochans, a local fishing hole where there's also an out-of-the-way driving range. I've hit balls here a few times just for the tranquility of the place. There's usually nobody else here, not even the proprietor. The idea is to put a few coins into a bin, which then drops golf balls into a pail. Basic stuff, and appealing for that.

Sometimes Nell and I ride our bikes out to Cyderhall and back. Returning, we reach Dornoch at Castle Street, the main drag. In the summer months, Castle is festooned with lush flower baskets that enliven the not-quite-gray, almost taupe stone homes and shops that line the street for a few short blocks. For Nell and me, Castle Street landmarks come to include Luigi's Café – where an espressochoc late in the afternoon replaces our Starbucks addiction – the friendly Eagle Hotel pub, a golf-talk-live kind of place, and the gourmet 2 Quail restaurant (on one occasion anyway), where well-heeled incomers and visitors, for the most part, savor fine food in an intimate setting that seems like the owners' cozy dining room.

Then comes the ironmonger (hardware store) and what's known locally as the "wee Spa" (the size of a party store). Just a block to the left is the "big Spa" (a fairly small grocery store to North Americans and Brits, who are used to jumbo-sized Meijers, Publix, Loblaws, Safeways,

Piggly Wigglies, and Sainsburys). The Spar chain of groceries – pronounced "spa" in these parts – is the IGA of north Scotland. Here we can get what we need, though sometimes the vegetables, imported from France or the Netherlands, look in need of resuscitation. Local people tend to grow their own in the summer. The "spas" really are party stores, stocking a full range of beers, some wine, and other liquor, including both single malts and the cheaper stuff. Early on, one of the White Settlers (the unflattering Highlands name for wealthy English who retire north to golf and booze and treat the locals as unenlightened savages, and that recalls condescending attitudes toward indigenous peoples in the days of empire; the appellation can be used in a wryly humorous way, but its undercurrents bespeak an ongoing tension in the Highlands) tells us that we should eschew single malts if a local buys us a drink: "They'll think you're toffs," he explains. "The Scots drink cooking whisky."

Just past the wee Spar, Castle Street opens up into the square, which is not actually square, but more an off-kilter oval with the Dornoch Cathedral near its center. Once more, history – writ large – impinges. Its old churchyard is across the street from our bookshop flat on the High Street. It forms something of a front yard – and a focal point as I look up from my keyboard and gaze out the dormer window from my third-floor study. It's hard to worry about missed putts when I'm reminded of the long view beneath the window, but that doesn't stop me from worrying when I'm on the course and away from the graveyard. Beyond the graveyard from my study I can see centuries-old stone houses, the castle, the Common Good Lands, the moody, windswept firth, and the Highlands to the south. But I digress.

Tradition has it that a sixth-century Irish monk named Finbarr established a religious community at the east end of this graveyard, which, as such, is out of bounds for archeological excavation. Finbarr and his monks may have been early Christian proselytizers in the

Highlands, but they were relative latecomers. There had long been human habitation in the area. The remains of neolithic cairns and brochs (unique circular towers) dot Sutherland and tell of a small hunting and tilling population that dates back about 4,500 years. At some point during the Iron Age, the Celts arrived; they were a fighting people who swept across a good chunk of Europe and appalled the Romans with both their ferocity and their penchant for human sacrifice. The Romans could never subdue the Celtic tribes in what is now Scotland. They called them Caledonii and, after centuries of raids, opted for the simpler expedient of walling them in. And out of Roman Britain.

Hadrian's seventy-three-mile Wall divided the whole island in AD 121 not far from what is now Scotland's border with England. Twenty years later, the Romans tried to push the frontier north by building a wall across the narrowest part of Scotland between the Forth and the Clyde. But the Antonine Wall was continually overrun by the tribes it was meant to pen in. The Roman walls evoke an empire that could never subdue the peoples of Scotland. Yet the walls also kept out the Roman influence that was to make a permanent mark on English law, language, customs, trade, and civic development. In this respect – as in many others – Scotland and its powerful neighbor to the south grew from profoundly different cultural and historical roots. I was reminded of just how fiercely the Scots maintain their uniqueness when I mistakenly wrote once of the "Englishman" Colin Montgomerie. Every Scot in Canada wrote me a fiery letter to remind me that Montgomerie, while he lives in England, is a Scot. I've never made that mistake again.

It's not known whether the Celts were the ancestors of the mysterious Picts or whether the Picts came from elsewhere (as did the original Scots). The Picti – the "painted ones" as the Romans dubbed them because of their wild blue tattoos – had a highly developed culture, though no written language. They left beautifully sculpted stones portraying strange fantasy animals, weapons, costumes, tools, and people.

After they were Christianized, the Picts combined these haunting images with elaborate crosses. During our hike around Tarbat Ness we came across an archeological dig – one of the most important in Britain – just outside Portmahomack, where an eighth-century Pictish monastery is being excavated.

The Picts fascinate historians, perhaps because they were a mysterious people. Timothy Neat, a writer and filmmaker, who also keeps bees and hunts mushrooms in the Highlands that he then sells to fancy restaurants, even has a theory that relates Pictish ways to golf. He's come to the Dornoch Bookshop on a signing, because the latest in his quartet of oral histories of the Highlands has just been published. I've been looking forward to his appearance, and find Tim in a corner of the bookshop with James Bell, Lesley's husband. They're talking about Tim's new book, *When I Was Young: Voices from Lost Communities in Scotland*, and also of an earlier one, *The Summer Walkers*. His method is to let people tell their stories, which are often about moving around in the Highlands, about people who, while at home in their land, also journeyed about to make ends meet.

"I quite like stories of the Travelers," James says. "They have such a wonderful relationship to the countryside, a deep feeling for it." Tim, a garrulous, bulky man who makes connections between far-flung elements, agrees. "That's true. They are naked people, aren't they? They're exposed." While James and Tim chat, I look at something Hugh MacDiarmid – a well-known Scottish poet - wrote. "It requires great love of it deeply to read/the configuration of a land." I'm beginning to appreciate that the configuration of the Highlands has often been twisted and tortured.

Before long Tim, James, and I are having lunch in the One-Up restaurant on the way to the golf course – summer vegetable soup, haddock and chips, a crisp Chilean white wine. Tim sits in his chair, gets up to make a point, sits down again, grabs my arm to emphasize an observation, then launches into his provocative theory that associates the Picts with the origins of golf.

"I was driving from Dundee to Carnoustie on the main road recently when the idea occurred to me," Tim says. "Suddenly it hit me why golf speaks to Scottish people. I came by an exposed souterrain, which is defined as an underground stone-lined passage and chamber, and is used to describe dwellings dating from the Iron Age. The Picts of the Pictish period, in eastern Scotland, lived in souterrains, in small villages. These collections of half-submerged, minimal structures of sand and gravel were probably roofed with turf and surrounded by swaths of 'lawn' grass and approached by various paths and cattle pastures – thus they have looked very much like the target areas of present-day golf courses. One reason why so many people enjoy the golf experience, I think, is that it echoes the age-old, and real, pastoral experience, especially in eastern Scotland. It represents the 'field of life,' and 'coming home.' So there's a complex Scottish tradition of living almost underground, especially in sandy areas where the grass is very short. The Picts lived like this. I noticed that the physical structure of old Pictish settlements resembles that of links courses. That is, they come out of a hole in the ground. The Picts hunted and fished in a dunes landscape, and then returned to the hole in the ground where they lived. It's the old life practice of living down in a hole. If you're going to have a game in the modern world that has historical antecedents, and golf is an old game, then you can begin to see the possible relationship. In golf you go out and hit the ball around. You swing that club, aiming toward a target, like shooting an arrow at a goose. Then you come back home. It's close to the lived experience of the Picts. There's something quite poetic here that could be explored. When you come to where the Picts lived, you find it looks just like a bunker."

James has been listening patiently. I've noticed that he's wanted to burst into Tim's soliloquy a few times, but has waited until he finished. It's his turn now.

"Have you seen those carved Pictish balls that are made of metal and have a slightly formalized appearance?" James asks. "Nobody knows what they represent, but they would have been used in some kind of game, play, or ritual, although some people suggest that they were a cooking utensil that helped heat water. But we know that there is a long tradition of play in Scotland. In the great houses people still play carpet bowls, using multicolored or patterned balls made of ceramics. This game is rather like boule, another game of western Celtic origin. The continuum in these kind of things here is very strong. I've seen one of these Pictish balls in the churchyard museum in Portmahomack, which traces the ongoing archeological dig there. It's about the size of a billiard ball, and as smooth. These balls are rare."

Who knows? Perhaps Tim's theory has some merit, although there's no evidence for it. Still, it makes for irresistible conversation. Golf and the Scots: it's hard to think of one without the other.

● ● ● ● ● ●

But the question of where the Scots came from remains. They came from elsewhere. From Ireland – around AD 500. They were an aggressive, ambitious tribe who came to mix it up with the Picts, as well as with the Angles and the Britons who had ventured north. By the eighth century the Vikings were pouring in, too, giving Sutherland its name – the land is southerly if your home is Scandinavia. The brooding land was roiling with tribal rivalries and blood feuds. In full flow already was the notorious Scots' propensity for internecine hostility and complex vendettas.

The word "palimpsest" insinuates itself here. A palimpsest is a parchment from which one layer of writing is overwritten by other layers. Many complex webs of writing may have been added to the parchment, making them devilishly difficult to decipher. The earlier layers never fully disappear. They remain beneath the present, specters from the past. Scotland in general and Dornoch in particular are palimpsests of peoples, cultures, and tragedies that emerge and etch themselves into the present. With that sobering image in mind, we resume our tour of the Royal Burgh of Dornoch. It is a burgh, too; we're reminded a few times not to forget that this is Dornoch's official designation. It's not a village, technically speaking, although that's how just about everybody refers to it here. It feels like a village.

Crossing the High Street in front of our flat and passing the Mercat (or market) Cross, we walk into the cathedral. Nell and I are hardly mavens of medieval church architecture, but we find this one surprisingly light and suffused with an unexpected warmth. It's devoid of the Gothic gloom that often attends such edifices. Dornoch Cathedral isn't large by cathedral standards, but its attractive proportions and glorious long-shafted windows give it an airy quality and an atmosphere of calm, dignified simplicity. Its turbulent history, however, does not reflect this tranquil spirit.

The cathedral dates back over 750 years to the 1220s, when it was built by Gilbert de Moravia, a kinsman of the Earl of Moray (the source of the surname Murray, which is so common around here) and of the first Earl of Sutherland. The powerful de Moravia family was of Norman origin, and the Normans were starting to make their mark in Scotland by the thirteenth century. (They'd crashed into England in 1066, of course.) Though as ferocious as many of the indigenous tribes and clans, the Normans had a leg up culturally. They were feudal in their political culture, and they could administer and think dynastically in a way that eluded their tribal rivals. Gilbert became the Bishop of Caithness in 1222, a position of considerable earthly, as well as heavenly, power in the thirteenth century. The bishopric was, naturally, attached to a huge whack of land.

Gilbert planned and supervised the building of the cathedral, consisting of the main nave with aisles, transept (the crosslike arms projecting out from the nave), and chancel (altar portion). The building also has a choir and a massive tower, supported by four clustered piers of local sandstone. On summer Saturday evenings, just before the weekly pipe-band parade, the cathedral opens the tower to the public. One Saturday, along with a jolly group of young and old folk, we climb the circular stone steps, fifty-three of them at one shot, to the at-home-with-Quasimodo bell tower of the church. From there we ascend a precariously high wooden stair and pop out onto the dizzying, mossy parapet of the cathedral – 120 feet above the square and the gathering pipers. We're startled by gargoyles set in the eaves, once thought to be evil spirits driven from the church and turned to stone by the sound of the bells. We gab with the others at the top – including a couple of local golfers debating the merits of the courses in Tain, Dornoch, and Brora – and survey the town, indeed the whole parish, spread wide beneath us. Then we wait in line to return to earth at Dornoch Cathedral.

The cathedral is a repository of communal memory of the past 750 years. On one hand, it reflects the treachery and violence that plagued Dornoch and Scottish history. It was sacked and burned, along with most of the village, in 1570 during a complicated clan feud between the MacKays of Strathnaver, the Gordons, and the Murrays of Dornoch. The MacKays won this particular round, and one of their lot proceeded to desecrate St. Gilbert's remains (he'd been canonized Scotland's last-ever saint after his death in 1245), scattering what was left of him with a foot. Legend has it, though, that the attacker's foot rotted and the man died after becoming "so lothsum that no man wes able to come neir him." The cathedral was rebuilt between 1614 and 1622, after the upheaval of the Scottish Reformation. Though the church retains its Catholic name of cathedral for historical purposes, it has been the Presbyterian church for the area for the past three hundred years.

The cathedral is also a repository of memories important to the community. Stained-glass windows on the south porch portray the contrasting moods of the Highlands landscape – its color, the changing light at various times, the natural world so far from the smog and pollution of the cities to the south. Other windows and memorials recall local people both mighty and humble, and the chancel windows remind us of the ways that Andrew Carnegie, who summered at Skibo, tried to change the world. One window recalls his love for music, another his efforts to promote international peace, and a third depicts the learning that he bequeathed the world in the gift of those three thousand free libraries all over Scotland. Nell and I are grateful to him; we've been spending pleasant hours at the Carnegie Free Library next to our bookshop flat. The library, Luigi's, and the golf course triangulate much of our lives here.

Several months after our season in Dornoch had come to an end, Nell and I would watch on TV in Toronto as the dignified old church became the site of the media frenzy that attended the christening of Madonna's infant son. There hadn't been such a siege since the MacKays rampaged through the town. We could only speculate about the various ways that the Material Girl might choose to leave a permanent mark on the building. There's already a Madonna and Child window in memory of a woman from nearby Ospisdale. O spare us, please, a conical brassiere!

Across the square from the cathedral is the sixteenth-century Dornoch Castle, which was originally built as a bishop's palace. The Gordons held out for a week in the large tower during the 1570 siege that also destroyed all the records of the castle. The fortresslike tower survived the siege, but the rest of the edifice lay in ruins for a long time. In 1813, it was fitted up as the county courthouse and jail; later it became the County Buildings. Since 1947, it's been a pleasant and unpretentious hotel. We spent many evenings at the small bar in the

Castle Hotel, warming ourselves by the large fireplace, talking golf and life above the dungeons and below the siege tower. Palimpsest.

• • • • • •

Our tour can take two directions here, but let's say we hop on our bikes and cruise north out of town toward Embo. We could also walk across the top of the course, past Gallowhill, site of Dornoch's last public hanging, past the mysterious grave marking the burial site of hapless cholera victims outside the burgh's boundaries in 1832, and past the Earl's Cross tucked into a field overlooking the fourth hole. In all likelihood, the Earl's Cross – a stone pillar in that open field – is a boundary marker, but it has the coat of arms of the Earls of Sutherland on one side and that of the town of Dornoch on the other side. And, therein, on our walk to Embo, lies another grisly local legend.

The legend – and historians debunk it roundly – says that the cross was erected in memory of the Battle of Embo between the Earl of Sutherland and the Norsemen in 1259. During this battle, the earl supposedly broke his sword in hand-to-hand combat with the Viking chief, whereupon he grabbed the severed leg of a horse that was nearby and smote the marauding Dane, sending his compatriots fleeing to their ships. This bit of epic, biblical-style violence endowed the Royal Burgh of Dornoch with the heraldic device that adorns its coat of arms: a horseshoe "in memory of this feat." The horseshoe also forms part of the golf club's crest, although I doubt that many visitors who spend small fortunes on logoed clothes in Andrew Skinner's pro shop know of the story behind it. A tale is told in the club bar to visitors looking for local color that one of the warriors in the Battle of Embo is buried under the hairy, homely protuberance that rises in the middle of the fifteenth fairway. Don Greenberg refers to this hump as a skybox, because the golfer who is lucky enough to find his ball on the top and in a good lie has a fine view of the green. But that golfer might shiver if he thought about what possibly lies under his feet.

Embo today is a quiet little fishing village that seems the most unlikely place for a battle. Its stone houses are set in rows perpendicular to the North Sea and its cold gales. Because of Dornoch's exposed position on the firth, and the Gizzen Briggs, a sandbar there, the local fishermen have for centuries lived in Embo rather than Dornoch. They sailed from Little Ferry, a tidal inlet just north of Dornoch that makes for tricky navigation. Embo's womenfolk not only used to carry their men to the boats so they'd at least set out in dry clothes, but they also followed the herring fleets down the east coast of Britain, forming the rugged crew of women who gutted and barreled the fish.

Embo also provided Dornoch with caddies for many years – when the club would allow them to work there, that is. The caddymaster in the club's early days preferred locals from Dornoch rather than from Embo. But Alexander Fraser, the first caddy from Embo, battled the club for the rights of his fellow caddies to work there, and finally prevailed. Embo caddies were so poor they didn't have shoes, and walked to Dornoch and worked there in bare feet – hence the term "the barefoot caddies of Embo." I'd read in John Macleod's club history that Alexander Fraser was Dawn Fraser's father; she had moved to Australia and represented her adopted country as a swimmer in the Olympics, winning gold medals in 1956, 1960, and 1964. She was one of the people who carried the torch to open the Summer 2000 Olympics in Sydney.

For us, Embo provided not only some historical links to golf in Dornoch, but also a humble necessity – a place to clean our clothes. Embo is the location of Grannie's Hielan Hame, a kitschy caravan park and family tourist trap that has a launderette. Our first attempt to find a place to wash clothes took us south on a forty-mile round-trip journey to the town of Alness, where we found a cheerful laundress who washed and dried them while we took tea on the High Street. But we needed a closer facility, and Grannie's in Embo, about three miles from Dornoch, was just the place. It's rough 'n' ready do-it-yourself, and we had to mix it up with tough Glaswegian mums who raced us to the two working dryers – our own Battle of Embo. At least the underwear was cleaned once in awhile.

Back on our bikes and several miles north, we arrive at Loch Fleet and Little Ferry, the tidal inlet between Dornoch and the next town north, Golspie (the seat of the Sutherland family at Dunrobin Castle). There's no longer a ferry at Little Ferry, because the A9 cuts north over the Mound, a remarkable earthen embankment built to carry the road around Loch Fleet. It also stops the North Sea from sweeping far up the Fleet River valley. The Mound opened up a lot of land for cultivation, but Thomas Telford's design also provided for fish, especially salmon, to get upstream. Great wooden valves close against the sea and open automatically to let the river flow. This was a remarkably eco-friendly dyke for the early nineteenth century, when Telford built it. The land and tidal flats at Loch Fleet are now a nature preserve, and the dunes – which I cannot help seeing as the prototype of a links – are home to a vast array of birdlife. Our first visit to Loch Fleet is merely a drive-by. We'll return to explore.

We do take note of a lonely, haunting ruin that overlooks Loch Fleet; it's the remains of a medieval fortress called Skelbo Castle. ("Bo" is the Norse suffix that denotes homestead; hence, names such as Skibo, Embo, Skelbo are common in East Sutherland.) Skelbo is haunting less for what happened there than for what failed to happen. The "Maid of Norway," as she was known, was the Queen of Scots by birth, the granddaughter of King Alexander III, one of the more capable Scottish kings who, unfortunately, fell off his horse and down a cliff onto the shore of the Firth of Forth near Edinburgh in 1296. Margaret, "the Maid," was also heir to the throne of Norway, since her mother, Margaret, Alexander's daughter, was married to Eric II of Norway.

The fearsome Edward I of England, known as "Longshanks" and the "Hammer of the Scots," proposed in 1290 that the Maid marry his son, then six years of age, to become Queen of England by marriage.

The Maid was seven years old when she left Norway on a ship that ventured out into the tempestuous waters of the North Sea, bound for Wick in the autumn gales. Edward I's emissaries had gotten as far as Skelbo on their journey to take charge of the child, but somewhere on the journey, perhaps near the Orkney Islands, the fragile little girl died, and Edward's dynastic designs were thwarted. What he could not gain through conjugal diplomacy, he tried to gain by force, and the long series of wars between England and Scotland began in earnest. The Maid's story still resonates in Scotland, particularly in the Highlands at the Skelbo ruin, as a symbol of the perils of children's lives at the time and of the enduring problems of succession in a monarchical system that led to so much bloodshed.

Scotland's earlier monarchs had succeeded to their thrones in a complex matrilineal system called "tanistry." This system resulted in numbers of claimants for the position of king. The job went to the last man standing – the guy who could kill off all his uncles and cousins. Thanks to Shakespeare's genius, we have a vivid portrait of Macbeth's murder of his kinsman Duncan. But the historical king Macbeth – who in truth was an excellent king for seventeen years – was killed by his successor, Malcolm III, in 1057. The downside of tanistry? Endless bloody feuds and sudden violent changes of leadership. There were thirteen Scottish kings between 859 and 1005; seven of them were killed in battle by their relatives.

The upside of tanistry? At least the man who would finally be king would be an adult. Another Norman innovation, primogeniture (the patrilineal legitimate firstborn rules) was to bring Scotland far too many child monarchs. The early Stewart kings, for example, included James II, who became king at six in 1406, James III, who succeeded at age eight in 1437, and James V, who became king in 1513 at the age of two. The succession of child kings only exacerbated the tendency of the magnates of noble families to war among themselves and to put their own interests above those of the monarch – or the nation. Scotland's earlier history is rife with treachery and intrigue.

• • • • • •

On our way back from Embo, Nell and I stop into Royal Dornoch's club-house to have a bite and a pint after our rambles. Over a cheese toastie and a pint of Royal Dornoch Club Ale, and after looking out past the course to the firth and north to Embo from which we've just come, we see the Carnegie Shield that sits in a locked trophy case on the upper floor of the clubhouse, near our table. The massive silver shield looks as if it could hold its own against Sigurd the Powerful. Andrew Carnegie presented it to the club in 1901, and since then generations of golfers have lusted after it – myself included.

Even a golf trophy is a palimpsest here, though, as emblazoned on the Shield is a scene of Charles I playing golf at Leith Links, an early five-hole course east of Edinburgh. The detail is taken from a famous painting by Sir Charles Gilbert. In the scene, Charles is receiving the message informing him of the Irish Catholic rebellion in 1641 that was part of the trouble that would result in the English Civil War, the accession of Cromwell, and Charles's execution in 1649. One account of the king's reaction to the news at Leith Links has him finishing his round – an authentic golfer, apparently. Another account suggests that he summoned his coach and sped off for Holyrood Palace in Edinburgh. Yet even in this version the monarch receives no quarter from the historian Sir Walter Simpson, who charges that the king acted "with his usual cunning – that at the time the news arrived he was being beaten, and that he hurried away to save his half-crown rather than his crown." Charles's other recorded golf game is as a prisoner of the Scots outside the walls of Newcastle-upon-Tyne. The king had surrendered to the Scots Covenanters in 1646 in the complex civil and religious wars of the era, but they turned him over to the English parliament and Cromwell in 1647 on the soon-broken promise that he wouldn't be harmed.

It's worth remembering that Charles himself was a Scot, born in Dumfermline in 1600 (as Carnegie was in 1835). His grandmother was the passionate, willful, Catholic, and ill-fated Mary, Queen of Scots, who lost her head in 1587 on the scaffold, at the orders of her more circumspect Protestant cousin Elizabeth I of England. It's also worth remembering that golf had a strange cameo role in Mary's tragedy. One of the charges against her was that she had been seen playing golf a few days after the murder of her husband, Lord Darnley. That she was a merry golfing widow, in the true sense, was deemed suspicious.

Mary's son, James VI, became Scotland's king at one year of age when his mother abdicated (or was forced to abdicate) in 1567. James succeeded to the English throne upon Elizabeth's death in 1603, effectively uniting the two kingdoms as James VI of Scotland and James I of England. It's said that James had learned the game of golf on the historic North Inch of Perth. What's certain is that he brought up his son Charles to play the royal and ancient game. Hence, the monarch's likeness on the stately Carnegie Shield gives us an opportunity to reflect on the fates of kings and queens over our cheese toasties and beer. The Carnegie Shield, which I've looked forward to competing in for months, is about to play an important cameo role in my season in the Highlands as well.

Refreshed by our stop in the clubhouse, we'll finish our tour of Dornoch by taking the long way back to our bookshop flat. We'll head down the road that divides the first tee from the rest of the hole (we pause as a few shots whiz across), heading for the beach. For those accustomed to beach life in more tropical climes, it seems strange even to contemplate the same at fifty-eight degrees north latitude. Yet Dornoch has a wide, sandy beach. The water is a bit on the nippy side if you are used to the Caribbean – about fifty degrees Fahrenheit. It gets up to fifty-five degrees in August, but no higher. Still, in the long sunny days of high summer (about three weeks in August, by our reckoning), kids play in the clean, shallow surf and dig castles in the golden sand. One Sunday afternoon, Nell watches as two women on horseback ride nearly across the firth to Tain at low tide. On another occasion she spots some frolicking seals out near the Gizzen Briggs.

The Gizzen Briggs is a local natural feature. The substantial sandbar in the Dornoch Firth lies just offshore of the golf course. Sometimes at very low tides, soon after the new or full moon, the Gizzen Briggs is visible. In relatively moderate seas, its position can be identified by white water swirling above. In severe weather, one can hear the crashing sound when the sea breaks onto the Gizzen Briggs – also known as the Noisy Bridge – with great ferocity. (The Gizzen Briggs is Old Norse for "leaky landing place," which goes back to when the firth was navigable and Tain was a port. The message is "Don't land here or you'll get your feet wet.") Shifting sandbanks beset the Dornoch Firth from its mouth here all the way to Bonar Bridge, thirteen miles to the west. So while there is small boating in the area, it must be done with a keen awareness of local tides, winds, and other sea conditions.

We stroll back toward town across the Common Good Land, passing the small grass landing strip, unmanned most of the time, with its jaunty wind sock telling us which way the wind blows. Then we walk along the lower Struie course, Royal Dornoch's second course. The holes are separated from each other by swaths of rough and thick gorse bushes; there's not much room to spray one's shots, which makes it fun to test one's accuracy here. Every so often during my summer, I encounter an old man in a kilt who plays the Struie most every day. He often hits shots backwards between his legs and has one of the most bizarre swings I've ever seen, nearly falling backwards onto the ground every time. I learn that this fellow once owned a bakery in the village, but that his golf came first. He used to put a sign on the door to the bakery that declared, "Closed for lunch." Rather than serve meals at lunch, he took himself off to the Struie. I enjoy running into him on the course. The man never finishes a hole, since he's out for recreation, and that's all. I never see him with anybody else, but that's his business. Meanwhile, the club is adding a few holes to the southeast of the course, nearer the firth. The Struie, named for the hill to the west from where Greenberg first saw Dornoch, is about to become longer and harder. I'll be out here frequently during the summer.

Nell and I return to Dornoch proper via what's called Littletown, a small neighborhood of cottages erected in the early 1800s to house crofters who'd been banished from their land in the Clearances. In Littletown, they were supposed to learn to fish for their livelihoods (Gizzen Briggs notwithstanding). The last cottage before the commons on Carnaig Street has a bonny front garden with a children's playground and toys; clean laundry is drying in the breeze. There's also a large stone marked with the year 1722. Incongruous in the setting – but congruent with the teeth in Dornoch's history – the stone marks the spot where the last execution for witchcraft was carried out in Scotland. Here, Janet Horne, a feeble old woman down on her luck, was burned to death for allegedly turning her daughter into a pony and having her shod by the devil. Hmm. Perhaps those Dornoch Cathedral gargoyles escaped a little further than the parapet.

We get back to our bookshop flat and start to cook dinner. Nell has bought some fresh haddock from the fishmonger who comes down from Golspie in a blue truck every Tuesday. She also picked up some "crumb dressing" (a.k.a. breadcrumbs), new potatoes, broccoli, and mushrooms at the "spa." So we manage to prepare a tasty repast with our two pans and two burners, as we sip some single malt out of our two glasses. After quickly washing up in a little dishpan – no dishwasher or microwave or any of the multitude of kitchen gizmos that we own in Toronto – I still have time for a few holes at 10 p.m. here in the endless summer evening of Dornoch, whose palimpsest – and teeth – are becoming apparent to us.

Chapter 7

The Captain's Pink Balls

"Pound on game or pound, pound, pound?" Don Greenberg had asked before we set out on our first match at Dornoch. He was asking whether we would play the match for a pound and no more. Or would Stuart and I prefer what is known in America as a "Nassau," where a pound would ride on the result of each of the front nine, the back, and the match itself? I like the idea of the match itself counting and nothing else. Club championship matches are usually scheduled for eighteen or thirty-six holes. That's the way the United States and British Amateurs are played. It's authentic golf, and so why bother with a Nassau? I often play matches for another small wager also, where the prize is a book or compact disc valued under twenty dollars. The loser chooses the prize with no input from the winner, and golf books are not allowed. Novels, poetry, non-fiction, and music from little-known artists: these are genuine prizes.

Today, however, I'm playing a different sort of match. It's the Curate's Egg, at the Brora Golf Club fifteen miles north of Dornoch, organized

by the James Braid Golfing Society. Why the Curate's Egg? Well, a reasonable response to the question, "How's life?", I'm told, is "It's a bit
like a curate's egg," which doesn't tell me much. Later I learn the term's
origin. Its meaning says a lot about how members of the Braid Society
feel about golf.

A curate is a junior clergyman in Britain, and doesn't have much
influence. The curate is at the bottom of the ecclesiastical pecking order,
akin to a caddy's role at most clubs or on the PGA Tour. He's there to
do the will of his boss – the vicar or parish priest. There's no job security. Still, a minister will occasionally deign to invite his curate into his
manse, which was the setting for a cartoon that George du Maurier did
for the November 9, 1895, issue of *Punch*, the satirical British magazine
of blessed memory.

Even a curate must eat, which the one pictured in the cartoon was
doing. He was having breakfast in his bishop's home, but the egg he
was eating was rotten. The minister said to the curate, "I'm afraid
you've got a bad egg, Mr. Jones." The curate, knowing his place, didn't
want to offend the vicar, and responded, "Oh no, my Lord, I assure
you that parts of it are excellent." Hence the term "curate's egg," partly
good and partly bad – like life. Like golf, as the golfers in the Braid
Society know.

The unofficial title of the Braid Society tells me more. Some non-
members call it the James Braid Veneration Society. Braid won the 1901
British Open at Prestwick, that old curiosity shop of a golf course in
the southwest part of Scotland, and then won the championship again
in 1905, 1906, 1908, and 1910, this latter victory coming at the Old
Course in St. Andrews. But Braid did far more than play golf tournaments, of which there weren't many for professionals in those early
days of the twentieth century anyway. Braid was the head professional
at the Walton Heath Club near London from 1904 until his death
in 1950. He was also an accomplished course architect, who was in

demand, especially after he all but stopped playing tournaments. He designed "minimalist" courses before anybody used the term that became fashionable during the 1990s. Braid moved little dirt while creating his courses, preferring to let the landscape dictate the holes instead. Braid had a light and inexpensive touch in those early days when golf professionals designed courses.

Braid also cut an imposing figure. He was six feet, five inches tall. His height, his handlebar mustache, and his long, graceful golf swing – "a most dashing one, with a very free loose knee at the finish of the shot, when he really went out for it," Bernard Darwin wrote – set him apart.

There's something appealing about contemplating Braid the golfer, swinging fully and freely and enjoying the motion. He traveled by train because he found it more comfortable than traveling by car, where he suffered from motion sickness. His method of working was to walk the property for a few hours, then to sketch the course routing and holes while on his return journey by train. Tom Watson likes to read putts through his feet by walking the ground. Braid designed courses by feeling them in his bones while walking the landscape. He would subsequently send in an invoice, rarely for more than £25.

Braid not only designed Brora, but also Golspie, a links in the village of the same name just north of Dornoch. Every village in the Highlands of any size has a links, and it's called, simply, by the name of the village. No embellishment, like the courses themselves. Braid's curriculum vitae includes highly regarded courses such as Carnoustie and the King's at Gleneagles in Scotland.

My introduction to the society had occurred the previous October, when I had dinner with Stephen Toon in St. Andrews, where he manages the Peter Thomson–designed Duke's course. Toon and his family have a cottage in Clashmore, near Dornoch. He told me about a round he had played at Brora one late September afternoon when the sun was setting. His companion was Thomson, a talented course designer as well as a winner of five British Opens. Thomson prefers the simple to the ornate, golf as the ground made it, not golf as the architect contrived it. Toon and Thomson chatted amiably as they made their way around Brora, a course where sheep still graze and electrical fences ring the greens and provide a harmless but noticeable zap to humans and sheep who come in contact with them. Golfers step over the thin wire fence while sheep pull back to graze elsewhere. The course is a classic out-and-in links, in which the front nine plays in a northerly direction except for the sixth, a par-three that crosses at ninety degrees to the west in the middle of the property. The back nine reverses direction, except for the twelfth, a short par-three that crosses to the east in the middle of the property. The course is exposed to the winds off the North Sea, and the clubhouse looks down on the links. Brora provides rugged, hearty golf, and the holes over which Jimmy Miller, who lives in the town, developed the game that won him ten Carnegie Shields at Royal Dornoch. The course is full of arresting green sites and bunkers so deep that, as one member says, "We need a physician to assess whether they can cause injury to older people who have to struggle to remove themselves." These are mean – nay, life-threatening – bunkers.

"Peter said that playing Brora reminded him of his days as a boy," Toon told me, "when he would climb over the fence of his local course and play until he was chased away, not keeping score, but just hitting the ball for sheer enjoyment. Nowadays he felt that many of the invitations he received to play had other motives behind them, and that it would be fun, a few times a year, just to play with friends for the fun of playing."

"Linksland cropped by sheep," Thomson, the president of the society, wrote in one of its newsletters, "with the sea in view from every hole, takes us back to a time when golf was played in a manner which emphasized the values of courtesy and fair play." Bad bounces? They happened because the ground and greens weren't manicured like today's courses, which seem almost ornamental by comparison. Good bounces? They occurred for the same reasons. Golf a fair game? Sometimes. Unfair? Sometimes. Be content, Braid advised. You're outdoors in healthy air with friends and foes. It's nothing fancy, this golf, merely a matter of hitting a ball from point A to point B.

Now it was time for the Curate's Egg. The format was a Stableford competition, or quota points, as it's also known. My five-handicap meant I could subtract a shot from my score on each hole on the Brora scorecard rated from the fifth most difficult to the most difficult. A bogey was worth one point, a par two points, and a birdie four points. An eagle – dream on – was worth eight points. I scored a supremely modest twenty-eight points, which meant that I hadn't played to my handicap. Had I gathered thirty-six points – an average of two, or par, a hole – I'd have matched my handicap. But I couldn't cope with the thirty-mile-an-hour Brora winds, a nor'wester that whipped into my face on the outward half as I strained forward to slam the ball against the wind. Then, on the ninth hole, I hit what I thought was a solid shot to the green. But the wind knocked the ball right down, deep down, into a thick cow turd. One of my playing companions, more familiar with such indignities, dragged the ball out with the head of his iron – adeptly, I thought – then rolled it around in the rough to clean it up as best as possible. "There you go," he said, "have a swing now." I elected to drop another ball, not caring if I broke a rule. Was this against the spirit of the society? I didn't mind venerating Braid, but a cow-turd golf ball was another matter.

After our round I had a pint or two in the bar, where I met Charles Shanks. Should I talk to a golfer whose surname represents one of golf's unthinkable shots? Unmentionable, too. To speak the word "shank" is to put the image into a golfer's mind of his ball hitting the hosel of his club and tearing off nearly at right angles to his intended line of play.

Golfers sometimes never recover from an attack of the shanks. Johnny Miller, the 1973 U.S. Open and 1976 British Open champion, once shanked a nine-iron and spent the rest of the year thinking he would do it again every time he used a short iron.

"I take a right rigging for my name," Shanks tells me. "It's the kiss of death. Once I was playing a tournament at Carnoustie and I hear a mighty roar from somebody who is saying, 'Look who I'm playing with, Shanks.' This poor man had spent six months getting rid of the shanks. Another time I played with a fellow named Harry Duff, so we were Duff and Shanks."

It's bad enough to duff a shot, but shanking one is humiliating. I linger with Shanks anyway. He's the secretary of the National Farmers Union of Scotland, and informs me of a recent meeting where the security of tenants on land was the issue. The subject of land use is never far way. Shanks explains that a person who pays rent cannot be evicted, and that a tenant can go to land court if the owner raises the rent. There he can argue that the rent increase is unfair. We go back and forth on whether the sheep should be allowed to remain on Brora's links. Can the golfers and the crofters whose animals graze on the course find a way to coexist peacefully?

That night the Braid Society convenes for dinner at the Royal Marine Hotel overlooking the links. I meet James Moreton at the cocktail hour in – what else? – the James Braid Room in the hotel. Moreton has written a book about Braid's courses. A driver that Braid made hangs on a wall in Moreton's home. Braid's plan of the Royal Blackheath course near London is on the wall above his fireplace. "Our educations are incomplete," Moreton says between puffs on his pipe. "There are so many courses." Asked if it's fair to call the group the James Braid Veneration Society, he answers, "Certainly."

• • • • • •

The James Braid Open, two rounds at Brora, one day. Fierce northwest wind, a wind that is more usual in winter. We can't see the Mannie, which means it's raining just to the north and that we'll get pounded soon – "full conditions," as the Scots say. I'm playing with Robin Wilson, a Brora member who is known as a "useful" player, in that he carries a five-handicap and plays to it most of the time. We head out, bodies bent to the cold wind snapping at us. By the third hole, the rain is a firing squad of needles digging into our faces. But it's okay; in Scotland we play in weather we'd never go out in back home. The idea is to stay in control and to accept the conditions and even to relish them. Somehow. Tom Watson maintains that one of the most gratifying days he ever had was during the 1979 Memorial Tournament in Dublin, Ohio, when he shot 69 the third round while everybody else was shooting in the high 70s and even the 80s. The wind chill was in the high thirties. Watson accepted the brutal conditions and soldiered on. Accepting what nature offers during a round qualifies as one of the game's highest arts.

But enough philosophy. Braid said, "Be content," not "Be tough." Maybe his trenchant advice applies not only to being satisfied with how far one hits the ball, but also with the conditions. It's helpful to remember this when things start going wrong on a nasty day, because then it's difficult to maintain one's equilibrium. Robin hits his tee shot into one of the malicious bunkers that front the sixth green. His first shot looks good, but just catches the top of the sod wall and ricochets back to his feet. His second never reaches the top and rebounds again, as if off the wall of a squash court. "Fucking bunker," Robin screams after his third shot from the bunker stays in there, and "Fucking criminal, put that in your book," after his fourth finishes back at his feet in the now thoroughly messed-up bunker. It looks as if a herd of cattle has walked through. Robin extricates himself with his fifth shot and is so hot he's aflame. As he walks to his ball on the green, he's raging at the golfing gods, recounting the time he played a county championship at some course, perhaps here, and started four, four, ten, two. No wonder the Scots play more match than medal play. It's tough, and harmful to any golfer's already fragile self-confidence, to have to post the numbers. Four, four, ten, two.

Gluttons for full conditions, we barrel our way forward. Some relief arrives when we turn around to play the back nine. Now the strong wind is at our back, but that only means it's next to impossible to stop the ball on the greens. A two-hundred-yard shot might require a nine-iron, whereas on the way out into the wind I couldn't hit a driver two hundred yards. It's also tough to stand still over a putt. On the eleventh hole I teeter and then I totter and I wave at a two-foot putt. The ball doesn't touch the hole. At the par-three eighteenth hole I wobble over my tee shot and come up short of the green and to the left, on the side of a hill. I feel wind-woozy, and I'm aware of the observers looking out from the clubhouse windows, no doubt chortling at my predicament. But I take a short wrist shot as if I'm playing hockey, and chip the ball onto the green. At least I've avoided the two new sinkhole bunkers on either side of the front of the green. Robin thought club officials were trying to reopen the coal mines that once operated in Brora when they constructed these new bunkers. Poor Robin. He's had a bad day in the pits at his home course.

After lunch we venture out for our second round. Again we're into a strong northwest wind. Alan Cameron, a scratch golfer from Fortrose and Rosemarkie, a links strung out on a narrow peninsula near Inverness, is playing with us. On the fourth I get a bit of a zing when I accidentally brush up against the electrified fence around the green. My ball is near the fence and I'm allowed a free drop no nearer the hole. Robin tells me that some golfers try to take advantage and move the ball so that, say, they don't have to pitch it over a pot bunker. They haven't moved the ball closer to the hole, but they've altered their angle of approach.

"But we think that's outwith the spirit of the game," Robin comments. "Outwith" is an old word that people here use frequently. I'm reminded that language often identifies people of a particular region. Keeping one's ears as well as one's eyes open amplifies the pleasure of traveling in a foreign landscape. Foreign to me, anyway.

We continue our appointed round, trying to avoid cow patties, electrified fences, and steep pot bunkers. I learn of a Brora trick, whereby golfers carry a few small pellets of cow droppings in their pockets and bring them out when faced with a bad lie. The local rule is that a free drop is allowed when droppings interfere with a shot. Come on. That trick isn't in the Brora spirit. Or is it?

I'm in a groove at last, making par after par on the back side after shooting 43 into the biting wind on the front nine. Three pars and I'll be in with 34, par for the back side. I'm score-conscious, the legacy of a life of medal play. I close with three bogeys. Alan is contending for the tournament, but finishes bogey, double bogey, bogey for 74. Robin is playing superbly, but he also puts in a finish guaranteed to send him to the bar for two or three pints. Or more. He bogeys the seventeenth hole and triple-bogeys the last hole, missing a one-foot putt to shoot 75. I've shot 84–80 in the James Braid Open, hardly what a five-handicapper would be expected to score. Or would himself expect to score.

• • • • • •

After the Braid Open I drive back to Dornoch and stop by the clubhouse. Don Greenberg is there, wearing his Spicy Cup sweater. The Spicy is an annual event that will take place this weekend. A team of Dornoch golfers plays a team of visitors, and between matches most of the competitors enjoy a Spicy Rum or two. Lagers and ales are also allowed. The prize is, well, the Spicy Cup trophy. I chat with the competitors for a few minutes, then leave and walk to the village square, where Nell is waiting for me. The Dornoch Pipe Band is in full kit and kilt. A couple of hundred people are milling about as the band plays. A woman walks in the square jangling a little tin that says, "Pipe band." I put some change in and enjoy the concert, which ends after thirty minutes. "On, follow," the pipe major commands his band members, and follow they do, through a lane and away from the square.

It's getting on to nine o'clock now. We're hungry, so we walk all of another three or four minutes back in the direction of the course, stopping at the Royal Golf Hotel that overlooks the first fairway. We warm up with glasses of Bunnahabhain single malt. The liquid gold hits my upper palate with a sting, then settles in the back of my mouth before cascading into farther reaches, like a space heater spreading its warmth throughout a room. Nell mentions that she can taste the clear Highlands water and the rich peat in this whisky. Nowhere else is the taste of Scotch whisky duplicated or approximated.

Dinner consists of smoked salmon sandwiches with salad and onion soup. We walk down the hill to our flat, read a while, and are in bed by midnight. I'm playing another competition as part of the Braid gathering tomorrow. Time to rest.

● ● ● ● ● ●

Today's event is a bogey competition, played for the Captain's Pink Balls. I'll be playing against the card at the Golspie Golf Club, and will get my five shots from the card. I've never played this sort of match-play competition, and decide to think of the card as a golfer who holds a scratch handicap. I'll be playing an invisible but formidable opponent. I'll try to do what Bobby Jones, who won the Grand Slam of the U.S. and British Amateurs and Opens in 1930, did in match play. His strategy was to play what he called Old Man Par, and to forget about his opponent. He figured he would defeat his opponent if he could match or better par.

Golspie's course doesn't look like much upon first sighting. Locals refer to it as a "satellite" course, not one visitors would think of playing, particularly on a first visit. Maybe so, but I remember playing here during my first visit to Dornoch. A boy named Alistair Shand rode his bike to the course to caddy for me. I wonder where life has taken Alistair. Satellite courses usually offer top-of-the-line crack, high-spirited enjoyment, that is. In Ireland the word is spelled "craic." Here it's crack.

The opening hole at Golspie runs down a field, into which has been cut a fairway and a green. The second hole cuts across the field toward the sea, and then the third and fourth holes run parallel to the first in the opposite direction. The feeling of being near the sea grows, and the fifth hole, a short par-four across a fairway with more warts, knobs, and bumps than a toad to a sunken green, gets the blood going. Now we're at the sea. The beach is a lateral hazard, in play. Hit onto the beach and you can play the shot if you choose.

After the fifth hole, the course turns to the west, moving inland and up to higher moorland dominated by yellow whins, trees, and views out to the empty lands, the mountains. It's that mixed environment to which Donnie Macdonald referred. The Mannie is in full view this sunny morning. I'm playing with John Moreton, the Braid expert. He notices me looking up to the Mannie. "It was basically a program of ethnic cleansing," he says of the Duke of Sutherland's Clearances. "There's not a strong enough word for it."

By the ninth hole I'm holding my own against the card. This is straightforward stuff. There wasn't any haggling on the first tee about how many strokes to give or get, or about the accuracy of handicaps. Scorecards are full of numbers, but they are powerful opponents anyway. I was realizing the Golspie scorecard was as authentic an opponent as a person. It embodied soul and spirit. I wanted to beat the damn thing.

I was even with the card as I teed off on the ninth, a long par-four where the fairway is an avenue between gorse bushes and heather. Alas, I hooked my drive a few feet into the heather.

The first rule when one gets into these thick, brutal bushes is to get out – the Greenberg Rule. Take an unplayable lie if necessary. If you have a shot, even going backwards, hack it out back into play. I was tempted to do more, because my lie was decent. But what was the point? I wasn't going to reach the green anyway. Jack Nicklaus advised that the golfer who wasn't comfortable with the club in his hand should keep choosing another club until he found one that felt right. His advice popped into my mind as I stood in the gorse up to my knees, getting pricked and prodded by the needles in the bushes, and I grabbed my wedge. My pulse rate dropped, and I hit a wedge to within eighty yards of the green. My next shot was a poor one, forty feet short of the hole. I felt the contours of the green in my feet as I walked to my ball, then rolled it in. Par. The card gave me a shot, so I was one-up. I felt a surge of power. I was on top now, affirming myself as a golfer against a piece of paper. Our group was cruising along, chit-chatting about all things golf.

"Who are the eight winners of majors with the letter Z in their names?" Moreton asked. Our group came up with not eight but nine names: Gene Sarazen, Vic Ghezzi, Roberto de Vicenzo, Babe Zaharias, Fuzzy Zoeller (a double winner with the letter in both his names), Nancy Lopez, Larry Mize, Jose Maria Olazabal, Lee Janzen. John also wondered if any of us knew the oldest club outside Britain. Easy – Royal Calcutta. And the oldest in North America – easy for a Canadian, because it's Royal Montreal.

While this quiz was underway, I lost three holes to the card. I was annoyed, losing to a scorecard. I wasn't losing only to the card, but to the architect. Braid, the man whose courses we admired, was the true invisible opponent. I was playing against him, the course, the card, and myself. I wanted to win this bogey competition. Old Man Par, hell. I was up against Old Man Bogey, and I was on the way out, soon down for the count. I lost 4&3, four holes down with three holes to go. We played the last three holes. All in all the card won five more holes against me than I did against it. Not one of the ten golfers in the competition beat the card. Braid, you win. Golspie, you win. Scorecard, you win.

But I couldn't very well congratulate Braid and Golspie and say, "Well done." I couldn't tip my cap to my opponent, or shake his hand, and I'd have felt silly in pulling up some turf in a symbolic handshake. I made the gesture that seemed appropriate. I walked over to the pin on the last green, took it out of the hole, and shook hands with the flagstick. I also bowed to the course, and presently followed my companions into the clubhouse for the lunch and the prize-giving. Prize-giving? Nobody beat the card.

No matter. Prizes were awarded anyway. The Captain's Pink Balls, a necklace of pink golf balls, decorated the table.

A couple of fellows win Thommo golf balls, made by a company with which Peter Thomson is involved. Alan Wilson, the captain of a cruise ship and one of the fellows with whom I played, wins the competition, having finished all square to the card. He picks up the trophy so that he can say, "I've held the Captain's Pink Balls." Moreton, who lost by a substantial margin, makes a few comments about playing in the spirit of James Braid.

Walking out of the clubhouse, I notice a framed invoice on a wall outside the bar. It's from Braid, to the club, dated November 28, 1927. It refers to "18th and 19th Nov., to Professional Services: 21. To Travelling and Hotels, 10." Braid had taken the train up to Golspie to lay out the course, and charged the club £31. Included is a copy of the check the club made out to him, which he has signed.

● ● ● ● ● ●

I return to Dornoch, where I meet Sam Kay in the clubhouse. Sam is a red-faced, portly man in his seventies, a member who also belongs to the lawn-bowling club next to the course. He was in the produce business in Nogales, Arizona, importing Mexican food, and he took a golf trip every September. Sam read that Tom Watson had become a Dornoch enthusiast, so visited the club. He was smitten, and returns for the summer season every year. He always stays for the Caddies Cup in mid-September, the last junior competition of the season. Sam is a big supporter of the juniors at Dornoch. He brings them golf bags, shirts, shoes, balls, whatever he can manage from home. His only rule is that the kids must write to him when he's in the States. He's also taken some Dornoch kids to the States for golf. Paul Martin, a teenager who is an excellent player and works in the pro shop, is one of Sam's charges. "I think of him like my grandson," Sam says.

"I never tire of this view," Sam tells me as he looks over the links, flowing in serial waves, burnished in the early-evening light. "My friends tell me that I must be sick, coming here every year and not going to other courses in Scotland. I tell them I'd be sick if I didn't come. It's a time warp here. You don't get this kind of golf in America, where the course is part of the town and where everybody knows everybody because of the golf. Yes, Dornoch is small, but that's its charm. If you need something, you try to get it here. If not here, then Tain. If not Tain, then Inverness. If not Inverness, then Edinburgh and Glasgow. You'll get what you need eventually. It just might take longer."

Or shorter. I'm making new friends every day. Andrew Skinner invites us to the annual Spicy Cup barbecue at his home. The place is crackling. I have a couple of burgers and a dram of Glen Ord whisky. The Spicy Cup awards are presented on the landing at the back of the house. The competition comprised four better-ball matches, and resulted in a tie. Dornoch had won the previous event, and so in the way of genuine competition – à la the Ryder Cup, say – the club retains the Spicy Cup. The awards are rum glasses, filled with Spicy Rum. Greenberg is aglow as he sips his rum from his Spicy Cup glass.

It's a soft Dornoch evening, little wind, kids playing soccer in the field behind Andrew's home. I feel an urge to get back to the links, never mind how tired I felt a few hours ago after the bogey competition at Golspie. I say good evening to my Spicy Cup friends, and zip over to the course. I flip my golf bag over my shoulder, hit off the first tee, and walk briskly down the fairway, dressed in jeans and sneakers. I play until after eleven, whacking golf balls into the pinkish night sky. I'm one happy golfer. Golf as play. It's an idea worth pursuing.

• • • • • •

I wake up the next morning at 5:30, and am on the course before six. Bobby Mackay is the course superintendent; he hopes to be here for the rest of his life, and he's only in his mid-thirties. "There's no better place on this earth than being out on this course at 4 a.m.," Bobby's told me. I haven't made it that early, but I'm sure happy to be here. What a way to start the morning.

"Up early, are we?" a woman cleaning in the clubhouse said, smiling. On the fifth green, a woman driving a greens mower says, "Have a good game." An elderly man out for an early-morning stroll greets me with, "Lovely day to be alive." I putt out on the last green just after eight, walk into the clubhouse, and see the woman who had greeted me two hours before. "Ye'll be awake now, I'm sure," she says. Awake, and invigorated.

Chapter 8

The Bookshop

It's impossible to walk onto the High Street and miss the Dornoch Bookshop. The shop is just about the widest building on the street, and its prominent position at the east end of the road encourages passersby to drop in on their way into the village center or to the beach.

The design of the shop also tempts one to enter and browse, and upon entering one immediately sees the counter where Lesley and her assistants are working. There's an inviting jumble of books on the counter near the back wall in the middle of the shop. There's room to move among the various tables where Lesley puts out books she'd like to highlight, yet the space is also small enough that it's easy to bump into fellow book-browsers and find oneself in a conversation. This is the art of the independent bookshop, where a kind of living-room-cum-library develops.

The building itself was constructed in the middle of the eighteenth century by James Boog. Boog was born between 1725 and 1730 in Perth, and in 1764 married Christina Ross of Tain, across the firth from Dornoch. A carpenter and an architect, he was working on Fort George, a defensive military installation on the Moray Firth near Inverness, when he met Christina. They had thirteen children and lived in Golspie for a time, where the Duke of Sutherland employed him to renovate Dunrobin Castle, a monster of a building devoid of charm. Dunrobin was then and remains the seat of the counts and dukes of Sutherland. The Boogs also rented and lived at Skelbo Castle.

Boog was a self-made man who designed many public buildings in the Highland counties of Ross and Sutherland; some of his descendants, who now live in Raleigh, North Carolina, have found in their genealogical research that Boog designed all the churches and manses built in Sutherland and Easter Ross between 1760 and 1804. Donald Sage in his *Memorabilia Domestica*, an account of life in and around Dornoch at the time, wrote of Boog that "He terrified all the schoolboys as well as every inmate of his own house by the violence of his temper and his readiness to take offense." I particularly relish Sage's use of the word "inmate." His baker's dozen of children and his poor wife might be comforted now to know that the man of the house's building on the High Street in Dornoch is now a bookshop, where those who visit are inmates by choice. But maybe the house has ghosts; could that have been Boog who caused part of the ceiling to collapse one early morning while Nell was still in bed and I was having coffee and reading the newspaper? Was it Boog's spirit that inhabited the building when darkness finally settled over Dornoch one midsummer night, a night when I was in a bus filled with drunken golfing Scots after a day's matches in a storm at the Gleneagles Golf Club? Nell, who isn't easily spooked, didn't like being alone in the rambling, creaky flat at night, and welcomed me as if I'd come back from military service when I straggled in after midnight. Meanwhile, the uncaring rain continued to smack the headstones in the graveyard opposite our flat.

James Boog died on March 6, 1810, in Dornoch, and is buried in Golspie. His wife died in 1817. Various descendants subsequently occupied the house. At one stage it housed a tailor's shop; the tailor married a woman from Cheadle, a village in Cheshire, England. Hence the name Cheadle House.

Cheadle House also had been home to a grocery and a newsagent, a Mr. Wills. In the late 1980s, Mr. Wills put his shop in Cheadle House up for sale. By then Richard and Brora Butterworth had arrived in Dornoch, and were looking for a place to settle after living in a village in Kent, England. They were in their late fifties. Richard had worked in educational publishing for years. An avid reader and a distinguished gentleman, who usually dresses in a jacket, checked shirt, and tie for his day's activities, Richard had arrived in Dornoch with a computer and fax machine. He went into partnership in a small bookshop just up the High Street, where his partner was the wife of a local surgeon. They expanded the shop, but the space was still too small for what Richard had in mind – a bustling, welcoming bookshop. In 1989 he took over the bookshop on his own, and went looking for more space.

Mr. Wills had happened to put up his shop in Cheadle House for sale, and after some protracted negotiations Richard purchased the downstairs space from the owner, my landlord, Sinclair Mackintosh. He didn't need the upper two floors, the space Nell and I would rent for our summer in Dornoch. Sinclair, who has a sharp eye for a building's details, had observed that the building just to the west of the bookshop had an archway through to a back garden. The bookshop windows were renovated to echo this theme. It was the right idea for the right place, because the arches say, "Come on in. Visit with us. Browse. You're welcome here."

"The happiest years of my working life were spent in the bookshop," Richard told me. He owned the bookshop until late 1999. (The unfortunate Mr. Wills, a curious fellow who used to walk up the High Street carrying a shotgun, was one day found in the street dead, leaning over his bicycle.) Then, having enjoyed his years at the bookshop, he sold it to the Bells, newly arrived from Kent themselves. But Richard couldn't stay away from the bookshop. He worked there when the Bells were moving their possessions north from Kent. He stopped by regularly. Many days when I popped my head out of the flat I noticed Richard across the road at the newsagent, picking up his newspaper. Then, invariably, he would peek into the windows of the bookshop to see what was on display. Once a reader always a reader.

"Dornoch is a reading village," James Bell told me. It sure is.

• • • • • •

The entire village sometimes seems to me like a bookshop, a place to learn. Tommy McCulloch lives past Golf Road at the other end of the village from Cheadle House, with his wife, Christeen. Their lounge is full of books, on British history, birds, nature, and golf. Christeen is an opera-lover, and when I visit their house her favorite music is always playing. Tommy sits me down in the conservatory just off their back garden, on a gray morning when the rain is heavy but somehow soft; this rain in the Highlands is referred to as a "smirr," and that's how it sounds and feels – almost soapy, sibilant. I like to visit Tommy, because here I learn about Dornoch's old days. He's seventy-six now; his father, Danny, was the professional at Royal Dornoch from 1923 to 1939. But when the war intervened, the club suffered; in September 1939, the club took in £700 in green fees, but a year later took in only £10. The club could no longer afford a professional, so Danny took a job with the Ministry of Food as its representative in the local abattoir, and did that until 1948. He worked in the club at the same time, for nothing. Things were so bad that it was impossible to get golf balls.

Golfers were loath to lose any, and so looked until they either found their balls or finally gave up on them.

Tommy's a quiet man. It takes time for him to open up and share his memories of a place he's called home for all his life. Gradually he brings out some gems – old *American Golfer* magazines, the tool his father used to stamp golf clubs that he made. Tommy whistles between sentences, and he talks sparingly. It's a matter of waiting for him to say something, of being patient. Highlanders can be reticent in this way, which I find attractive. They don't spill out their life stories to somebody they hardly know. Yet they warm up quickly once a common bond is established. Tommy can tell that I have a strong feeling for Dornoch, and that I want to hear about the life he's led, the place where he's lived. Most people I've met here have a great affection for the outdoors. Tommy's dad considered his house a place only to eat and sleep. Life was outdoors, on the golf course, playing hockey or curling on a frozen pond. He liked teaching golf, and chose his words carefully. To his son and other students he said, "You must appreciate what you have and add to it." He died when he was ninety-one. "The course and golf were his whole existence," Tommy says.

Tommy brings out two volumes of old *Golf World* magazines. A small bookcase nearby holds books by Joyce Wethered, Bernard Darwin, Bobby Jones, and Lee Trevino. Tommy served in the military during the war, then went to university in Edinburgh. He became a teacher, which was his profession in Dornoch until he retired. He and Christeen have three children and ten grandchildren, none of whom live in Dornoch. I'm learning that while many people retire to Dornoch – a fellow at the Central Garage around the corner from the golf club says the place is in danger of becoming a retirement community for golfers – most young people leave. Jobs are scarce; the big cities beckon. Tommy and other locals call this movement away from the village another sort of Highlands Clearance. There's a sadness in the air now as his wife's opera selections waft through the conservatory.

"They would all like to come back to Dornoch," Tommy says of his children. "But there's no work for them here. This is the story of the Highlands. We lose our young people. They don't come back. It's been going on for at least two hundred years, ever since the Battle of Culloden. The English decided people should be sent away and the young ones have been leaving since."

Tommy was clasping his hands and rubbing them together while he spoke on this troubling issue. He got up to remove an old golf club from a cabinet, and held it almost as a talisman. I soon left, and before turning for home, walked around the corner to the Struie course, where some kids were playing golf. Would they still be in Dornoch in ten years? Probably not.

• • • • • •

"Come over for a drink at about eight. We would love to have you visit," Richard Butterworth suggested one morning when I ran into him at Graham Sawyer's, the newsagent across from the bookshop. So that evening Nell and I drove the mile or so north along the western edge of the course and uphill into the countryside. Now we were surrounded by fields on one side, the Mannie up ahead – he was always up ahead, or behind – and the North Sea to our right. We reached the top of the road before the old fishing village of Embo and turned in at the low house looking out to the fields and the sea. This was where the Butterworths lived. They invited us in and told us their story over the next couple of hours, as the sun set over the western mountains. The sea shimmered in the play of light and the sky reddened.

Brora, Richard's wife, had known Dornoch since childhood. Born in Angus in 1930, she spent her summers here. Her grandfather, "mad about golf although he had one of the worst swings in Scotland," she said, had in 1900 bought a large house in Dornoch opposite the first fairway. He built a putting green in front of the house, and was never happier than when he was in Dornoch during the summers. The family was so enamored of the area that Brora was given the name of the town fifteen miles up the road on the sea. Besides, Dornoch wouldn't do as a name. "My given name was Margaret, but I've never used that," Brora said. She spent ten summers in Dornoch, until the Second World War. The house was then used for soldiers. Her grandfather died in 1944, and eventually Ross House, as it was called, became a boarding school for girls who lived on the west coast. There weren't any secondary schools on the west coast then, so the students came across to Dornoch. Not surprisingly, Brora played some golf during her summers in Dornoch. She remembered the barefoot caddies from Embo, who spoke in Gaelic while cursing the bad golfers for whom they worked.

Dornoch remained in the Butterworths' minds even while they raised their family in England. They had two daughters, Emma and Charlotte, and also adopted two of Richard's nieces. Their mother, Richard's sister, had married an American, but the marriage failed. The woman suffered from lupus, and died of the disease. The two girls were ten and twelve at the time that the Butterworths adopted them. "It went down quite neatly," he told us. The younger one, Kate, eventually married in the Dornoch Cathedral. In the meantime Richard and Brora had started coming up to Dornoch again in the summers, which they did for twelve years. During one visit they came across a house for sale in the countryside north of Dornoch, and eventually purchased it.

The house and property were perfect for the Butterworths – the spacious grounds, trees, gardens, a small guest cottage, views to the sea, Tarbat Ness, the mountains of Aviemore. The large front room in which we sat had those big windows that houses with a view should have, and the walls were filled with paintings and prints – landscapes, antique political cartoons, a 1654 map of Sutherland, a famous old print of Dornoch, a painting of the Dornoch Bookshop, done by Cyril Reed in 1999, which was given to Richard when he sold the shop.

"Dornoch is an extraordinary place," Richard continued. "People do find something here. It's difficult to explain."

Brora added, "As long as we have been here, we still are often surprised by what we find. You're walking and you come upon something beautiful, something you didn't expect."

But it takes a certain cast of mind to come upon unexpected things. One has to be open to the unexpected, and to want to learn. Brora's father collaborated on a book about, in part, the Battle of Culloden, the famous clash in 1746 where the British wiped out the Highlanders near Inverness. The British then engaged in a program to extinguish all things Highland – bagpiping, kilts, and any other symbols of Highland culture they could search out. The Highlanders considered this an act of genocide. (When I was with Tommy McCulloch I had discerned that same feeling in him.)

The book that Brora's father wrote was part of the British Battles series that the publisher B. T. Batsford put out. Her father squirmed at the histories already published, and so provided his own. The Butterworths remain interested in Scottish history, particularly that of the Highlands. Perhaps this accounts for the bookshop's strong collection of Scottish history. The subject goes with the landscape. Studying history is a way not only to learn, but also to enjoy, understand, and appreciate the places where one lives. Maybe it's why I wanted to spend a summer at a golf course where the game has been played for centuries.

By 1999, Richard was approaching seventy and, while still in good health, felt this was the right time to sell the bookshop. "The best time to retire is when you're still roughly in charge of yourself," Richard said. But to whom would he sell? He didn't want to turn it over to just anybody, because he had a personal as well as a financial stake in it. If he and Brora had become part of the community, so had the bookshop. People stopped by not only to browse and perhaps to buy books but to partake of something else – communication with like-minded folks.

The Dornoch Bookshop was a companionable resting place in the village, and, situated as it was beside the local library, formed a quiet corner of friendship and learning. The buyer needed to have a feel for Dornoch and a feel for books.

As these things sometimes happen, Richard found just the right buyer. After putting the bookshop up for sale, he soon got an offer. Richard told his lawyer that before he agreed to the figure he wanted to know who the buyer was. "It's Mr. and Mrs. James Bell, from Kent," he was told.

"I fell off my seat," Richard remembered.

James Bell had, during the 1970s, been an Anglican clergyman in Invergordon, twenty miles south of Dornoch, with additional responsibilities at the Episcopal churches in Dornoch and Brora, and so knew a fair number of people in the area. For the past seventeen years, he had been the senior chaplain and head of the divinity department at Tonbridge School in Kent. "That was my old school," Richard said, marveling at the coincidence. Richard had been a pupil there right after the Second World War, when James was just a wee boy. They met when James bought some maps of Dornoch and the area in the bookshop, after Richard noticed that James was wearing an Old Tonbridgean school tie.

Lesley Bell had been a nurse, social worker, and midwife. She wasn't quite the avid reader that her husband was, but she liked being around books and enjoyed people. James had decided to retire to Dornoch, while Lesley, who had also taken to the area, still wanted to work at something that would bring her pleasure and contribute to the community.

When Richard learned the Bells had made an offer, he knew he'd found the right people. They had taken control of the bookshop by the time we arrived there, and it wasn't a day or so before we were having tea and browsing there. Regularly.

· · · · · ·

We're heading for dinner at the Bells's home, high on a hill in Edderton, a hamlet to the south of the Dornoch Firth Bridge and just to the west. The house has a clock tower, so there's a whiff of romance about it. We're in Struie Hill territory, a landscape with a view. We turn off the road to head up a twisting path, soon arriving at the house. There's another world-opening view from here. James is waiting for us.

James and Lesley arrived in Edderton in April 1998, on a day of horizontal rain and abiding duskiness in the hills. "I thought, 'What have we done?'" Lesley recalls. "But it was gorgeous even in the storm."

Is Lesley kidding me about how "gorgeous" she thinks the area looks even in a storm? I don't think so. People in the Highlands manage to see beauty in weather I'd consider despicable. Just as Inuit have some forty words for snow, Highlanders have numerous ways of describing weather; everybody isn't so much an expert as a close observer of what's coming, what's already there, or what's just been there. Or maybe they need many ways to describe the weather because it's often perplexing. A typical forecast in the morning papers can confuse anybody. "Thursday will be a rather windy day with a lot of cloud and showers, although most places will have some sunshine." The conditions also work their way into the language. James describes a woman as having "a rather wintry smile."

The climate around Dornoch isn't too bad at all, though, because this area of Sutherland is on the lee side of the mountains to the west. These mountains act as a barrier to the storms that often pummel northwest Scotland, riding the prevailing winds out of the west. The process by which the air is rid of moisture as it falls to the windward side of the mountains and then blows dry on the lee side is called the föhn effect. The result is a quite pleasant climate for the area in which we're spending our summers. The average rainfall in the west approaches 120 inches, while Dornoch and vicinity receive only 30 inches, 11 inches less than Glasgow in the southwest. Locals use the word "microclimate" to refer to the weather in southeast Sutherland. It's an ideal climate for golf.

The main course during our meal with the Bells consists of an oval of thinly sliced meat called a Lorne sausage – named after an area of Inverness-shire called Lorne – that's been cooking since morning. There is also garlic bread; it's "wonderful for mopping," James exclaims. As we eat, he tells us of his time in the army. He's a student of all sorts of history, but particularly savors military history. He was an infantry officer in The Kings Own Royal Border Regiment from 1959 to 1965. I'm taken by his appetite for food, for riding, for reading, for landscape, for drink. A shock of white hair falls across his forehead and loops over his right eyebrow as he tells Nell and me about one of his best friends, the military novelist and historian Allan Mallinson. His horse Jessie appears in Mallinson's books, and a fellow named Bell, a colonel and a Scot, makes a cameo appearance at the end of his novel *Nizam's Daughter*. Mallinson is the current defense attaché for the British Embassy in Rome. He had signed copies of his novels at the bookshop in May. "He has a developing readership," James tells us.

"You will have another glass of wine, won't you?" James asks. Lesley brings out a big bowl filled with peaches, grapes, raspberries, and currants for dessert – a delicious concoction that James prepared. "You'll have to dig deep," he tells us. "There are lots of different things in there, bits of twigs. We're not American. We're not oversanitized."

We pick and eat and enjoy. Lesley informs us that she has already learned that the locals are such avid readers that she needn't worry about what to stock; they will tell her. We learn about a surgeon from Inverness who visits Dornoch primarily to stop in at the bookshop. The Highlands are full of well-stocked bookshops. During a drive to the northwest Highlands, in and out of the folds in the mountains, high above one loch after another, we stopped in at a craft village on an old, ugly abandoned military base, now colonized by artists – weavers, potters, painters. There's a terrific bookshop also.

Dinner is ending, although one course remains – cheese. First James invites us to have a whisky, and we accept; well, I accept. Nell says she'll drive home. James walks down a flight of stairs from the kitchen to fetch a bottle of fifteen-year old Dalwhinnie. He suggests a touch of still water to "cut" the whisky, or open it up. "All it needs is some good water and the whisky releases a lovely perfume." As rendered by Chairman James. "Whisky is wonderful, isn't it?" he adds. Yes, it is. Lesley informs us that when she was a nurse it was common to prescribe whisky for people who were ill.

This night refuses to end, or we don't allow it to end. Here comes the cheese: Caboc, a full, fat, soft variety, rolled in coarse-grain oatmeal and made locally in Tain; Bishop Kennedy, "a kind of Scottish brie which has matured and been washed in whisky," James informs us; and an organic Scottish blue cheese from Lanark, "wickedly delicious," James says, adding, "If you're pregnant, lactating or immuno-compromised, I have to warn you of the Lanark, as it is made from unpasteurized milk." Lesley offers coffee while James tells of the Beefsteak Club, a private gentlemen's club in central London to which he belongs. Members take their lunch or dinner at one long central table, where a steward seats them according to the order of their arrival in the club. "One then finds oneself in the most agreeable of conversations with people around and opposite," James says. Every member of the club staff is addressed as Charles, "an affectionate greeting, informally polite," says James, "without members having to remember each individual's name." James invites me to a meal at the club should we find ourselves in London at the same time.

It's time for Nell and me to leave. James suggests we leave by driving around the corner of the house and through the lower gate. "There's a rather large stone at the corner," James advises. "It would be a good idea to miss it. But don't worry if you don't."

We miss the stone, hit the road laughing and full of good feeling for our friends. We drive down the path to the road, glide through the clear, black night, cross the Dornoch Firth Bridge and up the A9. It takes us ten minutes to get home. We don't encounter a single car on the way, park in front of the bookshop, and walk upstairs to our flat. Some night. Some people, James and Lesley. Lifelong friends. We know that already.

Chapter 9

New Friends

The High Street is empty and still dark when Graham Sawyer pulls his station wagon into a parking lot in front of his newsagent's shop. It's not yet six o'clock in the morning, there's not quite as much light now in midsummer, but the sidewalk in front of his store is already loaded with newspapers. Graham arrives before dawn to organize the papers in his shop, because it won't be long before people show up for them. Many locals reserve papers, which Graham and his wife, Lorna, keep behind the counter. His store is small, maybe six hundred square feet, but it's the right size for Dornoch, a village big enough to support a store this size but so small that it couldn't support a major super-market. His store sells milk, soda, magazines, shelves and shelves of candy bars, stationery, and lottery tickets. I'm in there at least once a day for the papers.

Graham, a fast-talking, fast-walking man in his late forties, is the chairman of the Dornoch and District Business and Trades Association.

Lesley Bell is his vice-chairman. Most recently they considered a farmer's market in Dornoch, much like the one held in Tain. But they decided against it, reasoning that Dornoch is too small and the market in Tain is so close. Too bad, because there's not much variety to the produce in Dornoch. Graham, like Tommy McCulloch, is concerned that Dornoch is becoming a place mainly for older people. He has two kids of his own, but knows it will never be a place where kids stay. Graham and Lorna came up here eight years ago from the central belt; Lorna was returning, because, although she was born in Glasgow, she came to Dornoch when she was four and grew up in the area. Graham figures it was a stupid thing to do financially, because the prospects for earning much money aren't very good. But he and Lorna like the social life, the small talk of a village, the way the store has become a place where people meet. He also figures he'll never suffer from stress.

The store couldn't survive without the traffic in newspapers, for which there's a 25-percent profit margin. During the summer he sells 500 copies of the *Northern Times*, nearly 300 copies of the daily *Press and Journal* out of Inverness, and 180 copies of the *Record* and 130 copies of the *Sun* – both tabloids. *The Times*, one of England's national papers, finds 40 buyers a day, the *Guardian*, another national, goes to 15 or 20 readers, and the *Independent* to only 5 or 6 a day. The *Observer* finds 10 or 12 buyers each Sunday. The *Herald* and the *Scotsman* are the national Scottish papers, the former having its origins in Glasgow and the latter in Edinburgh. Graham finds that 25 copies of the *Herald* are sold each day, and 40 of the *Scotsman*. The *Herald* has the larger circulation, however, in Scotland at large.

Sundays are not fun for Graham, because the huge papers come in sections that he usually has to put together himself. They come fully assembled in London, but not in Dornoch. Meanwhile, for reasons Graham doesn't understand, his place has become a specialist shop for railway magazines. He also gets a couple of golf magazines, and *USA Today* and the *International Herald Tribune*. They're always available in the winter when visitors are scarce. But he can't get enough of the pub-lications in the summer.

Graham collects records, especially the blues, and has thousands. He also has a motorbike with which he zips around the Highlands. Though he knows he'll never be a wealthy man, he's made a home here. "The thing I'm proudest of," he tells me, "is that people come into the shop every day to meet other people. We know everybody who comes in, and if somebody didn't show up for a day or two we'd quickly find out why."

. . . . . .

I'd never lived anywhere but a big city except for two years when I was pursuing a graduate degree in Guelph, Ontario, which isn't a metropo-lis, but isn't a village either. Guelph is a small city, with a population of about one hundred thousand. Knock two zeros off that figure and you have Dornoch's population. Yet I remembered how easy it was to meet people the last time I'd visited Dornoch nearly twenty-five years before. The idea of walking out the front door of my flat and bumping into people on their daily rounds appealed to me.

One of the first people I usually saw every morning was Dona Matheson. Dona lived on Station Terrace, next door to Don Greenberg. Station Terrace was a wedge shot, and not a full one at that, from the flat where Nell and I were living. Dona lived there with her husband, Sandy, otherwise known as Pipey – the same Pipey I'd played with at Dornoch in 1977. I didn't realize we had played together then until I returned from my summer in Dornoch and consulted my notes from long ago. Greenberg had told me that I would have to meet Sandy during my visit to Dornoch, but, in fact, it would be impossible to not meet Sandy or Dona.

Dona was walking briskly to the newsagent for the papers this par-ticular early morning. Sandy, who did a little lawn maintenance on the side for homeowners in Dornoch, and who had caddied for years at the club, and who looked the part of a man who had spent the better part of his life outdoors – ruddy cheeks, rough hands – liked to do the daily crossword puzzle. That's when he wasn't watching golf on Sky TV or the BBC, following some golf at Royal Dornoch, or talking golf. Dona invited me to stop by the house that night. Sandy and Dona would be watching a PGA Tour event from the United States. Their son Kevin would be at home for a few hours that evening before going out with friends. I accepted their invitation.

Sandy and Dona were sitting in the lounge of their cozy home, watching the golf. I spotted them as I walked down the garden path that led to their front door. Dona opened the door for me, but that was the last time either Sandy or Dona did that. I was told to open the door myself any time during the summer, because, they said, I was welcome there any time.

"What are you doing wearing that sweater?" Sandy asked me, snarling through a smile. What sweater was I wearing anyway? I looked down and found the offending embroidery signifying the Old Course in St. Andrews. I should have known better. I'd learned already that just about everybody in Dornoch who had anything to do with the golf club wore a shirt or a sweater or a cap from the club. The Old Course? That was a world away. Dornoch was where one came for true links golf, Sandy said. Why, you couldn't even see the water while playing the Old Course, except for a glimpse behind a few greens at the outermost limits of the strange, flat layout. But never mind: Sandy was only half-serious. Or three-quarters.

I sat down beside Nell, who had come along to meet Pipey and Dona. He was called Pipey because his father had played in the Dornoch Pipe Band. But Sandy had also worked as a pipefitter. He had grown up on Ospisdale Farm, across from Skibo Castle. Now Margaret Thomson, the great-granddaughter of Andrew Carnegie, owned it and lived there. Sandy's father had been a plowman, the term for somebody who plows

– hence the term "plowman's lunch," a hearty variety of cheeses, pickles, onions, and meat. Dona was from Dornoch, and she and Sandy had lived there since they married. He had worked at many jobs besides pipefitting, driving a meat truck, for one. He'd also caddied at Royal Dornoch, "whatever I could do to earn a pound," he said. Dornoch was his home, and he was going to find a way to stay here.

A golfer couldn't do better than have Sandy as his caddy. He was the man the visitors wanted. Don Greenberg first met Sandy in 1985, and, he told me, has "nothing but fondness, respect, and admiration for one of the true characters in the Highlands." Don particularly likes it that Sandy treats royalty or his fellow caddies the same way. Sandy also helped Don find his home in Dornoch.

"Like me," Don said, "he is consumed by the total golf experience and I'm always amazed and entertained by his hilarious insights into everybody in the game, from the world's best players to the highest handicaps at the club."

John Stark, the long-time professional at the Crieff Golf Club and a great friend of Willie Skinner, told writer Michael Bamberger that "When you look at Pipey you are looking at the face of golf." Sandy has Bamberger's book *To the Linksland* at home and wonders if he should consider the declaration a compliment. That face knows the ups and downs of golf and human nature. It's a face that has registered the ways in which golf can drive a player nearly crazy; after all, Sandy had been as low as a four-handicap, although he said he never felt better than an eight. It's a face that belongs to a man, sitting in a comfortable little room in a snug row house in the royal burgh of Dornoch, who has followed golf and golfers for nearly every day of his life, and who knows the game. He has heard that I held a one-handicap not that long ago, and that I am a five now. He wants to know what has happened to my game, and implores me to keep my thoughts simple. Sitting in Sandy and Dona's home, eating their shortbread and drinking their whisky on a cool summer's evening, I know he is right. It would be helpful, perhaps, if Sandy were to caddy for me. But he doesn't caddy anymore. Sandy has smoked since he was fourteen years old, and suffers from bronchial problems. His doctor has been conducting tests, and has told him not to caddy. He's not allowed to get his wind up. Instead we will sit here often this summer, and I will listen to his stories.

Pipey once caddied for Bob Charles, the left-handed New Zealander who won the 1963 British Open. Charles is a severe man who rarely cracks a smile, even though he's been one of the best putters in the game for nearly fifty years. Pipey doesn't take any guff from people, even the supposedly high and mighty. I wasn't surprised to learn he and Charles had had a tiff or two.

"He wasn't easy to get along with," Pipey tells me. "On the fifth I told him he should use a nine-iron. He said, 'No, it's at least a six.' I blew my tip right there when I told him he was right if he turned the club around. It's a nine, I told him again. He hit an eight and his shot went over the back of the green. He didn't say a thing. Then on the fourteenth he was over by the ridge and I told him to hit a six. He hit it up four feet from the hole and said, 'Now we're finally getting along.' Not an easy man to work for, Mr. Charles."

Pipey pursed his lips and shook his head at the memory, then invited us to have another drink. "Would you like beer, or whisky, or a vodka?" he asked. "How about a wee dram?" Nell responded. "Och, a wee doch-an-doris," Pipey chortled, than sang us a song of the same name, about the "drink at the door," or one for the road. (Sir Harry Lauder, the celebrated Scottish entertainer from the first half of the twentieth century, popularized this song.) We listened, enjoying our wee drams.

Pipey was into another story now, about Darren Clarke, the successful tour pro from Northern Ireland. South African Wayne Westner was playing with Clarke at Royal Dornoch, and Pipey was caddying for the Irishman. Clarke was away, although already on the eighth green;

Westner was off the green but closer to the hole. Pipey knows the rules of golf – the golfer who is away plays first – and so he attended the flagstick while Clarke prepared to putt. Then he heard an angry voice. It was Westner's.

"Will you get out of there?" Westner demanded. "What are you doing?"

"Wha' am I doing?" Pipey boomed. "I'm attending the flagstick, tha's wha' I'm doing. It's not your shot."

Clarke stopped Pipey on the way to the ninth tee. He hadn't said a word to Pipey until then, but asked now, "Are you settled down yet?" Says Pipey, "From then on we had a lovely time. It was great crack all the way."

Sandy brings down a photo from the mantelpiece taken of him and Greg Norman at Dornoch. He didn't carry Norman's bag but did walk around with him all the way. "I had a veritable battle with him on every hole. He'd ask me for the line, I'd give it to him, and he would argue. On the third, in a wind off the sea, I told him to aim twenty-five yards right of the middle of the fairway, toward the right bunkers, and to hit a slight draw. He asked what would be wrong with aiming twenty-five yards left and hitting a slight fade. I said he should hit two balls then, and he did, one starting to the right with a draw and one starting to the left with a fade. They finished a foot from each other."

Sandy went down to the Old Course to watch Norman and Nick Faldo during the 1990 British Open. His eyes narrowed and his voice crackled. "Faldo leathered him, just leathered him." That was the year when Faldo and Norman were tied for the halfway lead at twelve-under par 132 and played the third round together in the last group. I followed the twosome around while Faldo whipped Norman, shooting 67 to Norman's 76. Faldo went on to win the championship. Faldo later won the 1992 British Open and the 1996 Masters; he erased the six-shot lead that Norman held after three rounds of that Masters, shooting 67 to Norman's 78 while playing with him.

Faldo soon went into a prolonged, baffling slump. Sandy was curious about why a champion could slip so badly. He remembered that he enjoyed caddying for Faldo at Royal Dornoch, but that the golfer was never satisfied with a shot. "Every hole he had to hit two or three shots," Sandy remembered. "And he fooled around an awful lot with his swing." Sandy chuckled, aware that golf, played over a lifetime, usually defeats all players, in the sense that very few maintain their form.

Sandy, Dona, and I turned to the telecast of the American tournament. Nell and I finished our whisky, cakes, and then our tea and said goodnight. "Have a good game tomorrow," Sandy said. "Make me some money. And keep those swing thoughts that you write about oot of your head. They'll do you no good. No good at all. I hear ye've a good swing. Believe it then yerself."

I walked the half-wedge distance back to the flat, where Nell and I read for a couple of hours. There wasn't a sound in the High Street. The only sounds in my head were the words Sandy had offered. Keep it simple. Trust yourself. You can play the game. You've shown that. It was sound advice. And for me anyway, hard to follow. Dornoch was asleep. I wished that were also the case with my hyperactive golfing mind.

· · · · · ·

Dornoch, Golspie, and Brora together are home to about five thousand people. There's only one stoplight in the whole county of Sutherland, and that's on the A9 that runs through Golspie; it's meant to keep people from zooming through the town at a high speed. The longer I stayed in Dornoch, the more I realized that these populated areas were the pictures in the frame – the frame being Tom Atkinson's "empty lands." I woke up aware of the vast lonely landscape that surrounded me, and in the silence of a Dornoch night on the High Street, with the waves breaking on the North Sea only a few hundred yards away, I felt small but not diminished. Small in a good way, because the proportions seemed right. While living in a city of four million people I had gotten out of whack when it came to thinking about the scale of things. I never felt in my skin the huge empty spaces of Northern Ontario, or the large area that Lake Ontario took up.

Man in the city was writ large, or so I felt. Landscape was writ small. For an appreciation of landscape we went to art galleries. Or we watched movies, an unreal way of confronting landscape. Landscape wasn't part of my life in any real way. I did feel it when I walked in the park near my home and, sometimes, on the golf course when I was on my own. But more often I was alienated from landscape. I didn't know it, either. I didn't know it until I drove across the Dornoch Firth bridge. I sometimes felt a few tears down my cheeks as I neared Dornoch. What did this say about my life back in Toronto, my real life, where I thought I was more than merely content? Was I really that alienated from landscape in Toronto?

These thoughts were often with me in Dornoch, perhaps because I had provided myself the time to indulge them. Sandy and Dona had lent Nell and me a couple of bicycles for the summer, and we cycled frequently up to Embo or along the Cuthill Road and past the Bennies' home all the way out to the firth. I'd cycled as a youngster but not much as an adult. With time on my hands in Dornoch, I thought of when I'd felt most myself – comfortable in my skin, that is. I'd started to think of these matters while back in Toronto during the spring prior to leaving for Dornoch. There was an afternoon when I took an old baseball mitt and an India rubber ball and went to a public school where I'd played hockey and baseball as a kid. I'd hit golf balls there, too, on summer evenings. This time, on a hot May day I simply threw the ball against a brick wall and reacted to it as it ricocheted back to me, or around me. Or by me. I worked up a sweat while purposely trying to throw the ball against the crevices between the bricks, so that I couldn't predict the way it would come back.

I threw that ball at the school wall for an hour, and was pouring with sweat by the time I finished. Pouring with sweat and feeling good. I was exploring the athlete that, obviously, still resided in me – the athlete that had been lost.

Marion Milner, in her book *A Life of One's Own*, writes about finding out what she liked. It seems an easy enough task, but as we age most of us lose sight of how we most like to spend our time. Conventions, expectations, social and personal pressures all contribute to a general loss of a sense of self. Milner, writing in 1926, began to record the things that made her happy, and was often surprised at how elementary they were: listening to a Schubert quartet, grasping a new idea, walking on a country road. Eventually she discovered a lost self, and decided to live more intuitively.

While reading this book before leaving for Dornoch, I'd realized there were reasons I had been enjoying golf less. I made a list of things I liked about playing the game, to see if I'd been ignoring them. I liked: playing alone on a course in the early morning or evening; hitting different shots according to what I saw and felt as I walked up to the ball; hitting the ball on the ground as well as in the air; playing not by yardages but by sight; playing with close friends; walking and carry-ing my clubs; playing with a caddy and chatting with him as we moved along; playing in a soft rain; playing in cold, nasty conditions while wearing layers of clothing; playing by the sea; hitting low shots into a strong wind; match play rather than medal play; playing worst ball, where the idea is to hit two balls on each shot and then to pick the worst result and play two balls from there – it's about the best prac-tice one can get in; practicing at the end of the range in the evening; hitting every club in the bag to a green from the same spot; playing a full round with half a set, or even fewer clubs; standing in a bunker for an hour and hitting a variety of shots just to feel the spank of the club into the sand, the sand spraying and the ball popping out and rolling along the green; putting check on the ball from the sand; making the ball spin in various directions; hitting different shots from the same stance.

It became apparent to me that I'd ignored most of what I had enjoyed about golf. I played most of my golf in pre-arranged games at specific times. I played for score and often I made wagers, however small, on the outcome. Although I preferred to walk, I found myself accepting invitations to play golf where riding in a cart was mandatory. Rarely did I play alone. This fit in with how diminished my participation in sports had become. I didn't play hockey anymore with my friends – something I had done for two hours a week from the time I was fifteen until I was forty. Instead I went to professional hockey games when I was invited, to sit in seats that cost $150, so that I could watch millionaire athletes whose names I didn't know. I didn't hike anymore, choosing instead to walk a few city blocks sometimes, and convincing myself this was recreation.

These ideas played on my mind in Dornoch. Marion Milner made the following entry in her diary early in her research: "I want a chance to play, to do things I choose just for the joy of doing, for no purpose of advancement."

I hadn't done much at all for no purpose of advancement. I would "work" on my swing because a club championship was coming up. And if I perceived it as work, well, it *was* work, and not play. Golf had become a way of testing myself; increasingly I had been having discussions with friends about the value of competition, and this while I followed professional golf as my work. When I went for a long walk it was because I thought it was good for me, that I needed the exercise. It wasn't for the walk itself, for the play of foot upon ground, the opening of the ears to the wind through the trees or the rushing of a mountain stream. To everything there was a purpose. Play had transmuted into effort, effort into work. Inexorably, I'd stopped playing for playing's sake. Why?

The wearing away of purpose-oriented life began the day I arrived in Dornoch, without my knowing it. Nell and I were cycling regularly. I golfed alone in the evening with one ball or five balls, carrying my clubs, and sometimes I walked the course without clubs, just for the pleasure of the walk. Nell and I hiked. The more I felt the big spaces around me, the more I wanted to explore them. Golf, walking, cycling, hiking – these all felt part of the same impulse to move. Any advancement was only that which came from motion; it was physical, and unrelated to improving my swing or bettering my career. It occurred to me that golf was a simple game in the sense that it was about moving a ball from point A to point B, wherever one was. It was about motion, and motion was what I cherished during my days and nights in Dornoch.

Chapter 10

The Clearances

Nell and I wanted to learn more about the Clearances. We'd read some books and were aware that the subject was a potent one in the Highlands. But the best way to learn about the Clearances was to explore the empty lands, so we decided to drive out to the western Highlands, a stark and frequently desolate landscape, rugged in the forbidding way that parts of Atlantic Canada are. Clinging to the rock in Newfoundland or Cape Breton would not have been a stretch for Highland émigrés. Sizable peaks such as Stac Polly and Ben More loom over lochs, sea cliffs, and moonscape terrain, though most of the peaks are hidden in misty clouds that hover over the area.

Ruins dominate these lonely windswept moors, jutting up like lighthouses on barren points. The ruins of Ardvreck Castle are said to be haunted by the ghost of the Marquess of Montrose, one of Scotland's tragic heroes, who was caught in the powerfully conflicting cross-currents of loyalties to the Catholic Stewart monarchy and to

Protestantism in the complex civil wars of Cromwell's time. In 1644–5, Montrose – a very capable military leader – had galloped all over Scotland in the campaign to restore the Stewart king Charles I (the ill-fated golfer on the Carnegie Shield, who was executed in 1648) to the thrones of both England and Scotland. The Marquess fled to the Continent in 1646, but returned to Orkney in 1650 in support of Charles's son, who had been proclaimed Charles II in Edinburgh. This second Charles was holed up in Holland, staying out of Cromwell's way. Montrose's small contingent marched south from Orkney, but met defeat at Carbisdale at the head of the Dornoch Firth; the battlefield, just west of Bonar Bridge, is another area where we have done some hiking over the summer.

After the rout, Montrose fled into the wilds of the west to Ardvreck Castle, where he was betrayed by Neil McLeod of Assynt (in the far northwest Highlands) for a small sum of gold. Captured, Montrose was taken to Edinburgh for execution, which he met, by all accounts, with courage and dignity. His executioners, not atypically in the brutal annals of Scottish history, chopped his remains into bits and sent chunks of him off to various cities in Scotland as an admonitory gesture. It's said that one can feel a strange curse that has hung over the stark lands of Assynt ever since Montrose was delivered over to his enemies. Though Assynt had long been riven by clan feuds and blood-shed, the Montrose débâcle occurred just as economic and political changes from outside Assynt generated the cycle of poverty and depopulation that plague this remote land even today.

Late in the first morning on our western swing, we reached Durness, the town on the farthest northwest coast of Scotland. Durness's nine-hole golf course is becoming a cult classic; each hole has two tees that create different angles to the green, which means the nine holes turn into eighteen. Three fellows who felt they had to drive too far from Durness for their golf designed the course, which sits at the edge of an ancient graveyard, Balnakiel. There's a memorial to Rob Donn, who grew up near here and is considered by many people the best poet ever from Sutherland. Donn lived on the beach here in his later life, and died in 1778. He was a man of the people, who loved the wild landscape in which he lived. In one of his songs he wrote: "I like the pennies and silver/But other things more/I'll take a wee dram/And the joys of the poor."

The threesome that built Durness wondered if locals would accept their course, or the very game of golf. They were concerned that the reaction would be, "Who needs this game?" But the golfers formed a close relationship with the crofters in the area, and the sheep and the course in the big hills of Durness coexist peacefully. The greenkeeper is a local fellow who had never played golf before trying his hand at taking care of a course. The club has one hundred and forty members. Stuart Morrison, Dornoch's assistant professional, is responsible for teaching juniors in Sutherland, and has helped some twenty youngsters here.

Golfers can pay their green fees at the local supermarket, through the letterbox at the front of the clubhouse, or inside. The course is strung along the high coastal promontories with immense views of ocean, dunes, lochs, and moor. To the north there's nothing but cold ocean between the golfer and the North Pole. I played the course, as Nell walked along in the mist, and we each hit a shot across a yawning gap in the cliffs on the par-three eighteenth at the edge of the sea.

After our round at Durness, we drove east and south around the long sea loch known as Loch Eribol, and across to the uncharacteristically green and wooded town of Tongue on the Kyle of Tongue. There another haunting ruin, likely Norse, Varich Castle, stands on a hill above the town. Our car climbed on the A836 as we continued our journey south toward Lairg through some of the emptiest land imaginable, but it was surpassingly beautiful at the same time. We drove past

Loch Loyal as the peak of An Caisteal (764 meters) and other mountains loomed above us. The sun appeared for the first time in our two
days in the west.

This inland expanse of deserted straths, forsaken glens, and desolate lochs is where the impact of the Highland Clearances is most
readily apparent. The Highland Clearances, we've learned, represent
one of those appalling historical epochs that scar the soul of a people.
Mention it even today in the Highlands – some two hundred years
after the events – and you'll most likely notice a slight narrowing of
the eyes and tightening of the mouth in your listener, similar to that
which happens when an Irishman is reminded of the Famine. Some
of the same political and economic causes were at work with both
the Clearances and the Famine. One of the consequences – the disper-
sion of people from their homeland to all corners of the globe
– happened in both Scotland and Ireland.

Most of the people who were "cleared" had lived traditional agrar-
ian lives in small settlements that were based on ties of family and
clan. The pre-Clearance Highlands supported a stable if never large
population, although it was growing by 1800, and revisionist historians argue that, if the Clearances had not occurred, the land could
never have supported the increased numbers. People engaged in
mixed farming, with cattle, horses, and small native sheep grazing the
hills, and small-scale cultivation of corn and hay in the straths, or
valleys. Small villages with schools and inns and pubs took shape.
Most importantly, a close-knit clan society shared ancient historical
traditions that included such elements as music and poetry in their
own rich language, Gaelic. It's sentimental nonsense to characterize
the world of these Highlanders as a tartanned rustic paradise; their
lives were hard, with fairly primitive housing, regular bouts of hunger,
and onslaughts of disease such as tuberculosis.

Yet this sense of their harsh existence is colored by the very different
standards of modern life. What the Gaelic-speaking Highlanders

found after being forced out to the slums of Glasgow or the coal mines of Cape Breton was an even harsher existence, but also one in which the deepest roots of their lives – clan, language, land – had been violently eliminated.

In tracing the origin of the Clearances, historians place a great deal of emphasis on the final English defeat of the Jacobite rebellions in 1746. Devotees of Scottish history (or popular song) will recall this as the abortive attempt to put what Highland, and many Lowland, Scots viewed as the rightful Stewart heir on the united throne of England and Scotland. This heir was, of course, Charles Edward Stewart, the "Young Pretender," Bonnie Prince Charlie.

Without going into too much historical background, suffice it to say that the Catholic Stewart monarchy retained a romantic appeal to Scots generally and Highlanders especially. But a Catholic king – with dangerous allies in France and Spain in these early years of empire building – was anathema to the English, whose parliament had secured the succession of the Protestant William of Orange in 1688. The Jacobites (so called for the Latin version – Jacobus – of the name of the last Stewart king, James II of England, who was also James VII of Scotland, 1685–1689) fought three rebellions borne out of their loyalty to the Stewart line as well as their age-old antipathy to the English.

The final rebellion in 1746 resulted in utter disaster: a military rout at Culloden, which is just outside Inverness. (We visited Culloden on a day trip to Inverness, but didn't last fifteen minutes there among the tour buses and jangling cash registers.) Twelve hundred Jacobites – mostly Highlanders – were slaughtered at Culloden, many of them brutally hacked up after their side surrendered. It was the last battle fought on British soil.

The consequences of the defeat at Culloden were horrific. With the help of loyal Highlanders, Charles himself escaped (to finish out a dissolute life in France), but the Duke of Cumberland exacted a ferocious vengeance on the people of the Highlands and nearly eradicated their way of life. Cumberland was to earn the epithet "Butcher" for the battlefield carnage, the executions all over the Highlands, hundreds of imprisonments, and transportations to the colonies.

It was as if this time the English had finally had it with their Scottish foes. They determined not only to wipe them out in battle, but also to crush them where they lived. The Highlands, remote even today, were virtually immune to invasion; there were no roads and little fortification to protect an invading military force. Undeterred, Cumberland took a naval frigate and unleashed his ferocity along the western seaboard, where whole villages were put to the torch.

Until the time of Culloden, clan members got protection in a patriarchal system where they were loyal in a filial way to their chief. In return, the chief got fighting men. Subsequently, parliamentary legislation effectively dismantled the clan structure (which is how this blood-soaked historical digression gets us back to the Clearances). One act destroyed the power of the chief to administer justice (rough or otherwise); another act disarmed the Highlanders and undermined their traditional identity by making it illegal to carry weapons or wear the kilt. It even proscribed the playing of what the English called "engines of war," the bagpipe. The Highlanders were forbidden their weapons, their chiefs, their language, their dress, and their music.

This cultural devastation had far-reaching effects, and the clan chiefs were far from blameless in what was to follow. Deprived of their traditional power, hereditary chiefs now lusted after newer symbols of power: wealth that would enable them to attain the ostentatious life of aristocrats of the time. Emma Wood puts it succinctly in her *Notes from the North*: "They discovered that to emulate the English landowning aristocracy they required quantities of cash for luxurious clothes, town houses in Edinburgh and London, foreign travel, educations for their sons and significant dowries for their daughters." The lairds extracted the cash by hiking the rents on clan lands, selling off land to newly prosperous English manufacturers who craved sporting estates, and – most notoriously – introducing larger Cheviot sheep onto lands that they emptied of people. These were the Highland Clearances.

Nell and I returned to Dornoch in the sober realization that, while economic, agricultural, and political changes would have altered Highland life in time anyway, the emptiness of these lands is the direct result of brutal human actions. An ancient and venerable way of life was swept away forever. The most notorious landlord of the Clearances stands high above us on Ben Bhraggie, leading us back, as it were, to Dornoch. The Mannie, constructed of white Brora stone, towers over the landscape.

Erected between 1836 and 1838, by his "grateful tenantry," the Stalinist-realist-style monument depicts the Marquess of Stafford, heir to a huge English fortune, who bailed out the floundering Sutherlands by marrying their countess in 1785. The Sutherlands date back to the thirteenth century, but the Earls of Sutherland were of local more than national importance. Lord Stafford was created first Duke of Sutherland in 1833, and became known for the forced clearance of his tenants from the glens and straths of his wife's extensive ancestral lands – and their replacement with sheep. He did attempt to establish some industries (Clynelish Distillery of Brora remains today), and some peasants cleared from the interior were either resettled in what were meant to be fishing villages (such as Bettyhill, near Thurso on the far northeast coast; Golspie; Embo; and, while it wasn't a fishing village, Littletown in Dornoch, near the course. Jimmy Bell, the local amateur historian, theorizes that Carnaig Street, which runs through Littletown, was so named because of people cleared from Strath Carnaig, northwest of Dornoch), or given passage to North America. However, the duke – and his effigy – remain a focus of anger and contempt for Highlanders the world over.

Chapter 11

Highland Music

One word often comes to mind while Nell and I move about the north of Scotland. That word is "lament," and here, where the emptiness and the reason for it leads to the word, it is inescapable. One hears it in the music, especially in the ancient and classical piping tradition known as *piobaireachd* (pronounced pea-broch), its proper Celtic name, or *pibroch*, as many people spell it. This is as far away from the bagpiping heard at Highland games in North America or tourist traps in Scotland as golf on overwatered, overmanicured, condominium-bordered, cart-pathed courses in America is from Royal Dornoch.

Piobaireachd is also known as *ceol mor*, or "the great music," and is said to have reached its Golden Age in the mid-1600s. The music was transmitted orally, that is, played without being written down, until 1762, when a composition was first written down, and none of it was published until after 1800; clearly, not all of the pipes had been taken from the Highlanders after the Battle at Culloden in 1746.

Whatever the accepted date for its origins, *piobaireachd* is Scotland's soul music, and it digs deep, even though it's hard to understand and appreciate, especially at first. *Piobaireachd* to the untrained ear – and mine is nothing if not untrained – sounds like screeching and wailing, but to discount it on first hearing isn't all that different from saying that golf is a stupid game because, after all, why would anybody want to whack a ball across a field toward a hole? Or to question curling, another Scottish sport, in which people slide along ice with a broomstick while sweeping alongside a moving stone that looks like a meteor that fell from the sky? To dismiss *piobaireachd* would be akin to dismissing much of what is intriguing in these Highlands. I am here to learn, to try to grasp why I was so attracted to this place and why I am still pulled here. The music pulls, but why?

Bridget Mackenzie, the author of the scholarly work, *Piping Traditions of the North of Scotland*, knows about piping and she knows about lamentations and she knows about living in the Highlands. She and her husband, Alex, live just to the west of Dornoch, near the hills from which so many Scots were cleared. In her book, Mackenzie, a thoughtful, energetic woman in her late sixties who studied Old Norse, writes of the clearing of Glencalvie in 1845; she refers to it as the "savage" clearance. Mackenzie writes that a man named Sandy Forbes composed a *piobaireachd* to commemorate the 150th anniversary, the "Lament for the Clearances of Glencalvie." During the event commemorated in Forbes's composition, crofters and their families huddled in the cold churchyard, close to the lands they were being forced to leave, and refused for some time to give up what was rightly theirs. They scratched notes into the windows of the church – lamentations on the lives they were losing.

Nell and I planned to visit the church later. Just now we were getting to know the Mackenzies. They'd stopped by our flat for some sherry, cheese, fruit, tea, and biscuits.

We felt we already knew the Mackenzies. We had communicated before our arrival via a few phone calls from Canada and e-mails through their son, Tom, the course architect who works with Donald Steel and spent a lot of time up here while working on The Carnegie Club at Skibo Castle. This job was ideal for Tom, because his parents live in the area and because he's been a member at Royal Dornoch since they moved here when he was seventeen. We were grateful to Tom's parents for inspecting the flat we hoped to rent, and had looked forward to meeting them in person.

Alex Mackenzie is a South African–born Scot who grew up in Durban. His father was in the Royal Scots during the First World War. His battalion was sent to Siberia in 1918 to fight with the White Russians against the Bolsheviks, and they were left there over a winter without adequate provisions. Later, when Alex was two years old, his father died of gut rot contracted during that period. Alex and his younger brother followed their genes home to Scotland when Alex was eighteen. He built a successful career as an engineer and did a master's degree at the Massachusetts Institute of Technology after being employed in an iron works in Toronto for a year in the mid-1950s. The Scottish genes of which he spoke led directly to an interest in the pipes. He and other members of his family had played the pipes in Durban.

Bridget is half-Canadian by birth, of Scottish descent, as her father came from British Columbia. He studied Old English and Old Norse at Oxford, where he was a Rhodes Scholar. There he met his closest friend, J. R. R. Tolkien, the author of *The Hobbit* and *The Lord of the Rings* trilogy. Here we are with the Mackenzies in our bookshop flat, and we are learning that the renowned writer and Old English/Old Norse scholar was Bridget's honorary Uncle Ronald. He was quite an irascible fellow, Bridget remembers fondly.

Bridget became an Old English/Old Norse scholar herself, studying at Oxford, and met Alex when they were both lecturers at the University of Glasgow. The family moved to Dornoch in the early 1980s, where they have pursued a wide variety of interests, including the Highland bagpipes. Alex works on the physics of the instrument, while Bridget, fascinated by Highlands history and how the *piobaireachd* tradition reflects it, discerned a connection between the structure of Old Norse poetry and the structure of the music – they share similar internal rhymes. The performer interprets the rhythm, so that the music doesn't have a regular beat.

Piobaireachd, as we had read, was handed down orally as songs for a couple of hundred years. Both Bridget and Alex feel it lost some vigor when it was written out, or put behind bars, as they say; they hear an order in the music that doesn't inspire them in the way the more instinctive music does. Alex tells of a friend who is one of the top *piobaireachd* players in the world, a man who learned to play from the written music. But now he's breaking out, "playing from the heart," Alex says. Hearing this, I think about my golf. I've become afraid to play from the heart and have, almost without knowing, become one who kneels at the altar of self-improvement by listening to "scientific" instruction. There are certain fundamentals to the golf swing that help one play consistently, just as there must be certain fundamentals to playing the pipes. But still there must be room for golf by the heart, golf that isn't put behind bars.

· · · · · ·

Around 1850, Pipe Major John MacDonald of the 79th Cameron Highlanders composed a march called "Dornoch Links." Did it have something to do with the golf course? If so, was it, too, a lament? "The best *piobaireachd* works are the laments," Bridget says. "Some are magnificent, and may last anything up to half an hour of playing time; some are short but poignant." I hope to find this piece of music, to hear

it and to understand it. Months later I read of a *piobaireachd* competition in which a Glaswegian piper who didn't win a prize said he made
a technical error. "It's like missing a three-foot putt for the Open
Championship," he claimed. "It's only half an inch from superstardom."

The Mackenzies leave, Nell and I finish our glasses of sherry and consider the visit we will make to Glencalvie. Enjoying the sherry and
contemplating a visit to this Clearances site don't go together. Such
is the dissonance I feel in the Highlands.

• • • • • •

Iain Strachan puts this dissonance into his music. He can't help it. Iain,
a social worker in the Highlands, and a locally well-known musician
and songwriter, has come by Alan Grant and Dot Bennie's home.
He and Alan are close friends, and Alan has told me that Iain is a man
with a musical heart and soul. "You'll want to hear his music before
you leave," Alan said.

"Have you read any of Hugh McIlvanney's writings on sport?" Alan
asked me. I had. McIlvanney wrote on boxing and golf for the *Observer*.
I'd read him frequently and liked the way he dissected the spirit of the
athlete; he saw a boxing or golf match as events in which the athlete
confronted the things he was afraid of, and tried to overcome those
fears by overpowering an opponent or a golf course. One of Alan's
favorite McIlvanney pieces was about boxer Johnny Owen.

"He wrote that Johnny Owen did nothing in his life but box," Alan
recalled. "The line I remember was this. 'The sad thing is that he was
articulate in such a dangerous language.' Well, Iain is a quiet man. But
he becomes articulate when he has a guitar in his hands."

Nell and I sit in the kitchen at Alan's farmhouse, eager to hear Iain.
Iain is shy, huddled in on himself at first, and he carries his guitar close
to him in a manner that suggests it's part of him. He sits at the cluttered

kitchen table, angling himself away from it so that his legs are out on the floor. Removing the guitar from its case, he hunches over and tunes the instrument, then starts to play. He's at home with his instrument and his music, in much the same way that many professional golfers are most at ease when they're playing the game rather than talking about it. I've found that the best way to get to know a player is by following him on the course and, perhaps, talking later about his feeling for the game. Jack Nicklaus and Tiger Woods both become most animated when playing shots. I once caddied in a PGA Tour event when Nicklaus was in our threesome. He was struggling to make the halfway cut, then had to hit a long fairway wood to a green on a par-five. He had to fade the ball around a tall tree, then carry it over bunkers in front of the green. Nicklaus felt challenged by the demands of the shot. I watched as he and his caddy, Angelo Argea, discussed the type of shot he wanted to hit; Nicklaus was turning into concentration itself. He hit the shot required, birdied the hole, and went on to easily make the cut. Years later I watched Woods hit a variety of unusual shots with a four-iron on a practice range in California. He opened the blade of the four-iron so that its loft was more that of an eight- or nine-iron, then cut underneath the ball so that it climbed over a sixty-foot-high fence only forty yards away. He was making the ball do tricks in the air. The best golfers become articulate with a golf club in their hands. Articulate artists.

Iain's head is bowed over his guitar as he picks at the strings. There's a note of melancholy, more than a hint of lamentation. Then the beat picks up as if to say, "Yes, there's sadness here. But we'll dance in the face of the sadness. How else should a person react?" A cab driver in Ireland once told me that the Irish dance at funerals and cry at weddings; the observation applies to Highlanders.

The kitchen is quiet except for Iain's music. He's playing a song that he wrote, off his first CD, called *Skelbo*, which is also the name of his band. His wife, Veronique Nelson, a fiddler and viola player, accompanies him on the CD. He and Veronique live in the hamlet of Skelbo, just to the north of Dornoch on the way to Embo and within a short walk to Skelbo Castle, or what's left of it.

Iain is now playing a song called "Under the Northern Lights." Alan has told me of the forces that converge on Dornoch, which make it a haven for artists of all descriptions. I hear these forces in this song as Alan sings.

Iain wrote "Under the Northern Lights" three years ago, after living life in the Highlands for six years. The music reflects his feelings for the landscape and the people – the hard days of working the land and the ways in which Highlanders mix and mingle and accept that theirs isn't often an easy life but that it is often a rewarding one. The hardships come out of the landscape, but so does the beauty. The gifts are the mountains, the lochs, the limitless sky, the sea, the hills, the straths. "After the day's work," Iain says, "people are ready for fun and craic. It only takes two or three people and a great night can be had."

Iain speaks of the power of nature in the Highlands, "with a depth of history superimposed on the landscape that is easily apparent wherever you look." Palimpsest again. He and Veronique once attended a *piobaireachd* recital that Bridget Mackenzie organized at Foulis Castle, a sixteenth-century mansion near Evanton, south of Dornoch. Three of the best pipers in the Highlands played a *piobaireachd* that Iain Dahl had composed a few hundred years ago, when he was the piper for the castle. Iain remembers the evening as being exquisite.

"A lament does have soul," Iain explains. "But the central word for me, and no word can suffice, is celebration. An air or a reel or whatever the form or style has to be played with some form of celebration. A lament is a celebration."

"There's a rightness about Dornoch," Alan Grant had told me. We had felt this rightness tonight, listening to Iain play his guitar, singing

"Under the Northern Lights." Now we also understood that dissonance – sorrow and beauty commingling in the Highlands – can also create something greater: a state of bliss, perhaps, a heightened awareness that results from the appreciation that life is fragile, and that so are we.

• • • • • •

Nell and I are driving to Croick Church, near the site of the Glencalvie Clearance. From Bonar Bridge we drive along Strath Carron for ten miles on an unpaved single-track road through the woods. A river is on our left, the hills to our right, and there's hardly anybody else out on this route today. We encounter only one other car, coming the other way, and have to pull over into a passing place to let the vehicle by. We drive on, slowly, knowing that we are about to come to the place where, Tom Atkinson writes in *The Northern Highlands*, "victims of the Clearances left one of the most poignant records of their misery." He was speaking of the messages that the people had scratched into a window at Croick Church. Eighteen crofter families had lived in Glencalvie, and all had been evicted – ninety-two people in total, according to the report of a *Times* of London correspondent sent to witness the episode, in May 1845.

After parking our car at the side of the track, we read on a commemorative stone that many of the victims had sheltered in the lee of the church rather than inside it because to do that might have seemed sacrilegious to them. But somebody had scratched "Not true" on the stone, meaning that the church had locked out the victims, not that they chose not to enter. Croick Church, built in 1822, is still a working church. Services take place at three o'clock on the second Sunday of every month. The inscription on an elaborate tombstone in the graveyard surrounding the church started with an arresting one-word remembrance: "Stalker." Of deer, of course.

Nell and I walked around the empty church, framed by the hills and aware of the bleating of sheep and the gurgling of the river. Just to the west of the church are the remains of a Pictish broch, evidence that people had lived in this area for centuries; until, that is, the area was cleared of its residents. We walked around the church twice, trying to find the messages scratched in the window, but couldn't make anything out. Then the angle of the sun shifted slightly, and the messages became visible – knife cuts in the glass. We strained as near as possible to the window and read the scratchings.

"The Glencalvie people was in the churchyard here May 24th 1845 . . . The Glencalvie tenants resided in the kirk grass May 24, 1845 . . . Glencalvie people the wicked generation . . . Glencalvie is a wilderness under sheep." Transfixed, we read these words, and peering through the glass into the church we tried to imagine what it must have been like to be thrown out of one's home. We couldn't. It was beyond us.

"Of the eighty people who passed the night in the churchyard with most insufficient shelter," the *Times* correspondent wrote, "twenty-three were children under ten years of age, seven persons were sickly and in bad health, and ten were about sixty years of age. About eight are young married men. There are a few grown up children and the rest are persons in middle life from forty to fifty. . . . Eighteen families of ninety-two individuals supporting themselves in comparative comfort with not a pauper amongst them. That they owed no rent and were quite prepared to pay as much as anyone in rent for the land which they and their forefathers had occupied for centuries but which it seems is now to be turned into a sheep walk."

• • • • • •

A land-use issue is also alive at Royal Dornoch, generated by the road that crosses in front of the first tee and provides access to the beach.

It's of local significance only, perhaps, but demonstrates that the matter of how land is used in the Highlands remains complex and controversial. In the latter part of 1930, the town council decided to build the road on a rough old cart track, but didn't consult the club. John Macleod in his history of the club wrote that the building of the road constituted the worst controversy in the club to that point. At the same time another road that would pass to the south of the main course and through the Struie course was under consideration. Eventually both were built, but it is the road that crosses in front of the first tee that has provided ongoing controversy for seventy years. Walkers don't pose much of a problem to golfers on the first tee, although the golfers are a potential hazard to walkers. Cars, however, create not only tension but also potential havoc, even those moving slowly. No accidents have happened as yet, but the possibility and even likelihood is there. Many members of the golf club would like to divert the road behind the first tee, or simply close it without providing an alternative.

Residents of Dornoch who aren't golfers want the road to remain where it is, believing it's their right to get to the beach via that route. After all, it is on Common Good Land that belongs to the people of the village. The fact that there's another road south of the main course and well away from play isn't the issue. The issue is the right of way that the road constitutes, and the message that removing it or diverting it would send. That message is simple, to Dornoch's residents anyway. It says that the golfers come first, and that access to the beach for the population at large is a secondary issue. Diverting the road touches a core value in the Highlands: the land belongs to the people, not to special interests. At the same time, Dornoch people know that the golf club makes the village thrive. Dornoch would be much the poorer without the club. But that hasn't stopped the controversy that began in 1930 from persisting into 2000 and beyond. The discussion hadn't resolved anything, as far as I could judge by the time I left Dornoch.

"It deeply divided the community," John Macleod wrote of the matter of the road to the beach. It did then and it does now. Land matters here. It's apparent in the music. It's apparent in conversation in Highland towns. It's apparent at the golf courses. It's history, and yet it's current. In the haunting silence at Croick Church these matters reverberate in my mind. Nell and I drive home, slowly, silently. What is there to say?

Chapter 12

Linksland

There were many evenings when I played a few holes on my own, or with Nell walking along with me. One night when I was alone and playing quickly, the sky suddenly shifted from a deep blue to an alarming charcoal. The bruised sky highlighted a series of lonely bands of late light that engraved themselves on the hills around Tarbat Ness and on the other side of Loch Fleet to the north. The rain started and didn't stop. I put my head down and played up to the High Hole, the sixteenth, stopping there to listen as the surf pounded the shore and to watch as the high winds flung the marram grass back and forth. The dune world held fast, protected by the sturdy grass. I putted out on the green at the High Hole and considered walking directly to the clubhouse from there. By now the sea was roiling, and the back of my neck was being attacked by rain as sharp as a razor blade. Weather is just that, however. Weather. We think of it as good and bad, but maybe there's just weather. I played on.

I finished my round as blackness set over the links. The wind was so loud I couldn't hear my clubface contact the ball when I hit up to the last green. Soaked, I traipsed into the clubhouse and locker room, dried off, and went upstairs for a pint, where I sat at the window overlooking the deserted links. It didn't resemble a golf course just now, not during this fierce storm. It was a piece of ancient ground, deposited here by the receding sea, transformed into a golfing linksland during the last few centuries. A few centuries – a blink in geological time.

· · · · · ·

The dune world that produced the linksland of the Royal Dornoch Golf Club is always in motion. The physical nature of the land changes, as winds off the North Sea shape the dunes, altering their form in small and large ways. The shifting sands add or subtract from the humps and hollows, knobs and crests, that make up the turbulent ground. Forces of geology over billions of years have created this landscape. Change is constant, because the sea and gale-force winds are only yards away.

This gently curving linksland captivates both golfers and non-golfers. The terrain mimics the contours of the ocean waves. The land swirls, the ground moves, sweeps, and rolls. One needn't be aware of the historical forces that formed the links, but a little understanding can help one appreciate the environment. At the same time it is important not to lose sight of a basic and intuitive meaning of the word "links" – land that, as Donald Steel writes in his book *Classic Golf Links*, "links the sea with the more fertile plains that may be only a couple of hundred yards distant. It is land with no agricultural value. The only vegetation it supports are the fine, wiry grasses that, on top of a sandy base, make an ideal playing surface, especially for iron play."

Steel and a handful of other writers provided me with a limited understanding of linksland before I arrived in Dornoch. I knew that the sea had receded from higher ground over the ages and left behind what Sir Guy Campbell, a golf historian who wrote in the early twentieth century, called "channels" between features such as ridges and furrows. The tides, he explained, moved forward and back along these channels. He added that rivers, streams, and burns naturally sought these channels as they flowed to the sea. Sutherland is flow country, because of the volume of water that moves from the higher, western areas that get so much rain, through river valleys, down to the sea. This accounts for the broad curves in the hills, the ways in which they sweep this way and that. Mass glaciation over millions of years scraped away the uneven angles from the landscape. The word "flow" also applies to the shape of the land.

In time, shorebirds nested and bred in the channels, and the manure they deposited, Campbell wrote, mixed with seeds blown toward the sea from inland. Vegetation resulted from the fertilization and covered the channels – the tight turf of today's links fairways. Only hardy plants survived on dunes, principally the tough marram grass that is the essential ingredient for stabilizing them. Marram thrives only in areas where sand is blown in regularly, because it gets its nutrients from the diluted salty solutions and minerals that are dried on the surface of the sand particles. If a golfer, walking in the dunes to get a view of the sea, pulls up some marram grass, he is cursed, or so I decide to believe. He will never lower his handicap, because he has disturbed the coastal ecology. The wind will always push his ball away from his intended target. Putts will lip out, not in. The links golfer must be an environmentalist, else risk the wrath of the golfing gods.

It also helps to be environmentally sensitive and not to want to change things, because it's more interesting to accept the ground the way it is and to play it as it is. Some better-known links have been tarted up to attract the coddled golfer accustomed to immaculate, unnatural conditions, but it's preferable and more in the spirit of the game to accept the ground as it is, leave it as it is, and play it as it is.

Golf at a links is all about how the player deals with the humps and bumps and rises and falls in the land. Dunes are dynamic, and golfers who choose to play on a links must be resilient to handle the changing conditions. Links are also meant for walking, given that most are flat. The undulations in linksland provide a gently rolling landscape, with just enough movement to ask the golfer to play from sidehill, downhill, and uphill lies. But a links hardly has the dramatic and sometimes ungainly rises and falls that are often built into modern courses, or that are natural on mountain courses. The golfer walks and feels the ground beneath his feet. There's a sensuality in links golf that connection to the sea, contact with the ground, and a sharp awareness of climate help foster.

• • • • • •

If golf at a links is all about how the player deals with the humps and bumps and rises and falls in the land, it follows that a golfer/geologist might have a deep interest in such an environment. Robert Price, a Welshman considered an authority in glacial environment, has turned his hobby – golf – into some of his work, and has studied the factors that influenced the formation of courses in Scotland. He hasn't let that interfere with his regular Saturday-evening four-ball during summertime at his golf club, however. That's sacred time.

In *Scotland's Golf Courses*, Price writes:

> Scottish links land occupies a relatively narrow zone (often less than one mile wide) along the coast. Since the source of the sand is the adjoining beach and the mode of transport is on-shore winds, the distance the sand extends inland is not great. It tends to accumulate in dune ridges which are usually ten to thirty feet high, and, on average, blown sand rarely

occurs higher than seventy-five feet above present sea level. There are limited cases, however, where blown sand occurs between 200 and 300 feet above sea level. The links land is, therefore, a narrow zone paralleling the present coastline where sand has accumulated in the form of ridges, hummocks and spreads. The zone is usually about half-a-mile wide and the ridges rarely more than thirty feet high. . . . Golf course architects have often taken full advantage of the sequence of ridges and depressions to be seen on links land. The fairways are found on the short grass of the inter-dune system (slacks or valleys) while the dune ridges and their tough marram grass form areas of "rough."

Price's important work was published in 1989, and since then interest in linksland has only accelerated. As changing coastal ecosystems, links continue to attract attention from scientists. Dr. John Pethick of the University of Newcastle in England provides a challenging way of looking at a links. He refers to the ground that constitutes a links as a fossil sand-dune ridge. Blown sand from the sea creates dunes that become stabilized by coastal vegetation that in time binds them. These dunes prevent the further migration inland of sand. The result is that the ground inland from the seaside dune system becomes starved of sand, as Pethick wrote in a paper called "Links Courses and the Challenge of the Rising Sea." This area actually deflates because it's starved of sand, and turns into a lower landscape – the links. It is a fossil ridge, because the dunes that intervene between the golfing ground and the sea have arrested its growth. However, enough sand does blow across the dunes onto the ground that in time becomes the golfing terrain, acted on by natural forces – such as rabbits, other animals, fertilization, and germination of grasses.

Pethick claims, though, that global warming is changing the ecology of links courses. Sea levels are expected to rise, which will mean that the shore will move inland; the dune world will advance, which will change the character of links courses. Pethick predicts that the outer dunes that separate the links from the sea will be eroded as the shoreline advances inland. The result will be a migration of the links where golf is played. Holes will be altered, and in many cases lost.

Dune migration is already apparent at some links. I've played at Ballybunion in southwest Ireland, where the club had placed fences along the shoreline in hopes of holding back blown sand. The seventh green at Ballybunion sits on a cliff above the Atlantic, and has been pounded many times by violent storms. The club uses an alternate green from time to time, when coastal erosion has put the proper green out of play. There are many other examples, too. Dune erosion has occurred at Aberdovey, a Welsh links that the British golf writer Bernard Darwin loved. Royal Portrush in Northern Ireland, a glorious, wild-looking links, has had erosion from the wind and sea, and also from people who, by walking in the dunes, have destabilized them. The Jubilee course in St. Andrews, not far from the Old Course, saw three meters of linksland collapse due to sea incursion recently. "It fell away so fast, it frightened the life out of us," Peter Mason, the external-relations manager for the St. Andrews Links Trust, which oversees the Old Course and four other courses nearby, told Mike Aitken of the *Scotsman*. Royal Dornoch has had some coastal-erosion problems on the ninth, tenth, and eleventh holes, all of which are hard by the sea, and also the sixteenth tee, which is adjacent to the dunes.

Do global warming and rising sea levels mean that links courses are doomed? Will links last only a few hundred years, or fewer, to be overwhelmed in the end by massive assaults of seawater and blown sand? Will the links where golf is now played become dunes? And should we consider the changes that could occur as assaults? Or are they, again, just weather that must be accepted? The idea of links golf is to accept the conditions, isn't it? A links course is different every day, and often from one hole to the next. Nobody who knows links golf goes out on the course without a set of waterproofs and a strong umbrella, no matter how fair the day might be to start. Conditions can change in a minute. Veterans accept this. I walked with then–*New Yorker* writer Herbert Warren Wind during one round of the 1984 British Open at the Old Course. The day dawned sunny and mild, and was still that way when we went out to follow the play later. Herb wasn't about to be lulled into believing the good weather would remain, however, and in addition to wearing an extra sweater, he carried an umbrella and overcoat.

Golf on a Scottish links consists of enduring and even welcoming the conditions, allowing them to influence the shots one plays. To play links golf is to acknowledge that nature, not the golfer, dictates play.

This is an ideal attitude that most golfers adopted before modern maintenance procedures and machinery allowed for the manicuring of courses – the golf course as a lawn. Professor Pethick points out that efforts to hold nature back on links courses are usually futile, and that golfers of earlier times understood that. "Golf as it originated was a game that made a positive virtue of a random course landscape – that is why links were the chosen environment," he writes. "Changes in the course caused by wind blown sand or rabbit burrows or footpath erosion were seen as a challenge, not as a curse."

Professor Pethick's solution is that those charged with overseeing links courses, and the golfers who play them, should acknowledge that nature takes away and that it also gives, and that they should allow courses to migrate with the dunes. I wasn't able to appreciate what he was saying until I grasped the fact that a links is a changing, moving landscape. It was difficult for me to project myself into a future where, for instance, the sixteenth tee at Royal Dornoch would have been over-taken by a rising sea rather than exposed by a receding sea, as it had been, or when the ninth fairway could be inundated by coastal forces.

These seemed like fantastical scenarios, calling to mind the supposed lost city of Atlantis.

But then I thought of what I had seen at Ballybunion, and even on beaches in southeast Florida, on the Atlantic Ocean. One day there's a beach and the next day, following a storm, there isn't. It's migrated inland. What to do? Pethick argues that new dunes are created as sand is blown more inland, and that therefore on the other side – further inland – more links, more golfing ground, is created. Donald Steel has seen this happen at Rye, a rugged old English links, at Royal West Norfolk (known also as Brancaster) in the tidal area known as The Wash in England, and at Portmarnock near Dublin. But it's not always possible to develop golf holes on the newly created linksland, which environmental agencies often designate as untouchable.

"It is recognized that the solution advocated here is not an easy one," Pethick wrote. "Migrating with the shoreline would mean the loss of ancient greens, regular changes to handicap, problems of land owner-ship, and sand, sand and more sand. The alternative is a short but futile battle with the sea and eventual loss of our priceless asset – the links."

Pethick does not support those agents of change who would try to hold back the coastal influences. Yet today, golfers, most course archi-tects, and most engineers who consult with clubs feel they can deal with any challenges that nature poses. If the sea is invading the linksland, well, add seawalls, rock armor, stone gabions, and fencing. Introduce vegetation to hold back the sea, plant trees along a coastline, build boardwalks in the dunes to encourage people to walk there rather than on the fragile landscape itself, or fence along coastal lines.

Golf clubs concerned about losing their links – the more enlight-ened ones that take the problem seriously and that have a longer time perspective than tomorrow – have held meetings and symposia on the matter. One such meeting was held at Brancaster in October 1999, another at Royal Aberdeen in Scotland in January 2001. The Royal and Ancient Golf Club of St. Andrews, worried about what was happening, and could happen, to its links, had struck an advisory committee to learn about the various issues. The R&A acknowledged that it required expert help.

"Coastal erosion is extremely worrying," Donald Steel told me. "More links have a problem than don't." He added that clubs that are taking remedial measures find them expensive, and not always successful – more prevention than cure – and that they may well in the end have no option but to be guided by nature.

One afternoon Nell and I took a walk with a ranger from the Highland Service to the southeast of the links, where the sea last receded some 6,500 years ago. It left a long, wide stretch of beach, protected by dunes and the grasses that hold them in place, inland of which is a grassy plain. We were in sight of the course, and in the presence of natural history, hoping to better appreciate the forces that have created this landscape.

Starting inland from the coastline, we moved toward the place where land meets water, separated by the beach that curves in a half-moon from the Dornoch Firth, and along which, raised fifty feet above sea level, lies the golf course. We were walking on Dornoch's Common Good Land. On Dornoch's links.

The qualities that define a linksland were clarified for me during this walk. I pulled on a clump of marram grass near the beach to sense its resistance; it was as if the grass were nailed into the dune. No wonder the dune systems are relatively stable. Relatively. But global warming and rising sea levels compromise that stability.

Here, close to the course, was a naturalist's laboratory. We spotted kidney vetch, a yellow plant that takes nitrogen from the air and is itself food for common butterflies. There was Scottish bluebell. The species of wildflowers and plants that we had seen on the grasslands farther in from the coastal dunes weren't evident here, because we were entering a world where life was tougher. The dunes and beach can be arid, so that species need to be able to adapt and find water. One reason that marram grass thrives in the dunes is that it rolls its leaves together, which helps prevent water loss. Marram grass also grows low into the dunes, and so isn't affected unduly by the drying wind. It's this drying feature of the wind that also accounts for how quickly a links course can be played after a downpour. One morning I sat with Dornoch's greenkeeper, Bobby Mackay, in the clubhouse and watched a deluge over the course. Hollows in the first fairway filled with water, making those areas unplayable. At least a couple of inches of rain fell that morning, but after the drying winds came in the afternoon and the sandy soil absorbed the water, the course was playable. It would have been impossible to return to an inland course as quickly.

The dunes at Royal Dornoch are visible from everywhere on the course. They are immediately to the golfer's left on the ninth through the sixteenth holes, and invite the player to step up and look at the beach and the sea. The dunes here are set back from the shore, perhaps thirty yards inland, and act as a barrier between the shore and the playing area. But the dunes are not the first line of defense against the sea; fleshy plants such as sandwort, sea rocket, and frosted orache survive close to the high-tide mark, taking their nutrients from seaweed that is washed ashore. Their deep roots keep the sand from moving so rapidly that a dunes system would not have time to develop. "The curving slopes, the gullies, the ridged surfaces of the dunes all carry the impress of the sea winds," Rachel Carson wrote in "Our Ever Changing Shore" for *Holiday* magazine in 1958.

I've rarely thought of these matters while playing golf for years at various links. But my season in Dornoch is sensitizing me to the fragility of coastal ecology. There's more than seaside golf at stake here. Non-golfers enjoy this landscape and could also suffer should coastal erosion develop into a major problem; they too will be pushed inland. I think of Dornoch, St. Andrews, Gullane, Carnoustie, all towns that are very near the sea, separated from them by the linksland. Could global warming and rising sea level flood and overtake the links and inundate the towns? This is a horrible scenario to contemplate, but science suggests this could happen. Global warming is a cause for concern around the world, but we live in the moment and rarely think about what can happen down the generations. It has to be said, too, that scientists are still debating the effects of global warming, and that it's not certain that links will inevitably be flooded.

Out golfing or walking on the links in Dornoch, I wonder how one should behave. I try not to disturb the dunes, and that seems about the only practical response I can muster. I'm attracted to the seashore; we all are. It's difficult to conceive of how humans can be kept from the shore. We belong there. We feel good there. Common sense is probably the most reasonable response to the problems that we bring with us.

* * * * * *

John Macleod and I sat in the Royal Dornoch clubhouse one afternoon, talking about the club history that he wrote. Looking out at the links, he told me a story that stands in my mind as the definitive example of golf on a links when the weather is wild, when one can feel desolated and yet invigorated.

The conditions were brutal one winter evening when John and two of his fellow club members were trying to finish a round. The three golfers had a rule during the winter that they would play no matter what the weather. This time the rain was so hard and the winds so strong when they came off the sixteenth green that they had to put their umbrellas in front of their faces or be blinded. The conditions were so harsh that even they, dedicated winter golfers, knew they couldn't finish. They turned and walked toward the clubhouse, leaving the shore behind, but not the gale-force winds and the rain driving into their faces, blinding them. They couldn't see a foot ahead. One fellow walked directly into the wall in front of the Royal Golf Hotel. Another finished to the left of the clubhouse beside the first tee. John had the right line. He walked into the flagstick on the eighteenth green, nearly impaling himself. Nature won.

Chapter 13

The Golf World Comes to Dornoch

Club members become frenzied when the best golfers play their courses. Ernie Els, the winner of the 1994 and 1997 U.S. Opens, played Royal Dornoch twice prior to the British Open this summer. Els carried his own bag, a fact that interested most people, because he's a touring pro and members of that group usually don't do that. Still, even the best golfers enjoy playing golf or participating in it in basic ways from time to time. Tiger Woods caddied for his friend Jerry Chang during qualifying rounds for the 2000 United States Amateur Public Links Championship, four days after he won the U.S. Open. Pro golfers are most relaxed when they're just playing the game. Late Saturday evening, prior to the last round of the 1998 British Open at Royal Birkdale in Southport, England, Woods and David Duval amused themselves hitting shots on the range so that the balls would cross one another in the air. Nick Price, a right-handed golfer, and Robert Baker, a left-handed player and a teacher, traded drivers one afternoon at the Medalist Golf

Club in Hobe Sound, Florida, and engaged in a long-driving contest. The more the pros can *play* golf, the more they relish it.

Els was no exception. He showed up in the middle of the afternoon with his father, his friend and former U.S. Open tennis champion Jim Courier, and his manager. Els was a few minutes late for his starting time, and some wag in the clubhouse looking out toward the first tee said that Els should be assessed a two-stroke penalty for being late. He didn't hit a practice shot after he got out of the van that had delivered him to the course, but simply took his clubs out, hopped up a couple of steps to the first tee, and signed a few autographs for kids waiting there. Macarthur Bennie greeted Els, who then took his big easy swing with a two-iron – he's often referred to in print as "The Big Easy" – and sent his first shot well down the fairway. Els parred that first hole – easy all right.

I decided to follow Els for a while. Pipey Matheson was out on the links, and Bennie came along too. Els hit a beautiful six-iron right over the flag on the second hole, where the pin on the par-three was set to the back left – greenkeeper Bobby Mackay set it there because he knew Els would be playing this afternoon. His ball stayed in the air a second too long, though, and carried all the way to the back of the green before rolling over and down the steep hill. Tom Watson has said that the hardest shot at Dornoch is the second to the second, but Els made it look, well, easy. He popped his fifteen-yard shot high in the air, and then the ball landed softly on the green and rolled six feet past the hole. That was as good a result as he could have wished. "That's the bread-and-butter shot of the pro," Pipey said after Els's flop shot. Els then rolled the putt in for his par.

Conditions were calm, which always means that a links won't play nearly as difficult as it can. Wind, which the course architect Robert Trent Jones, Jr., calls the "invisible hazard," is about the only defense left on a links course when the touring pros play it. A links course doesn't have trees, although it can have plenty of rough in the way of gorse bushes, whins, and high fescue grasses. The championship committee of the Royal and Ancient Golf Club of St. Andrews, which conducts the British Open, naturally wants to test the pros. It always hopes for a good, healthy wind, and likes to narrow the fairways and let the rough grow high and thick. That's what it did during the 1999 Open at Carnoustie, across the Firth of Tay from the Old Course. Some fairways were only twelve yards wide in the landing area, and the rough had been allowed to grow very high. A premium was placed on accuracy. Fair enough, most of the time. But the R&A acknowledged during the Open that it had been too zealous in letting the fairways get so narrow and the rough so penal; by then it was too late for the R&A to make the conditions more reasonable. It's an open question as to what extent a golfer should be tested. Is it fair to ask him to hit a driver into a fairway only fifteen yards wide when the penalty for missing the fairway is a shot out of knee-high steel-wool rough? Golfers had one shot and one shot only to play out of that rough; they tried to slash the ball back onto the fairway, and often they weren't able to advance it even that far.

Still, golf is a game of the elements, and the wind doesn't always blow. It didn't blow during the 1990 Open at the Old Course in St. Andrews, where Nick Faldo shot a record eighteen-under par score of 270 to win his second Open Championship. It did blow during the first round of the 1997 Open at Troon, where Justin Leonard had to pitch out of rough frequently to within wedge distance of the green on his incoming nine the first round. The stern wind was making the incoming holes exceptionally long, and blowing balls into the rough. Leonard accepted the conditions and got up and down from one hundred yards on many holes coming in, to shoot par-thirty-five, and 69 for the round. He went on to win the championship, having proven himself in the wind.

The most thoughtful golfers know that golf is about so much more than hitting standard golf shots where they simply dial in a yardage. "Okay, one hundred and seventy yards to the hole. Seven-iron. I'll fly it one-sixty-two and it will roll eight yards, give or take a yard." But it's not possible to play golf that way on a dry links course, even when there's little wind, never mind a strong wind. A golfer will need to use his imagination, a faculty required less and less on immaculately groomed courses with their perfect fairways and soft greens. A links is best when it's really firm and when the wind is really up. Els knows that. He's come to Dornoch to play links golf in a wind.

But it's calm today at Dornoch, and Els is disappointed. "I want to see this place in a gale," Els says as he turns the corner from behind the second green and emerges on the other side of the bushes to the third tee, where the course sweeps away in all directions. This is Dornoch – golf holes everywhere, the sea in view, greens perched on ledges, tucked into hillsides. It's a painting. Ah, but where's the wind? Without it, the course won't be difficult for Els, but at least it's starting to rain and getting chilly.

The harsher the conditions, the more Els likes it. He knows that choice is an important part of golf, and that a links course asks more of a player because it provides more options. Els has hit his second shot on the third hole just to the right of the green. He's ten yards off the green and a bunker is between his ball and the hole. The hole is cut on a portion of the green that rolls from left to right, though. Els can choose to hit the ball up in the air over the bunker directly at the hole, planning for a soft landing and a roll of a few feet up to the hole. Or he can run the ball along the ground left of the bunker, so that it will take the slope on the green and run down to the hole.

"In America you'd be hitting the ball way up in the air," Els says, smiling. Patrolling the scene, he decides on the run-up shot. The ball scuttles along the ground left of the sand, then takes the tilt of the green and nudges up near the hole. Job well done. Satisfaction gained.

By the fifth hole, Els is in full play mode. He's having fun on the course, as Tom Watson did when he first played here in 1981. Watson said then that his experiences at Dornoch constituted the most fun he had ever had on a golf course. He and his friend Sandy Tatum played one morning in front of a crowd, when rain had started on the back nine. The club held a modest party for them after their round, but it wasn't long before Watson was thinking about going out again.

"After fifteen or twenty minutes in there," Watson told me when I asked him about his experiences at Dornoch, "it was raining and blowing hard. I said that I'd love to play again. So we went out with just the two caddies and got soaked. I beat Sandy in the morning, but he beat me that round."

That was the day when Watson met Donald Grant, Alan's great-uncle. Donald had just turned ninety-two. He and Watson chatted for an hour, and Donald told Watson that he had played Pinehurst #2 a few times. Donald Ross always gave him his own clubs to use there. Uncle Donald and Watson talked about Ross; about Byron Nelson, who had often helped Watson; about young Tommy Morris of St. Andrews – an Open championship winner; about Bing Crosby, who had played Dornoch; about Herbert Warren Wind; about earlier incarnations of Dornoch holes – golf talk from two men who were enamored of the lore of the game and the links of Scotland.

Yet Watson didn't like links golf when he first played it prior to the 1975 British Open at Monifieth, a course near Carnoustie, site of that year's championship. He hit what he thought was a perfect drive on the second hole, or so his caddy said it was. But the ball rolled fifty yards into a pot bunker. "I grew up playing target golf, where the ball stops quickly," Watson told me. "I didn't like the luck of the bounce at first."

Watson didn't like the luck of the bounce even though he won that 1975 British Open, and won the championship again in 1977 at Turnberry on the west coast of Scotland. He didn't like the Old Course when he first played there during the 1978 Open. But he succumbed to the charms of links golf in 1979 during the Open at Royal Lytham and St. Annes in England.

"That was a revelation to me," Watson explained. "The sixth and seventh holes are par-fives. On the sixth I hit a driver and three-wood and a five-iron as hard as I could hit it to reach the green. On the seventh, downwind, I hit a driver and then had a choice of an eight- or nine-iron for my second shot, which was two hundred and ten yards. I decided to hit the nine and land it thirty yards short of the green. I did that and the ball rolled up ten feet from the hole. I made the putt for eagle. That nine-iron shot was totally by feel. I told myself to quit fighting the conditions at a links course and to accept it. I changed my mind right then and there, that I would deal with the bounces by liking that part of the game instead of not liking it. Those feelings were solidified when I played with Sandy."

Ben Crenshaw, like Watson a links-lover, played Royal Dornoch in 1980 prior to competing in the British Open at the Muirfield Golf Club. More than any modern golfer, Crenshaw has studied golf-course design. His library at his home in Austin, Texas, contains every book worth reading on the subject, and Crenshaw has read them. He and his design partner, Bill Coore, are already making their mark in course design, and the two-time Masters champion could well make the most significant contribution of any modern player in that area. Crenshaw loves big, sweeping landscapes, options for shots, huge, undulating greens. He and Coore prefer to move as little dirt as possible when designing a course. It came as no surprise to me when I learned that Crenshaw pronounced Royal Dornoch "a great natural golf course" after playing it.

Crenshaw hasn't returned to Dornoch since his lone visit there twenty years ago, but he often thinks about it. "It's one of the most serene places on the face of the earth," Crenshaw says. "It's pure golf. The people who live in the village know so well that they have a wonderful asset there. The course is part of the fabric of the village and part of their being. It's all connected. The golf course is relatively unadorned, yet it's majestic in its natural beauty. And to know that this is where Donald Ross and John Sutherland grew up makes it all the more remarkable to visit there. Donald Ross carried what he saw at Dornoch to the courses he designed in America, so that the influence of the course has spread far beyond the Highlands."

Els has similar feelings for links golf. That was apparent by the way he was stimulated by the choices available to him on that little shot beside the third green. He's challenged again at the fifth hole, which is only 354 yards from the elevated back tee. Three bunkers protect the front of the green, which is raised about twenty feet above the fairway. The ground slopes off the ridge to the left, moving toward the sea; that's the general run of the land at Dornoch. The play is usually a shot up the left side to take the slope of the fairway, and then a pitch over the bunkers to the green that is fifty yards long. But Els had a different idea, and why not? He was having some sport with the course. The hole was playing downwind, and so he took out his driver.

His driver? But what about those fierce bunkers in front of the green, which appear about as deep as a coffee mug and not much wider? What of them? Els wasn't playing a tournament. He was out for a casual round, and so he decided to go for the green. The design of the hole lets him do that, because there's a space of two or three yards between each of the frontal bunkers. A golf course that didn't reflect links principles – that is, most courses – would likely have one vast bunker running right across the front of the green. That would take the driver out of play on the days when it might be possible to reach the green here. And although the hole is 354 yards, the wind can get strong enough to allow golfers who don't hit the ball miles to give it a go. Choices. Possibilities. The narrow opening between the bunkers introduces the possibility of a shot that will hit the ground running, scoot between them, and run up and onto the green.

Els makes his usual sleek swing, its various hip and shoulder turns and arm and shaft planes so connected that it appears effortless. The ball soars up the left side of the fairway, lands short of the bunker at the extreme left, punches its way up the bank, and just catches the edge of the bunker before dropping in. "I thought I could get lucky," Els says as he walks up to the green, pointing to the inviting-if-narrow strip of ground between the bunker to the left and the one in the middle. Now Els has a hard shot. He's four feet back of the lip of the bunker, which is four feet high. "I need practice at these shots for St. Andrews," Els says. The pin is well back on the green, so that Els has to hit a high, hard one. Slap, the bottom of his sand wedge thunks into the sand. The ball comes out high and with good force. Thud, it lands on the firm green – so firm the sound of the ball hitting the ground is audible. The ball rolls up to within ten feet of the hole. Quite a bunker shot.

"You should turn pro," I suggest to Els. He tosses his head and chuckles, then rolls the ball in for his birdie. Easy game.

The odd thing is that this sort of golf – paint-by-choice, not by-numbers golf – appeals to most people who give it a chance. Golfers back home who can't imagine they would like golf played on the ground in wind and sometimes nasty weather, and on courses that aren't green from start to finish, find they soon warm to it. Maybe a golf course is like a piece of music or a piece of art in that it's important to open oneself up to the work. English writer Colin Wilson, in his book *New Pathways to Psychology*, wrote of two ways of looking at something: what he called the immediacy-perception and then the meaning-perception.

The immediacy-perception is the way one might see something for the first time, perhaps the view that Watson had of links golf when he first encountered it. "That's ugly, that brown turf. And what kind of a fairway is this, with its knobs and ripples and lumps and bumps? And you mean I'm meant to hit this four-iron only one hundred and forty yards along the ground, or putt the ball from fifty yards off the green? Come on. Look, I hit a perfect drive, then it bounces and runs, and now it's in a bunker that I have to play backwards out of to get back into play. This isn't golf."

The meaning-perception comes later, after exposure, after the opening up. "Meaning-perception shows us what is important," Wilson wrote. "Immediacy-perception shows us what is trivial. One is a tele-scope; the other, a microscope." Marion Milner said she noticed that her happiness often depended on the view she took of an experience or object. She wrote that the wide view was preferable to the narrow view. The wide view is another way of referring to the meaning-perception, as if to say, in a golf context: "It's fun learning to hit the ball along the ground, and to use the ground. Putting the ball fifty yards is a challenge; I've never done that before. When back home would I think of hitting a forty-yard slice with a four-iron into the wind to catch the slope of a fairway and run the ball into a green? These old Scottish architects knew what they were doing. There's more to golf than the way I've played it at home or seen it on television. I'm beginning to see what the game is all about here."

Seeing what the game is all about here. Perception. A wide view. An opening up. The grand scale of the landscape with its uninterrupted views enables the awakened golfer to experience Dornoch in a way that will expand his enjoyment of the game. Els said as much on the seventh tee, on the higher ground of the course. From here the golfer can see so much – the Mannie, the cleared hills to the west, the North Sea, Dornoch to the south. The course itself is an empty space that golf holes alone cannot fill, nor should they. The vastness carries the golfer forward. A links by its nature is without trees for the most part, which promotes distant views, far-reaching gazes, even wistfulness.

Donald Ross learned about these artistic elements of course design while walking the ground at Dornoch. Seminole, in Juno Beach, Florida, on the Atlantic Ocean, testifies to his feeling for spaciousness. Much of the course sits in a bowl, with some greens set on high points. All eighteen holes are exposed to the ocean breezes, and, except for a few palm trees, there's no cover to block the winds. Ross at Pinehurst #2 in North Carolina, his best-known course, designed for openness. Photographs of the course in its early days show its lack of trees. Trees were planted and grew over the years, closing some views and generating a feeling of constraint rather than freedom. But a trimming program during the late 1990s started to open up the course again without giving it what Ross called "a barren, devastated appearance." Dornoch redux, at least in a small way. Ross would have approved. As he said in *Golf Has Never Failed Me*, the collection of his writings, "As beautiful as trees are, and as fond as you and I are of them, we still must not lose sight of the fact that there is a limited place for them in golf."

"At least here you can see what's going on in front of you," Els says on the seventh tee at Dornoch, looking straight north down the fairway of this 463-yard hole. "You can see much more here than you can at most other courses."

Seeing far and wide is a fundamental part of golf. In this regard, I like to associate the Augusta National Golf Club and the Old Course in St. Andrews, which look so different from one another. But they play similarly in numerous ways. As many trees as Augusta National has, it's the openness of the course – its spaciousness, its roominess – that catches the attention of most visitors. Bobby Jones was influenced by the flat, treeless Old Course in the design of Augusta National. Two courses couldn't look more different, yet share as many architectural principles. The space to drive the ball; the need to find the right part of the fairway to create the most favorable angle into the section of the green where the hole is cut; the rolling terrain around the green that kicks the ball many ways and that also allows the player to use it for pitch and chip shots; the huge, contoured greens that also deflect the ball and thereby require a shot hit with the right shape and spin. Dornoch also has these features, which is why Els has come here to play.

I followed Els through seven holes, then turned back to the club-house and returned my umbrella to Captain Bennie, from whom I had borrowed it. A steady rain had sent some other Els-watchers back to the clubhouse. There, people were regaling one another with stories of what they had seen of Els's play the last couple of days. "I understand he reached the turn in thirty-one yesterday." And another: "He missed the green at the first yesterday. I don't know how he did that." Yet again: "He took a six at the twelfth. That's a shame. An eagle was on there."

I left the club and walked home. A young girl in the village square was clutching a copy of the latest Harry Potter book, which had just been published that day. The bookshop window – the right side – was full of J. K. Rowling's Potter books. I popped my head in to the shop. Lesley said it had been another banner day for Rowling and the sorcerer Potter. Books had been flying out of the shop. Later I read that the newest Potter – or should that be the latest Rowling? – had sold 372,775 copies on its first day. I had no context for such a number. Narrowing my focus, in opposition to what Marion Milner suggested, I had a cup of tea and thought about other matters of sorcery – how to post a low score at Dornoch, for one. All I needed was an Ernie Els swing. If only. But even Els was still learning. David Thomson at The Carnegie Club had played with Els during his visit to the Highlands, when they discussed the swing. Thomson, forthright as always, dis-cussed the bad shot that Els sometimes hit under pressure – every golfer seems to have a bad shot particular to him, and for Els it's the one that goes left. He drove left on the last two holes of regulation play in the 1994 United States Open, and fell into a playoff. Els won the playoff, but the shot to the left lurked. He and Thomson discussed what Els did in his swing to make that mistake. Els liked what he heard, and invited

Thomson to the next tournament in Scotland to work with him. The search for improvement continues, at all levels.

Els didn't have any problems with his bad shot after seeing Thomson. He cruised on down to the European Tour event at the Loch Lomond club north of Glasgow, and won. Dornoch was good for his golfing soul, and Thomson, apparently, was good for his swing.

Chapter 14

Swing Thoughts

When David Thomson said he could find another thirty yards for me with my driver, it was like offering an expanse of grassy pasture to a hungry Highland sheep. We were on the twelfth tee at The Carnegie Club, and David, the pro there, had seen my usual brand of reasonably accurate and relatively short golf. "Given the mistakes you make and the limitations in your game, it says something about your athletic ability that you play to the high standard that you do," he said in the tantalizing yet subtly sadistic manner of the golf teacher. I'd once asked David Leadbetter what he thought of my swing and he answered, "It's the finest of its kind."

Walter Hagen, one of golf's most colorful players ever, supposedly made a similar observation when asked his opinion of a course he had just visited. "This is without doubt the finest course of its kind I have ever seen." Leadbetter probably tells everybody what he told me, but that didn't keep me from remembering the comment.

By the time I met David Thomson I was moving in the wrong direction from my five-handicap. I was also feeling like a weakling on the course. My drives carried only 220 yards. They were usually straight, but I was prematurely short and fed up with being thirty and forty yards behind my golfing friends. "You have too many leaks in the system," David said, "starting with your set-up. But we can fix those things. You do get into a superb position coming into the ball, and we will want to preserve that. I don't see why we can't add thirty yards to your driver and improve your length with the other clubs correspondingly. Power and accuracy go together up to a point. You're nowhere near that point."

I was trapped, willingly. David was promising me nirvana – power and more accuracy. Maybe it was fate. I had come to Dornoch to immerse myself in the sort of golf I appreciated, and if thirty yards more would come along in the bargain, well, why should I decline the offer? Besides, the Carnegie Shield was coming up. It wouldn't hurt to hit the ball a little farther. Or a lot farther. Sheep – and golfers – get hungry. Chomp, chomp.

David was in the pro shop when I arrived for our appointed lesson a couple of weeks prior to the Shield. I hit a few balls on one end of the range before he came out to have a look. I'd been through this routine many times with innumerable teachers (I'd rather not say how many, but it's one of the hazards of my profession that I meet instructors, write about them, and receive unbidden – and also ask for – their advice). I enjoy writing about the swing and have written books with George Knudson, Nick Price, and David Leadbetter. But was there an unwritten law that I had not only to write about the swing, but try everything teachers suggested? It wasn't as if I hadn't played well in tournaments before. I'd won the 1974 Eastern Ontario Amateur when I shot 74 – 69. I won the 1984 Golf Writers Association of America's championship with a 74 on a cold, raw day in Myrtle Beach.

Still, how could I decline suggestions from Knudson, Price, and Leadbetter? Or from Jack Grout, who had taught Jack Nicklaus and from whom I'd had a lesson in 1985? Or from Claude Harmon, father of Butch – Tiger's teacher – when I ran into him at a driving range in south Florida years ago? I came away from every session with these teachers figuring I was on my way to consistently good golf. I played my best golf after writing the book with Price. That lasted six months, but then the Price material I'd incorporated into my swing vanished and Rubenstein reappeared. I had so many swing thoughts that the hard drive of my golfing brain was surely corrupted by now. But my vision of better golf remained. I also couldn't remember anybody offering me thirty yards while saying that my swing was already useful. David stood to one side, watched as I hit a few middle irons, and then spoke with conviction.

"The first thing we need to do is provide a structure for your swing," David said. "We won't even concern ourselves just yet with the swing itself, and, as I say, it's not too bad. Not too bad at all. But you don't support it from your address position. You're what, six-three, and you're hunched over at address. Your posture is poor, which means that you aren't giving yourself a chance to create as big an arc as you could. You're cutting yourself off from the start."

David showed me how to stand to the ball in what he called an "athletic" position. Rather than hunching over the ball with my rear end stuck out toward the middle of Scotland, I was now standing taller and letting my arms hang from my shoulders. "I want you to feel deep when you're over the ball," David said. "The deeper you can feel the better. The idea is to use your height rather than compromise it. Why would you want to be shorter over the ball than you need to be? Yes, you need some bend forward, some tilt, just to get down to the ball. You can get that with some knee flex. That will give you a spine angle and not a bent-over set-up where you're so rounded in appearance. The bottom half of your back will be straighter and your neck will be more on top of yourself, instead of overhanging the top of your chest. The neck position you've had keeps you from making a full turn away from the ball. Your left shoulder runs into your chin. So let's see you set up this way."

Immediately I felt liberated from myself. I pictured tall golfers: Tom Weiskopf, Nick Faldo, Ernie Els, Davis Love III, Tiger Woods. Woods stood tall to the ball; his posture over the ball was always a proud one. He didn't cut himself off at the start, so why should I? George Knudson had spoken of using one's height. "Never do anything at the expense of balance," George advised. Stand proud. Use yourself. David was echoing these thoughts.

Once we improved my posture, David considered my tendency to take the club back to the inside. I did this, he said, for the same reason that I couldn't make a full backswing: my left shoulder ran into my chin, because I was hunched over at address. To compensate for this, I inadvertently took the club back to the inside and was off plane right away. Now I was dependent on timing alone to square the clubface at the ball. David stood behind me and asked that I swing the club back to a halfway position along a straight line away from the ball. I felt that I was taking it back far to the outside, which showed just how much to the inside I'd swung before. From the halfway back position in this drill, where the shaft of the club was parallel to the ground, David wanted me to spin my left hip to the left to start the downswing, and said I would feel as if the club were cutting across the ball. The idea was to try to fade the ball, to impart a slight left-to-right spin. It did worry me that Bill Davis, a highly regarded teacher at the Jupiter Hills club in south Florida, had encouraged me to set up in a way that would promote a hook. I'd also had the pleasure of a round with Chuck Cook, who had worked with the late Payne Stewart. "Don't ever try to do anything but hook the ball," Chuck told me, without my even asking for advice. But David saw things differently. So had David Leadbetter and Nick Price when they inspected my swing while I worked on their books. Confused? Who, me?

"You've been taking the club back so far to the inside, and then when you've come into the ball you've either come over the top and pulled the ball or, on the other hand, returned on nearly the same path and hit the ball to the right," David said. "Your good golf has come when you've managed to use your hands to square the club up at impact, which is an iffy thing at best. Your hands and arms and body haven't been working together. It's all down to your set-up."

David placed a golf ball three feet in front of the one I was hitting and asked that I try to make my shot start to its left, while not allowing the clubface to turn over. This would get me moving through the ball with my body, while keeping the club in front of me; my hands, arms, and body would work together instead of against one another. I would be using more of my body and less of my hands. The swing was a chain reaction, and the set-up provided the first link – it was the foundation upon which the swing rested and depended. I'd lost my way right there.

David left me to work on what we had discussed. I returned to the range for a few sessions to practice and soon was looking forward to the Carnegie Shield. David watched me hit balls one late afternoon and offered enough encouragement to keep me chomping. "Now you look like a golfer. Look at those shots. They have character." I was taking full swings with every club. My clubface was rotating in tandem with my body. I wasn't flailing at the ball but rather was making an athletic, aggressive move through it. I'd also gained distance, as David had promised. When I'd had that first round with Don Greenberg, he had said that my swing was unorthodox, but that it worked. It repeated. I got the ball around the course. He was right, but what he didn't know was that sometime during the last few years, I'd stopped feeling like a golfer. I was playing with what Canadian pro Moe Norman, perhaps the straightest hitter of the ball ever, said was "hope and fear." Moe told me more than a few times, "People see hope and fear when they look down the fairway. But it's a big fairway, a big fairway. Look, the ball fits the Moe Norman way, the ball fits the Moe Norman way."

The Moe Norman way was to take the club straight back and straight through in as much of a single-axis pendulum motion as possible. He didn't like the rotary swing that modern professionals used, and there wasn't much rotary motion in his swing as he hung on to the club through impact. His clubface pointed at the sky when he finished, and didn't go behind him. "Everybody swings around the course, around the course," Moe said in his usual, double-barreled way. "Why don't they swing through the course, through the course? That's what I do. I swing through the course."

David wasn't teaching me a Moe Norman action. But he was showing me that it was helpful to keep the club on line away from the ball and through impact and beyond. Lee Trevino did this beautifully. Tiger Woods took the club back on a straight line away from the ball until to go any farther without turning would have compromised his balance. Bobby Clampett, a golfer who, it was predicted, would be the "next Jack Nicklaus" when he turned professional in 1980, and who studied the swing like a research scientist and advocated an approach called The Golfing Machine, spoke of a "line of compression" before impact. The longer one's line of compression, the more sting one could impart to the ball. The line of compression extended through the ball, as Moe knew intuitively. Tiger did, too. He had worked on a shot he called his "stinger," where he uses a two-iron off the tee to hit a low line drive that will get out there some 250 yards. Tiger extends through the ball a long way while hitting this shot, holding the clubface down the line through impact. He's swinging through the course, not around it. David wanted me to do this as much as I could: my shots started to have some spank to them. I felt as if the ball were sticking to the clubface a long time instead of squirting away, which happened when I slapped at it with my hands. Now the ball was penetrating through the air and carrying and holding its line. The winds didn't affect its flight nearly as much as before. This was a good thing. I was in Scotland, and the winds blew here.

David and I talked for hours about the swing. We dismantled the swing as if we were in a science laboratory, and I suppose we were. After working with him, I'd nearly fly back to Royal Dornoch to play a few holes and test out the ideas. I committed to what he had shown me, and started hitting quality shots. I began to feel that, notwithstanding human frailty and human error, I was bound to hit mostly good shots if I followed his advice. I was seeing the results on the links. I felt powerful over the ball with my new athletic set-up. I felt like an athlete on the course, not just a slightly-out-of-shape middle-aged man playing a game that some people didn't consider a sport. To me, golf was becoming a sport again as I zipped around Dornoch. I felt like an athlete because I had adopted an athlete's stance. I'd never hunched over like a ragdoll while playing first base as a youngster, or flopped downfield while running a pass pattern in football, or slumped while carrying the puck down the ice. But I'd slunk into the ground while playing golf, a stationary-ball game in which one stands in place and moves only within a tight, confined area – the limits of one's swing.

"Feel like you're making a 'big' swing," David suggested. Here in the empty lands it felt like the right thing to do, and I did it on the range and on the course at The Carnegie Club and at Royal Dornoch. I was a little concerned that I might lose any flair and feel I had for shotmaking while I introduced new mechanics into my swing. But I had veered wildly between being enmeshed in the mechanics of the swing and the opposite pole of favoring feel alone. I hadn't found a balance. Here I thought I had a chance, perhaps because I felt so spirited while practicing and playing. The professional golfers of whom I had been writing also struggled with the opposite poles of golf by mechanics or golf by feel. This was a significant issue when it came to my own golf, and it wouldn't vanish because I had come to the Highlands, far from video machines and computer analyses of swings, or, from the mental side, sports psychologists and gurus who claimed that visualizing a good shot all but guaranteed that one would produce a good shot. I had hoped that, in time, I would be able to open up to the game here, having understood and internalized the fundamentals David was teaching me. Fundamentals, then feel.

"You're more talented than you want to believe," David said. "I can see how you were a one-handicap not that long ago. But I can also see how your game can slip. That doesn't have to happen."

I was hopeful because of my work with David, and felt unburdened. Nell and I had often discussed the ways in which golf could affect a player's mood. I try not to bring my golf home with me, but she can read me in a moment. One example kept coming to mind, when I'd been playing well prior to a club championship but, during the event, I came up with a sorry round. That night at a dinner party with friends I was determined not to let my misery affect the evening. No chance. Nell and our friends still talk about how dejected I appeared. We show how we feel in small ways. People who know us read our body language: a sentence that trails off to nowhere; a slumping in the chair; a faraway look; no interest in cheesecake. Its opposite, too: the overpowering sense that all is right in one's world after one plays well; the feeling of, now, finally, beating the game if only for a day or a tournament; the sense of having come through and met the challenges the game presents.

It's all absurd, because we are speaking of a sport, a recreation. Why should I let my success or failure at a recreation define me, even if only for the moment? But so often the definition has lasted for much longer than the moment. I try not to let this happen, but it does. My self-concept is tied up with how I play the game. And that hasn't changed much even as I have gotten older and, supposedly, developed a more mature attitude toward golf. I had hopes that this would change during my season in Dornoch. In the meantime, I was working toward the Carnegie Shield, coming up in two weeks. Dornoch was already getting Shield fever. Overseas members had started to show up for their annual visits. Friends and acquaintances I ran into at Luigi's would ask if I had entered for the Shield. Don Greenberg and the boys were telling Shield lies in the club bar.

But I also needed a break from thinking about the Shield. It didn't feel right to be paying it so much attention when it was still two weeks away. Sure, some anticipation was useful. But this was just a golf tournament, even if it was the storied Shield. There was more to Dornoch than a golf tournament, or to golf itself. I felt in danger of sinking into a tournament frenzy, and wanted some respite. Nell and I walked and walked in the village, taking in the place and the people.

One evening we visited the Wilds – Peter and Sally – in their cottage just off the High Street. We'd met the Wilds once before during a dunes walk, when I overheard Peter, looking at the course, remark, "That's a silly game, golf. I can't understand why anybody would play it." But we chatted amiably that afternoon despite our differences. Sally, an artist, had done some illustrations for the Dornoch Heritage Society and owned a flock of small sheep that grazed on eight acres in the Dornoch meadows; she rents the land from the golf club and the current Duchess of Sutherland. Sally had grown up in Wick, on the far northeast coast, and, like most people we were meeting, had a strong feeling for the landscape here. This no longer surprised us in a landscape where the average population density is eight people per square kilometer. The average density in continental Europe is sixty-five people per square kilometer. Sally often tells people, "It's worth a lot of money to have the privilege of living here."

Nell and I also visited the Clynelish Distillery in Brora, where we had been told to look up Liz Miller, wife of the famous Jimmy Miller – not that he would call himself famous. Liz showed us around the distillery, which has a view of the sea. She's a golfer and was proud of the links in Brora, where she and her husband played frequently. Like Jimmy, she likes a links to be firm and fast.

"It's getting to be a proper links again," said Liz, who knew whisky-making in as fine a detail as David Thomson knew the swing. "It was getting a bit porridgey for a while." While Liz spoke, Nell and I were enjoying a dram of twenty-eight-year-old Brora whisky that Clynelish makes. I enjoyed it, but kept saying the word "porridgey" to myself. Now there's a word I've never heard to describe a golf course.

● ● ● ● ● ●

One pre-Shield night, Nell and I walked up to the Burghfield House Hotel, high on a hill overlooking the village, and settled in at the cozy bar. It was a fine place to settle. There we met Euan Currie, bartender, raconteur, and Highlander to the core.

"Butterworth could find any book," Euan says of Richard Butterworth from behind the bar at the Burghfield ("Buddafield, if you please," he adds when I mention I'd been here on my last trip to Dornoch). "I would ask Richard for a rare Robert Service and he would find it." Euan always wears a kilt when tending bar, is always smoking a pipe, and often recites poetry. He's worked here for forty years, all of that during a period in which his family owned the hotel. But Euan and his brother finally sold it to American interests. Euan still tends bar, and it takes only a minute or two to realize this is a kind of home for him; what better place than a bar in the Highlands for a man who loves the place and who knows its literature and also wider Scottish literature? He keeps works by Robert Service, Robbie Burns, and other poets and writers in a nook behind the bar. Visitors send Euan books from all over the world, and when he wanted to make his own purchases he used to consult Richard Butterworth. He'll likely do the same with Lesley Bell at the Dornoch Bookshop.

"I let the world come to see me," Euan says in his rollicking, rolling burr of a voice. "There's a magic about the Highlands. It's the lack of population as much as anything. If Royal Dornoch were in Glasgow or Edinburgh, it would be played out of sight. I think that's why people come here from all over. They can get a game at one of the special courses in golf. They're gone by the fall, but some come back for Christmas and New Year's. Why, you should see New Year's Eve here. It's evil. They don't allow me to go to bed."

Nell and I are at one edge of the bar, and within an hour we're on our third brandy. We aren't heavy hitters when it comes to drinking, but we are drinking more in Dornoch than we would at home; still, we're only keeping up with many of the locals. Between the bar at the club, pubs at the Royal, Burghfield, and Eagle hotels, a whisky to end the evening, and nights like this that go on for some time, we're more than occasional drinkers now. But, we have yet to reach the state that James Joyce called "tighteousness," and don't plan to get there. Cheadle House is only a five-minute walk from any of the watering holes, though, so we're not concerned about having an extra brandy. Or two.

Euan is clearly the director of this show. He brings out some huge old tomes from behind the bar, including one that contains, he says, "some Robert Service poems you won't see anywhere else except in this." Euan begins to recite a Service poem. "Tramp, tramp . . ." His voice is quaking. Euan is a Service devotee, even if the poet didn't live all his life in Scotland. Service, who was born in Preston, England, grew up in Glasgow, where he worked for a time at the Commercial Bank of Scotland. He despised the drudge work and used it only to make a few dollars and because it offered enough dead time so that he could read. He walked the floor at the bank reading Robert Browning and John Keats any time he had a chance. Service eventually emigrated to Canada in 1895, when he was twenty-one years old. He lived in British Columbia, and soon followed the gold rush to the Yukon. Later, when Service was working in a bank there, an editor at the *Whitehorse Star* asked him to write about life in the Yukon. Service continued working at the bank while taking long walks for exercise and exploring the countryside in the Yukon. He also wrote poetry.

Euan's hands are trembling and his eyes are misting as he thumbs through what he calls "some absolutely classic bits" in the old volume he's produced. A sweet silence has swept over the room. Euan is about to recite and bring Robert Service into the bar. He's looking for another poem to recite, and while he turns the pages over he says, "Boom-boom, boom-boom" – a personal mannerism. It's a poetry all its own. Euan's love of poetry dates back to when he was seven or eight years old and attending the Dornoch Academy. Nellie Bubbles, his teacher, sat at the front of the classroom at her desk with a duster in her hand, banging it on the table and sending chalk dust flying as she recited William Wordsworth's famous poem "I Wandered Lonely as a Cloud." Euan didn't sense that Miss Bubbles was in love with the poetry, but he did discern the music in the words, their rhythm, the songs that were in the poetry.

"Ah, here it is," Euan says. " 'The Spell of the Yukon.' The poem applies as much to the Highlands as it does to the Yukon. I tried to get the tourist board here to adopt the poem, but they wouldn't do it. Boom-boom, boom-boom."

This is life in the Highlands. We come into a pub for a drink and we find a fellow in a kilt behind the bar who recites poetry – the Bard of the Bar. Behind us lies the links, while to the west are the open, mostly uninhabited, mountainous areas. We feel dwarfed but also enlarged. How can these feelings coexist? Maybe it's the brandy. Things seem in their proper proportions. Euan recites. We're in a literary citadel for the moment.

There's a land where the mountains are nameless,
And the rivers all run God knows where;
There are lives that are erring and aimless,
And deaths that just hang by a hair;
There are hardships that nobody reckons;
There are valleys unpeopled and still,
There's a land – oh, it beckons and beckons,
And I want to go back – and I will.

Later I looked up the poem, and took down the following lines.

There's golf and it's haunting and haunting;
It's luring me on as of old;
Yet it isn't the gold that I'm wanting
So much as just finding the gold.
It's the great, big, broad land 'way up yonder,
It's the forests where silence has lease;
It's the beauty that fills me with wonder,
It's the stillness that fills me with peace.

Of course the right word in the first line I'd taken down should have been "gold" and not "golf." I felt proud of this Freudian slip. The golf here is haunting and haunting, and lured me back as of old. I was trying to find the golf in my swing with David Thomson. I was trying to find the golf I believed in while playing out on the bouncy seaside turf at Dornoch.

Nell and I remain at the Burghfield until midnight, then walk back to the flat under a clear, starry sky. The path through a wood takes us down to the High Street. It's high summer, so there's light in the sky, a glow. We hear the rustling of the leaves on the trees, notice the way the village lies low, between the sea and the higher woodland. There's a serenity here I didn't know I needed. The concrete jungle in which I live in Toronto can't provide this feeling – even though, as concrete jungles go, it's an appealing one, because ravines wind through the cityscape, and it's easy to get away from the noise, if not the pollution. Now I cherish not only the air, but also the summer serenity that Dornoch provides.

We emerge from the wooded path near our flat and run into a fellow known to us only as Young Bob. He's had a drink-filled night himself. Young Bob, teetering, asks where we're from.

"We're locals," Nell says.

"No, you're not," Young Bob retorts.

"Yes, we are," Nell counters, laughing, enjoying the repartee. "We live there," she adds, pointing to our flat.

"You'll never be locals, not in twenty-five years," Young Bob shouts. "And your grandchildren won't be locals. Och, but it dinna matter. Are you enjoying yourselves?"

"Yes, we are," Nell says, dancing in the street.

"That's good," Young Bob remarks. "That's good."

It is too. Very good.

Chapter 15

The Scottish Amateur

Who is that? This is the question I ask myself when I come across a golfer swinging so slowly that I could turn my eyes away on his backswing and still catch his downswing. I walk up to the fourth fairway while checking the sheet for the draw in this, the first round of the Scottish Amateur. The player is Craig Watson, the 1997 British Amateur champion. He's on the fourth green when I reach him, a tall, thin man in his mid-thirties. This should be good; I've come across a champion golfer, and follow him for a few holes.

Watson's swing is the slowest I've ever seen. I'd freeze in place if I swung that way. But the pace of his swing works for Watson, who is two-up after six holes in his match and goes on to win. Watching him has been one of those unexpected treats that amateur tournaments sometimes provide. The British Amateur was once considered a major championship, so I'm glad to run into Watson.

I played in a British Amateur myself, in 1977, at the Ganton Golf Club in Scarborough, England. I was two holes up with three holes to play against Huw Evans, a Welshman who had represented his country inter-nationally. That day, as I stood on the sixteenth tee, I thought, "Well, even if I lose the last three holes, I'll still have lost only one-down. My friends back home will read the result and know I gave my opponent a good match."

I lost the last three holes.

• • • • • •

The Scottish Golf Union started in 1920. Representing amateur golfers, it conducted the first Scottish Amateur, now the SGU's flagship event, two years later. The venue was, appropriately, the Old Course.

If you study the roster of Scottish Amateur winners, it's immediately obvious how few "famous" names one finds, especially through the mid-1980s. By "famous" I mean golfers who have come to the golf world's attention, and in modern golf that means professional players. Colin Montgomerie won the 1987 Scottish Amateur and went on to a highly successful professional career, leading the European Tour seven years running from 1993 to 1999. Graham Rankin won the 1998 Scottish Amateur and turned professional in 2000. Not many players remain lifelong amateurs. Amateurs who have succeeded at high levels want to test themselves against the best players in the game. That means on the pro tours.

At the same time it's pleasant to recall when golfers remained ama-teurs, and to seek out any members of the increasingly rare species. There was a time when Jack Nicklaus considered remaining amateur, and going into the insurance business. Tiger Woods kept people won-dering when he would turn pro; for a time it seemed he might finish his degree at Stanford University first. But nobody was surprised when Woods turned pro in the late summer of 1996, having won three con-secutive U.S. Juniors and then three consecutive U.S. Amateurs. "Hello world," he said to open up the press conference where he announced that he was turning pro. The world already knew about him.

Of lifelong amateurs, I think of Marlene Stewart Streit, Doug Roxburgh, and Nick Weslock in Canada; Sir Michael Bonallack in Great Britain; Vinnie Giles, Bill Hyndman, Bill Campbell, and Carol Semple Thompson in the United States. These players have all won national championships. It's difficult to say whether any of them would remain amateur if they were young today, when the lure of the pro tours is so powerful. That's all the more reason to celebrate amateur golf, and why I was pleased to learn that the Scottish Amateur would be held at Royal Dornoch during my stay. Amateur golfers care as much about how they are playing as do tour pros. The career amateur with game enough to have turned pro does exist, but it's not easy to find him. Jimmy Miller in the Highlands never turned pro. He's at Royal Dornoch this week, working for the Scottish Golf Union as a rules official. Jimmy is also a selector for the SGU's junior golf teams. While following the play, I run into Jimmy at vari ous points.

After following Craig Watson, I need water, and hie myself back to the trailer that the SGU is using as its press headquarters. This isn't the British Open that was held recently at the Old Course, so there aren't concession stands all over the course. Anybody watching the golf has to bring his own supplies or return to the clubhouse.

Stewart McDougall, who works in golf, is the press officer this week for the Scottish Amateur. He held the same position at the British Open, so he's gone from the massive Open at St. Andrews to this small affair, which is fine with him. To Stewart, the Scottish Amateur matters.

"This will get a lot of coverage in the Scottish papers," Stewart tells me. "Not as much as the Open, of course, but still impressive. The good thing about amateur golf, at least for me, is that I can see the players going forward. The Scottish Golf Union is trying to identify players as young as fourteen who are talented. We can follow their progress at these championships."

There's a sharp contrast between the British Open and the Scottish Amateur, and between St. Andrews and Dornoch. St. Andrews was the center of world golf during the Open, which Tiger Woods won by eight shots. Some 2,500 golfers entered the Open, the vast majority hoping to get past the qualifying rounds, while a select group got into the championship by virtue of a variety of criteria – the most obvious being their recent play. There were a couple of hundred entrants for the Scottish Amateur, fewer than had been anticipated. As the deadline for entry approached, some players withdrew because they didn't want to make the trip up to the Highlands. Dornoch remains remote to many players, which to them evidently means "not worth the trip."

It's quiet here during the Amateur, so much so that locals might not know it's on unless they care about the championship; it's very much an outside affair brought to the club. But St. Andrews during the Open was a Goliath of a championship, as Nell and I learned while staying there for the week. There, Stewart McDougall and his associates presided over a massive press center that held some nine hundred journalists. Here, his small trailer has a couple of tables, a few chairs, and is home for the week to half a dozen writers from Scottish newspapers. Small but friendly. Manageable.

• • • • • •

"I wish the greens were a little faster," Royal Dornoch's greenkeeper Bobby Mackay is saying out on the links. "We've had just enough rain that the green speed has been affected. I'd like them faster. Today with some sunshine the greens should begin to dry out. You do want some wind. Most definitely."

The course is too green for Mackay's taste. He'd prefer it shading to brown, as would Jimmy Miller, a links aficionado. Mackay believes that a links plays best when its turf is thirsty, which creates the brownish look he wants. Hard and fast conditions put the bounce back into golf.

"I could happily go a whole year without rain," Bobby says. "We have a watering system, but we use irrigation not to grow grass, but to keep the grass alive. It's traditional greenkeeping. I believe that what we have out here brings with it an immense responsibility. What we have out here should not be touched. The Scottish Golf Union left me alone to set up the course as I see fit, and I respect them for that."

Here's hoping for sunshine, wind, and drier conditions. For linksy golf. For demanding, championship golf.

• • • • • •

Back on the course, I meet Charlie O'Hara beside the thirteenth green. He's using binoculars to follow his son, Stephen, and other golfers also. Stephen is a tall, lanky twenty-year-old Glaswegian, who won the 1998 British Boys' Championship. He works with Ian Rae, the coach for the Scottish Golfing Union at its new base in Drumoig, near St. Andrews. He made it through the first qualifying round for the British Open, then shot 70–70 in the final qualifier. That wasn't good enough.

Stephen has been getting the support from the SGU and friends that young golfers need. Members at Cawdor Park, where he plays, gave him £1,000 to help with his tournament expenses. A lottery fund provided another £3,000. He's headed for the Walker Cup next year, and then will probably turn professional. Stephen started to play when he was ten years old. He's played golf for half his life, and he's just out of his teenage years.

I walk along with Charlie O'Hara and learn more about his son – where he'll be playing, how competitive the Scottish and international golf scenes are. Stephen is playing decently today in his first match, and takes a three-up lead after ten holes over Ben Freeman from the Crieff Golf Club. He develops putting problems, though, and after fourteen holes the match is even. Stephen wins the fifteenth and sixteenth, three-putts the seventeenth green to lose that hole, and halves the final hole with Freeman. He gets through, one-up.

• • • • • •

Barry Hume walks onto the first tee. I've been waiting for his match. Hume, eighteen, is Scotland's finest young player. He plays at the Haggs Castle course three miles from Glasgow's city center. Hume has already won the Scottish Boys' Championship, by a record thirteen shots, and later had three second-place finishes in the Scottish Men's, Youths', and Boys' Stroke-Play Championships. He also won the Young Masters in Italy when he was fifteen. He's in the early stages of what he hopes will be a golfing odyssey to the game's highest levels. Hume won his first match here. Now this serious young man is on the first tee in his second match of the Scottish Amateur.

"This is match number forty-nine," says Hugh Ferguson, a Royal Dornoch member and starter, who is helping out during the Scottish Amateur. "On the tee, Gavin Cooper."

Cooper, Hume's opponent, is a stocky fellow in his mid-twenties, built like Darren Clarke, the burly professional from Dungannon, Northern Ireland. He tops his tee shot and laughs. Cooper gets away with the bad shot because the ball bounds down the hard fairway a good distance. Hume's shot now. He turns behind the ball with a full backswing, drops the club into the slot coming down, drives forward with his legs, and hits a first-class shot.

It's a delightful morning. A sea breeze from the south and east will influence play. When the wind blows from this direction the first eight holes play downwind, which makes those holes shorter but also means that it's harder to keep shots on the greens. Hume and Cooper halve the opening hole with pars, and then both miss the second green. Hume comes up only a little short and a little to the right of his line, but that's enough. His ball bobbles into the bunker at the front right of the green. He shakes his head and drops it in annoyance. If I'm not mistaken I'm seeing some petulance in the lad.

He's looking at another classic Dornoch challenge. The sod wall face of the bunker is six feet in front of his ball, and it's nearly as tall as he is. He has to hit the ball hard and high enough to get it out of the bunker, because the last thing anybody wants to do is leave the ball in the sand. Anything can happen then. Tommy Nakajima putted into the Road Bunker at the seventeenth hole during the 1984 British Open at the Old Course, then proceeded to hit shot after shot trying to extricate himself. He made a nine on the hole, and some wags started calling the Road Bunker "The Sands of Nakajima." Jack Nicklaus couldn't get himself out of Hell Bunker on the fourteenth hole at the Old Course during the 1995 Open, and made a ten. David Duval bashed around in the Road Bunker during the last round of the 2000 Open, while playing in the final group with Tiger Woods, and concocted a tangy quadruple-bogey eight. These golfers failed to meet the first requirement when faced with a shot from a deep sod-wall bunker: get the ball out.

Hume lashes at his ball, and knows he has hit it too hard. He's got the ball out of the bunker, but it's headed through the green and down the hill on the other side. "Bite," Hume yells. He can't see the flight of the ball because the high face of the bunker is in his way, but he senses there might be trouble. He knows the ball is on line, though, and hears it slam into the flagstick about halfway up and drop right down into the hole. Birdie, just like that.

Hume is poker-faced. Come on, I think. Fair is fair. You were irritated when your ball bounced into the bunker, and showed it. Now you act as if it's your birthright to get a good break. At least laugh a little at the vagaries of the game. You're too young to be so tight. I'm watching with some other spectators, and we're all disappointed that Hume is stoic; he seems almost anhedonic. But never mind. Hume wins the hole when Cooper doesn't make his chip shot. Hume is one-up through two holes.

"I'm sure he's pleased with that one, although he's not showing it," Hume's dad, Jim, says as we move to the third hole. Hume wins the hole after Cooper drives to the right into the thick rough, looks for his ball for a few minutes, and declares it lost. Hume, two-up. "I don't know what I'm doing today," Cooper mutters. "I hit it good yesterday."

Hume is four-up after five holes. This match is all but over. It ends officially on the thirteenth green, where Cooper runs out of holes. Hume betrayed no emotion all the way round. There was only that one flicker of a reaction on the second tee. Otherwise, nothing.

Hume first played golf when he was eight years old, during a family trip to Myrtle Beach in South Carolina. Soccer had been his first sport, but he developed some physical problems and was advised to stay away from soccer for eighteen months. He took up golf seriously then, and that was it for football. Jim McAlister, the professional at Haggs Castle, followed the youngster's early development. "Don't touch anything with his swing," he advised Hume's father. "Just keep him interested. Maybe have him hit trick shots to do that. But his swing is wonderful. There's no need to do anything with it."

Hume hits the ball high, long, and either straight or with just a little right-to-left curl. It's a pro's ball flight. Everything about his game makes me think "tour professional." His ball takes off, soars from impact, and stays in the air a long time. Nell once watched from the back of the tee at the Bay Hill Invitational in Orlando as Tiger Woods hit his drive. "I've never heard a sound like that," she said. Woods's ball explodes off the face of a club – a firecracker. Other pros create similar sounds, but none that booms quite like his. The sound that Hume makes when his club contacts the ball is in the upper register – approaching Woods's. The kid seems made to play golf. He walks into his stance over the ball as if that's his natural way of moving. He doesn't so much set or plant his feet into an orthodox golfing stance as simply assume the pose. But it's not a pose. It's a personal attribute.

Walking back to the clubhouse after his match concludes, Hume still seems tight. I ask him about his self-containment on the course. "I usually get quite down and hard on myself," he says. "But I'm learning not to. I want to have Tiger's mental strength. If I had that I could probably go on tour now. When Tiger drops a shot it doesn't bother him so that it affects his next shot. I'm not there yet." Woods wasn't there when he was eighteen, and he still shows emotion on the course; nothing wrong with that.

• • • • • •

I walk home to have some lunch between matches. John Duncan, Royal Dornoch's club secretary, has parked his bicycle in front of the library. He's waiting until the library reopens. "I'd like to get some quiet reading in," John says. Things are hectic back at the club during the Scottish Amateur, so what better place to get away from it all than in the library? I look in on Lesley at the bookshop, which is full of browsers, then go up to the flat. The early-afternoon sun is warming the village. People are walking in the High Street. There's a constant flow in and out of the newsagent's shop. I make some tea, have a sandwich, read the papers, and feel content. I'm a five-minute walk from my favorite course. Nell is out for a bike ride, whizzing up past Embo to Loch Fleet. A national championship is on at Royal Dornoch. I'm starting to feel too comfortable here. Things are getting dangerous. I find myself looking in store windows at ads for real estate.

• • • • • •

The matches have reached the semifinal stage. Craig Watson went out in the quarter-finals against Stephen O'Hara. Graeme Dawson, a twenty-two-year-old student at St. Andrews University, has been one of the most compelling stories in the tournament. Dawson was born without a left forearm and hand, yet plays to a one-handicap at Ranfurly Castle in Glasgow. He plays by putting the club into a piece of garden hose that is attached to a prosthetic limb. A rule of golf doesn't permit a player to use "artificial devices and unusual equipment," but the Royal and Ancient Golf Club of St. Andrews and the United States Golf Association, golf's ruling bodies, decided that Dawson's device was acceptable. Dawson reached the fifth round before losing on the eighth extra hole.

The four semifinalists include Hume, Craig Heap, the defending champion, Stephen O'Hara, and Stuart Wilson, a twenty-three-year-old university student. The two semifinal matches will take place this afternoon.

It's the afternoon Bobby Mackay craves. "It's nice to see the wind blowing from the west," he says. Royal Dornoch plays its toughest in today's southwest wind, because the inward holes, except for the seventeenth, are into the wind. "That's the way the course should play," Bobby adds. "It's transformed almost overnight. I've been concerned all week as to where all the grass was coming from. There was too much growth and we also couldn't get the green speed as we wished. But now the ground is firm and also brown in many areas." Walking out to the middle of the course, I feel that firmness in the ground. The course has gone quickly from green to brown. The only green patches are in the hollows, to which water drains.

Craig Heap seems well on his way to victory in his semifinal match. He's two-up through thirteen holes and hits the green at the fourteenth, while Stuart Wilson misses it. Heap goes on to win; he's headed for tomorrow's scheduled thirty-six-hole final match.

I continue up the course and catch up to Hume and O'Hara at the twelfth, where the match is all square. Something seems amiss. The golfers are moving erratically, at the wrong speeds. Hume has played a poor third shot to the green at the par-five; he's left with a thirty-foot putt for birdie. He hardly took any time at all with his putt, and is wearing a look on his face that says, "I've been wronged." A Scottish Golf Union official mutters, "Come on, Barry, you're not even trying." What's going on? I'm perplexed.

As it turns out, there's been a rules dispute on the eleventh hole. O'Hara drove left of the fairway, possibly into a lateral hazard – the beach. He wasn't sure if his ball had gone into the hazard and there was a chance that it was lost in the rough ground between the fairway and where the hazard starts. He decided to hit a provisional ball from the tee, knowing that he would be able to see his ball if it were in the hazard, which would have meant that it was in play. If he couldn't find it in the hazard, or elsewhere, then his tee shot would be declared lost; hence the provisional. The rules of golf allow a player to hit a provisional when he's not sure of where his initial ball went.

O'Hara's original ball was found, and that, not his provisional, became the ball in play. He was able to play back to the fairway. Hume believed that O'Hara was required to play the provisional ball, and was upset when an official ruled otherwise. The ruling was correct, however. O'Hara played a superb long third shot from the fairway to within four feet of the hole. Hume, angered and feeling the victim, hurriedly played the hole, in the end lying three through the green. He didn't play his fourth, electing to concede his opponent's putt for a four.

"Now he just wants to go home," his father, Jim, tells me. "You can see by the way he's walking that he doesn't want to play. I think maybe he's feeling that O'Hara is the Scottish Golf Union's favorite. He really needs to calm down. I've never seen him like this."

Hume two-putts the twelfth green for par. O'Hara, just off the green to the left in two, chips to within six feet, but three-putts. Hume walks off the green and whacks the ground with his putter. O'Hara, his red face getting redder as he fumes following his three-putt, throws his putter a good ten yards when he walks off the green. The match is degenerating. Hume is one-up.

Both golfers hit good shots on the par-three thirteenth hole. They halve the hole, so Hume is still one-up. But there's too much tension in the air, and it's not the tension that a close match generates. It's the tension that is generated when a golfer feels aggrieved. Most often golfers feel this way when putts lip out, or a ball bounces the wrong way. This time Hume is feeling that the rules officials are against him.

Hume and O'Hara hit long, well-placed drives at Foxy, the memorable fourteenth hole, where a shoulder juts into the fairway from the right, blocking a view of the green on that side. The plateau green runs across the fairway, angled from left to right. There's not a bunker on the hole, which only goes to show that superb land doesn't require embellishment. Hume, who is carrying his own bag but who could use the calming influence of a caddy, is on the right side of the fairway a few yards ahead of his opponent. He sits on his bag with his back facing O'Hara and holds his head in his hands. The thirty people who are watching are taken aback by his behavior. O'Hara hits what appears to be a good shot to the green, and then Hume, taking no time, hits his shot and in one motion returns his club to his bag and starts walking. His choreography is that of a golfer who has decided to lose.

Both golfers have hit their approaches through the back of the green. Hume, first to play, pitches up fifteen feet short of the hole after not bothering to walk on the green and inspect the shot he faced. O'Hara hits a fine shot to within four feet of the hole. Hume putts without looking at the line of his putt, and misses. He concedes O'Hara's par putt, though it was hardly a gimme. I know and every other spectator knows that Hume's antics are tantamount to his throwing the match. There's no other way to put it. I'm saddened by this turn of events. Hume is a gifted young golfer. He's played plenty of competitive golf. He should know better.

Hume's dad stops him on the way to the fifteenth tee, and speaks to him. Hume listens but doesn't say anything. A friend of his says to me, "You can't let yourself be beaten by a ruling. Good or bad or indifferent, you have to be big enough to take it on the chin."

The fifteenth hole is no better for Hume. He bats his forty-foot birdie putt twelve feet by the hole, misses the next putt, and then concedes Stephen's ten-foot birdie putt. He's one-down now. O'Hara drives into the quarry to the left of the sixteenth fairway, double-bogeys the hole, and concedes it to Hume, who is on the green in two shots. The match is all square again.

"How often do you have a chance to reach the finals of the Scottish Amateur?" a golf-watcher asks. "If you're going to let this happen you've no chance of moving forward." By now seventy-five people are following this curious match. Macarthur Bennie is among the group. The club captain shakes his head, as if to say, "This isn't the way a golfer should conduct himself."

Hume has the honor on the seventeenth tee, and hits the worst shot I've seen him play. He tops the ball a few yards forward into the gorse. O'Hara plays down the right side of the fairway. Hume plays three off the tee after declaring his first ball lost. O'Hara wins the hole and takes a one-up lead to the eighteenth tee.

"He's beating himself," somebody says. "He's thrown away the whole week. He might as well have done this on Monday." Jimmy Miller remarks, "It's best he go down the road. You don't want to see a Scottish champion behaving like that. The ruling was right."

But then Hume regains his golfing senses, and takes his time on the eighteenth tee. He hits a first-class drive. Maybe he listened to what his father said between the seventeenth green and eighteenth tee. Or maybe he realized he had only been hurting himself. Whatever the reason for his revived sense of purpose, he's still in the match. O'Hara follows his drive with a good one of his own.

"I know a couple of the Scottish Golf Union officials, and I told them this is not Dornoch," a club member says as we move down the last fairway. "This is not the way we play golf here. I'm sure the officials will give the players a talking-to later." He's disappointed in Hume, and also in O'Hara, who not only threw his putter after leaving the twelfth green, but had smacked his ball away in anger after missing a three-foot putt on the ninth green.

It's O'Hara's shot from the fairway. "Here's his moment of glory," somebody says. His shot looks good, and finishes twelve feet left of the hole. Hume's second finishes thirty-five feet left. He needs to hole his putt to have any chance of squaring the match. Hume examines the line of his putt, looking from behind the hole and from the side his ball is on. He hits a good putt, but it just turns left at the hole. He takes his cap off and concedes O'Hara's birdie putt. The match is over. The sorry mess concludes. Hume walks briskly to the car park, followed by his father and a friend. He won't talk to anybody. A writer for one of the Scottish papers tells me that Hume's play has developed in one year to the standard of a golfer who could represent the country internationally in important events. The writer is also concerned for Hume's future. Who wouldn't be after what he showed today?

• • • • • •

The next day, Saturday, I walk over to the course after noon to follow the final match between Stephen O'Hara and Craig Heap. Stephen's dad, Charlie, is filling his car with petrol for the drive back tonight to their home in Motherwell, a Glasgow suburb. He'll caddy for O'Hara this afternoon. I ask him about his son's match yesterday against Hume.

"It was shocking," he says. "I told Stephen during the match that he was going to win it. Barry was beating himself."

But that was another day, another round, another match. O'Hara and Heap have finished the first eighteen holes of their scheduled thirty-six-hole final. O'Hara is two-up after the morning round.

There's a strong wind out of the south, which makes the green on the short par-four first hole reachable from the tee. The Scottish Amateur trophy sits on a green-and-blue plaid cloth on a table at the back of the tee. Heap, first to play, drives through the green. O'Hara comes up thirty yards short of the green in the dry wispies. They halve the hole with pars, then miss the second green downwind. Jimmy Miller isn't impressed. "They should be on the green. They're only hitting eight-irons. It's not as if it's a short green." The second green must be forty yards long.

This is old-time golf-watching. Seventy-five people, including John Duncan and Andrew Skinner, are following the match. No power-drunk volunteers are bellowing, "Quiet please," just as a player begins his swing. We're watching top-flight amateur golf. Both O'Hara and Heap get up and down for their pars. O'Hara remains two-up through twenty holes.

The afternoon is brightening. It's a perfect links afternoon – sunny and breezy. I think of the observation that the Honourable Arthur Balfour, a British prime minister, made more than a century ago. He wrote: "A tolerable day, a tolerable green, a tolerable opponent supply, or ought to supply, all that any reasonably constituted human being should require in the way of entertainment. With a fine sea view and a clear course in front of him, the golfer may be excused if he regards golf, even though it be indifferent golf, as the true and adequate end of man's existence." This is true not only of playing golf on a links, but of watching golf. This final match promises better than indifferent golf.

There's a cold logic at the heart of match-play golf. At the beginning of the week it seems impossible that anybody could win seven straight matches – which the winner will have to do. The odds are long, the matches tiring, the course relentless. But one person, obviously, will go all the way through.

Through twenty-seven holes O'Hara remains two-up. The atmosphere is dramatically different from what prevailed during O'Hara and Hume's match yesterday. Stuart Wilson, the fellow whom Heap defeated in his semifinal match, is caddying for him. Heap and O'Hara walk together, chat, then move to their shots. O'Hara needs to hole a twenty-foot putt for par on the tenth to halve the hole and remain two-up. He drills the putt in. The golfers reach Foxy, with O'Hara still two-up.

O'Hara drives just into the right rough at Foxy, while Heap smashes a long drive down the middle, twenty yards past his opponent. "Tremendous drive," Andrew Skinner says. O'Hara sails his second thirty-five yards to the right of the green. Heap's second with a wedge finishes twenty-five feet from the hole. O'Hara pitches up thirty-five feet from the hole, and two-putts. Heap is trying to lag his long putt near the hole. He starts walking toward the hole as the ball is still rolling, expecting to tap it in when it comes to rest. He needn't bother. The ball drops for a birdie. Heap is within one hole of catching O'Hara.

Dornoch members stream out of the clubhouse to follow the players in. Where's Don Greenberg? He'd rather participate by playing or caddying. He's not a golf-watcher, and waits in the bar, where he will hear the final result soon enough.

The golfers halve the fifteenth hole, and then Heap drives left on the High Hole, the sixteenth. O'Hara lays well back with an iron to take the quarry on the left, which drops down to the beach, out of play. Heap finds his ball in the quarry's steel-wool rough. The ball is well below his feet, and he has to brace himself by bending his left leg at almost a ninety-degree angle to the ground. He bashes the ball back to the fairway from there.

Heap, however, has played out of turn, because O'Hara was away. It's another potential rules brouhaha. Heap realizes he played out of turn, and walks back toward O'Hara. He looks embarrassed. A referee is talking to O'Hara and explaining his options. O'Hara has the right to ask Heap to replay his shot – a choice the American side would make just ten weeks later during the women's international competition, the Solheim Cup, forcing Annika Sörenstam of Sweden to replay a chip shot she'd holed for birdie. O'Hara chooses to let Heap's shot stand.

"It's a very generous thing that Stephen did there," a club member says. Another old-timer who has seen it all remarks, "The young man offered to play his shot again, according to the rules. Stephen said there was no need to. That's all there is to it." Well, there still remained the matter of finishing the hole. O'Hara missed the green, hit a poor chip, and bogeyed. Heap holed from six feet for bogey, and halved the hole. "A brave five," somebody notes. He and O'Hara halve the seventeenth with pars. O'Hara is one-up with one to play.

Each golfer hits a big drive on the last hole. Macarthur Bennie is impressed. "They each give the ball a good dunt, don't they?" O'Hara's second from the light rough to the left finishes behind and to the left of the green, some ninety feet from the hole. Heap's second is over the flagstick, but rolls through the green. "Just a tad big. It wouldn't stop," he says.

O'Hara hits a well-judged long chip and run that stalls three feet short of the hole. Heap putts from seventy-five feet, and will probably need to make it to square the match. What are the chances? He comes up a couple of feet from the hole – a heck of a try. O'Hara is three feet away from his first Scottish Amateur win. He lines up the putt from both sides of the hole. His father is holding the flagstick off to the side. O'Hara takes his stance but is concerned that he might be standing on Heap's line. Heap tells him not to worry, and O'Hara settles in again. He holes the putt and offers a modest fist pump with his right hand, then shakes hands with Heap and embraces his father.

"That was a superb final," the Scottish Golf Union's president Colin Wood says. "It was played in the true spirit of a championship."

Charlie O'Hara slips into the clubhouse to make a phone call to his wife. "Hello, Kathy. Stephen won on the last hole, one-up. I can't talk long. The presentation is on in a few minutes. We'll see you this evening."

Meanwhile, O'Hara and Heap are in the pro shop, buying some goodies. Heap grabs a big chocolate bar and says, "I've been waiting for this all week." O'Hara pays the bill for the sweet stuff. "We'd better go," Heap says. "They're starting the presentation."

Macarthur Bennie and John Duncan are wearing their club ties. Willie Skinner, John Macleod, and Charlie O'Hara are taking photos. Sandy "Pipey" Matheson is seated on the bench in front of the pro shop with his wife, Dona. He sums up the final match. "I didn't think the tee-to-green play was all that good. But the up and downs were very good." As rendered by Pipey.

The medals are handed out. Barry Hume isn't here to receive his bronze medal for reaching the semifinals. Craig Heap, who will return to his studies in architecture, is given the silver medal. Stephen O'Hara gets the gold, and speaks highly of his opponent. "I'd like to say unlucky to Craig. He'll tell you that he only plays twice a week, because of his architecture program. Don't believe him."

That night Nell and I attend the pipe-band concert in the village square. The square is full of people. Andrew Macleod, who will be my caddy in the upcoming Carnegie Shield, assesses the final match. He's in the camp with Pipey – the camp that believes the golfers had their short games in tune, but that their long games were ragged. "They both putted well," Andrew concludes. "Stephen is a very worthy champion." The Scottish Golf Union will later name him its golfer of the year.

The pipers play. We chat with locals, then head to the Eagle for a pint. The bagpipes fade away behind us. I can't help but hear them as melancholy sounds, and think of Barry Hume. I hope he'll learn from his experience. "He'd better learn," Colin Wood told me. "Otherwise he could put his career in jeopardy."

I hope that doesn't happen. Hume didn't win the Scottish Amateur, but he's the golfer I'll remember most clearly from the championship. (A year later, while working on this book, I will be pleased to learn that Hume has won the 2001 Scottish Amateur.) He's brilliant technically, but golf is about more than swinging the club properly. Much more.

Chapter 16

The Carnegie Shield

There it is, bigger than the trophies for the U.S. and British Opens and the PGA Championship, more striking than the Inuit carvings that Canadian Open winners used to receive. It's the Carnegie Shield, and it sits in a locked trophy case on the upper floor of the clubhouse at Royal Dornoch. It comes out once a year when the captain of the club presents it to the tournament winner. There's no missing the trophy, which Andrew Carnegie presented to the club in 1901 for a new annual tournament; that was the same year Carnegie sold his steel company to the United States Steel Corporation and retired. Carnegie also donated £100 to the club, which was to invest the sum in order to provide the winner with a gold medal.

The format for the inaugural Carnegie Shield was medal play over thirty-six holes. Local baker Thomas E. Grant shot rounds of 80–85 off a three handicap, good enough to win the Shield, which was then a net competition. Grant had lost his left thumb while apprenticing as a baker in Glasgow, and adapted in golf by turning his left hand to the right until it was almost on top of the clubshaft. This encouraged a roundhouse hook, which he accepted. Grant's shots started well right, but curved back toward his target. He also played "off the left foot" in the Dornoch manner, as it was called; Dornoch golfers tried to hook the ball and hit it low, a useful style in wind and on firm turf. His address position had the ball well forward near his left foot, so that he could make a strong move at it with his body. His shots not only flew right to left, but low to the ground. There was one further embellishment in his swing: Grant shifted his right foot six inches back and to the right, just as he started his swing. This gave him a longer swing and added to the amount of draw spin on the ball. Grant was a real Dornoch golfer. He was full of idiosyncrasies in the service of hitting the ball where he wanted it to go.

The Shield didn't stick to the medal-play format for long. Match play was the usual format for competitions in 1901, and soon was put into place at the Shield. Sixteen golfers qualified over thirty-six holes for eighteen-hole matches. The competition's popularity increased over the years, until now more than two hundred golfers enter annually. They play in qualifying rounds, and are then streamed into one of three match-play divisions, each with thirty golfers. The sections are the Carnegie Shield itself, in which the matches are conducted at scratch – no strokes are given even if one player holds a higher handicap than the other. The next thirty-two low-handicap players who don't qualify for the Shield section play for the Davidson Trophy. The high-handicap group qualifies in a separate competition for the E. C. Fraser Cup. I'm in the low-handicap division; my goal is to qualify for the section that will play for the Shield.

● ● ● ● ● ●

David Thomson is putting me through a pre-Shield checkup. We're on the range at The Carnegie Club, where a strong east wind is making it hard to stand, let alone hit balls. But a strong wind is ideal for working on my balance. Good balance begins with good posture, something David has impressed upon me. He comes over after I've warmed up.

"Your posture is much better," David tells me. "I like what I see. You're standing taller to the ball, and I can see that your hands have that 'deep' look that I like. You're looking like a golfer now."

I was taking full swings, moving the club on a straight line back from the ball to as far as I could take it, given my flexibility. My hands then came up, my wrists cocked on their own, I turned behind the ball, shifted my weight forward while spinning my left hip out of the way as quickly as I could, held on to the clubhead through the ball, and finished with the shaft behind my neck in a more or less horizontal position parallel to the ground. The swing felt tighter, more efficient, more athletic. A golfer's swing. Controlled, not chaotic.

David stuck a shaft into the ground a few feet ahead of me and, as in our first lesson, asked that I try to start my shots left of that. We worked on my takeaway, so that I could achieve more width; a wider arc is a more consistent arc and should produce more coil behind the ball and hence clubhead speed, and also accuracy. I developed a pre-shot routine that would give me the feel of where I wanted the club to go during my takeaway. The routine comprised my taking the club back along the ground a few inches and then cocking my wrists. That's all. "Good idea," David said. I then placed the clubhead behind the ball again and went directly into my takeaway. From there I felt as if everything happened automatically, as long as I kept in mind the image of the ball starting left of the shaft in the ground.

"It's starting on line," David said of the ball. "There's just a hint of fade, which is what we're after. Most good golfers don't curve the ball very much. Their shots fall either right or left a little."

But there are times when a golfer needs to hit the ball with a pronounced right-to-left or left-to-right flight. David showed me a new way to do this – at least it was new for me. My target was 150 yards straight away, and I was imagining that I had to hook the ball around some trees to get it there. The ball would have to start well right, then curve back to the left. I had always hit this shot by closing my stance, pulling my right foot well back from the straight-on line, aiming right, and manipulating the clubface into a shut position at impact. David felt this was too complicated.

"Set up to the right, but not with a closed stance," he instructed. "Now turn the face in at address so that it is aimed at the target. Then swing normally." No clubface manipulation, that is. It's all physics and aerodynamics, he said. I'm facing to the right and the clubface is turned in. When I hit the ball it will start off to the right but will then curve left because of the turned-in clubface. That was the plan. David preferred a swing in which the golfer shouldn't feel his hands working.

"If you feel your hands working, they're not working properly," he said. "And if you don't feel them working, they're working well." Golf teachers do like a well-turned aphorism. But I knew what he meant. The hands should just go along for the ride in the modern swing. But what if I couldn't develop a modern swing, since I had learned the game in pre-modern times – well, in the 1960s, when golfers still consciously used their hands and not many people thought of the "big-muscle" swing.

My shots flew right to left on demand. They flew left to right on demand. They flew high and they flew low. David pronounced me fit to play in the Carnegie Shield. Buoyed by his show of confidence, not to mention the penetrating trajectory of my shots, I went back to Royal Dornoch for my last game before the Shield's first qualifying round. Kevin Morrison, Tom Mackenzie, and Neil Macdonald, a former Shield winner, were waiting for me on the first tee. I striped my opening tee shot and played well most of the way around, using my tight, hip-spinning, body-controlled swing. I shot 39–41 after three-putting the sixteenth and eighteenth greens and losing my drive into the whins to the left on the seventeenth. I wasn't thrilled with my mediocre finish to the round. Still, as I noted on my card, "I hit the ball quite well. Encouraging."

· · · · · ·

"What a gem of a morning," Andrew Macleod says as he greets me on the first tee for my maiden Shield appearance. The temperature is sixty-five degrees, the winds are light, and the sea is calm. Andrew, the seventy-nine-year-old club vice-president, weighs 155 pounds and stands as straight as a one-iron while he carries my golf bag. He has the body fat of a sixteen-year-old sprinter, and has been retired for fifteen years from his lifelong job as a housepainter. Andrew played in his first Carnegie Shield in 1933. Don Greenberg had introduced him to me on the High Street early in my visit.

I'd chatted with Andrew occasionally after our first encounter, and asked if he would caddy for me during the Carnegie Shield. "That will be fine," Andrew said, using a minimum number of words. "I'll have a look at the draw sheet when it's posted and meet you on the first tee a few minutes prior to your starting time."

I liked his economy of words, the way he said only what was necessary. Andrew was careful with his words and gestures. He was comfortable in his own skin. He was Andrew Macleod, and he didn't see why he should try to be anybody else.

The Carnegie Shield itself tells quite a tale. It's a history lesson, although I'm sure that's the last thing golfers in the Shield think about when they're over a four-footer for triple-bogey on Foxy.

Carnegie was evidently pleased to learn that Charles I – royalty – liked golf, but the representation of Charles I playing at Leith Links isn't the only element in the Carnegie Shield. Carnegie commissioned another four panels around the central one. There's Skibo Castle, Carnegie's summer residence; Dornoch Cathedral; the Bishop's Palace, later the Dornoch Castle; and Dornoch itself. Carnegie's monogram is also in view, as are the American eagle and the Scottish lion. Carnegie also included the Scottish and American flags. The Carnegie Shield cost £120 in 1901. The value of the silver alone in the Shield was set at £25,000 in 1980, while, as John Macleod notes in his club history, it's impossible to calculate the value of the workmanship. It's also gold to anybody who wins the competition. Golfing gold.

● ● ● ● ● ●

Nobody has made a bigger mark on the Shield than Brora's Jimmy Miller. He won his first Shield in 1965 and his last – his tenth – in 1983. His name is spoken with golfing reverence all over the Highlands. "The best golfer the North has ever had." "I remember him as a young lad, when he would sometimes wear a cowboy hat." "Ah, Jimmy Miller. What a man. What a man," Barry Hume's father, Jim, said during the Scottish Amateur.

Miller's first Shield win was memorable. He and Willie Skinner, then Dornoch town clerk and secretary to Royal Dornoch, came to the eighteenth hole all square. Willie holed from fifteen feet, giving him the advantage. Then Jimmy made his putt from the same distance to send the match to extra holes. The playoff went back and forth, one shot to the next, one hole to the next. Willie looked out of it when he hooked his tee shot badly on the twentieth hole, but Jimmy three-putted from the edge, so the playoff continued. Jimmy looked out of it at the twenty-second hole, but hit a short bunker shot near the hole to keep the playoff going. Willie duck-hooked his drive on the eighth hole, and couldn't get to the green, the farthest from the clubhouse. Jimmy, having driven well there, hit his wedge second shot on the green and putted up for a sure par-four after Willie had played his third within twelve feet of the hole. Two hundred spectators had accompanied the players to this remote edge of the course, and now watched as Willie faced his putt to halve the hole and keep the match going. But he missed, and Jimmy had won his first Carnegie Shield. Nine more Shield wins followed.

"Open that second drawer there," Jimmy, a tall, red-haired man, told me at his home one day. I found a medal there. "The club gave me a lovely gold medal last year in recognition of my ten Shield wins. It was very nice of them to do that. They didn't have to."

No, they didn't. But nobody will win ten Shields again. The young golfer who wins two or three will probably be good enough to turn pro. Jimmy's been a lifelong amateur. As a housepainter, he's kept his time his own. Nearing sixty, he's not playing much competitive golf with younger players anymore, but he is a member of the British Seniors' Society and plays some of their events. Later this year he'll visit Australia with a twelve-man Society team and play matches there. The games will all be foursomes or alternate shot matches – "a wonderful game," Jimmy says. "Aye, you find out your strengths and weaknesses. You play two rounds of foursomes, it's a wonderfulday's golf."

Perhaps Jimmy enjoys foursomes golf because he likes to be put under pressure, not only for himself, but for a partner. He's not afraid to have to hit a shot, and it's been that way for as long as he can remember. In the Highlands people still talk about the time Miller beat another Miller – Johnny Miller, the virtuoso golfer who would go on to win the 1973 U.S. Open and the 1976 British Open. Johnny was at Dornoch with his Brigham Young University team, and Jimmy beat Johnny 4&3. He was that good a golfer. But Jimmy didn't play much competitive golf away from the Highlands, and Scottish selectors for international teams didn't like that.

"It was difficult to attract their attention," Jimmy remembers. "People forget that it wasn't easy to travel south then. I couldn't get to Edinburgh in less than eight hours, no matter how hard I tried."

Highlanders don't particularly mind that they're often considered outsiders, even in most of Scotland. Jimmy wasn't all that interested in going further afield anyway. "There's more to life than golf, isn't there?" he asks, rhetorically. Jimmy found that out early in his golfing life, when he was in his mid-twenties. He had some back problems and learned he suffered from mild spina bifida. Surgery helped but kept him out of golf for two years, and, he says, "finished me for traveling." He and his wife, Liz, have a son and two daughters. He's a Highlands man who was born here and stayed here.

Some people, though, think Jimmy didn't have the self-confidence to succeed in the bigger arenas of competitive amateur golf, and maybe that's part of why he didn't test himself to the limit. Then again, he hit the shots in the Highlands when he had to.

"To be a good golfer you have to play well under pressure," Jimmy says. "To me, the definition of a good golfer is one who can play when he has to play. A lot of golfers can hit a five-iron on the green when they're in a bounce game. But can he do it when he has to?"

Maybe I'm a bounce-game golfer and I shouldn't bother trying to become a tournament golfer. But maybe not. It's possible that I've yet to try my best to handle whatever emotional pressures I let build inside. I also know, though, that I don't have the trust to compete with a swing more feel-oriented than mechanics-oriented. That's why I've been working with David Thomson. I'm playing in a big tournament. It's a big deal. It's why I wanted Andrew Macleod to caddy for me. I planned to give myself every chance in the Shield.

• • • • • •

I'd heard voices while having my breakfast prior to meeting up with Andrew Macleod for the first qualifying round in the Shield. This wasn't an encouraging development.

Voice one: "What do you think you're doing, trying a new move in the biggest tournament of the summer only two lessons into the change? Are you crazy? It takes time to learn a new language of the game. Maybe this wasn't such a good idea. It's not like you were playing so badly before."

Voice two: "Yeah, but you really didn't like the way you've been striking the ball. It felt weak, more of a slap with your hands than a swing. And you promised yourself you'd work hard on your game this summer, which is what you've been doing. You're going to have to test the new feelings sometime, and the best place for that is in a tournament. You've already played a few rounds with the moves, and you like the power you feel, the tightness, the athleticism. Put the action to the test. That's the only way to find out if it will work for you. Just think of those solid swings you made the last couple of days, a three-iron over the flag on the second at Dornoch, a six-iron that covered the flag in a hook wind at the thirteenth, when you brought the shot in from the right as if you were reeling it in. Come on, have some confidence. Toughen up. Stick to what you've been working on."

"Lorne Rubenstein, National Golf Club, Canada," Hugh Ferguson announced. Show time. As I stood over the ball, a queasy feeling grabbed me in my stomach, traveled into my hands, and I blanked out just before I swung. I remember waggling the club as I'd done on the range with David, then setting it down behind the ball and swinging. It wasn't the most aggressive swing. No, it was full of fear of where the ball might go if I really gave it a ride as I'd hoped to. Instead I held back at impact, and hit the ball with all the force of somebody gingerly taking apart an electrical appliance for fear it would blow up in his hands. But I somehow made contact and looked up to see the ball fluttering down the right side of the fairway, disappearing presently over a hummock. I hoped it was in short grass there and it was. The queasy feeling remained, but I was in play.

My second shot, an over-the-top, chopped eight-iron, rose quickly and headed on a direct course for the bunker at the left front of the green. But it stopped short, and I then putted from off the green within ten feet of the hole. Ten feet short of the hole. Already my mind was filling with images of where I didn't want the ball to go rather than where I wanted it to go. How do the professionals keep these thoughts and images out of their minds anyway? Maybe I should do some breathing exercises, take self-hypnosis, read books on positive thinking. Who am I to say these approaches won't work?

I made the putt, but I wasn't feeling good about how my body was reacting. I felt tense. My swing felt small and I felt tiny, overwhelmed by my grandiose plan to change it. Dornoch was so pretty today. What a shame I couldn't see its beauty. How could I even think that a golf course, any course, even a links, was a beautiful place? That funny, familiar feeling of waiting for something horrible to happen was sneaking into me; Hopewell, reaching into the golf course. But I had a plan. I had a swing. I had worked hard. I deserved good things today. I'd looked forward to the Shield for months.

Onward, to the second hole. The hole was cut in the back left of the green, and I definitely didn't want to go over the green and down the steep hill there. Nor did I want to go to the right of the green and down the steep hill there. Nor did I want to hit my ball to the left of the green and into the hellish bunker there, from which Adrian Bagott, the fellow who had taken that marathon cycling trip, had made a twenty-three during one Shield qualifying round when he couldn't get out. The bunker looked like a war zone after Adrian finally emerged. I could miss this bunker and go into the bushes and lose my ball. Or I could come way over the top, pull my shot, and go over the fence and the footpath near Bill Gifford's house, where I'd find his well-stocked golf library. Maybe if I hit that shot, I'd retire from the Shield then and there and read for the rest of the morning.

But I composed myself somewhere in this nightmarish golfing fantasy and asked myself three fundamental questions: Where do you want your shot to finish? What sort of shot do you want to play? What club should you use?

These were helpful questions. I wanted my shot to finish short of the hole in the middle of the green. I wanted to play a slight fade, starting the ball in the left center of the green. And I believed a six-iron was the club. If I hit a five-iron flush, I could hit my ball over the green. A six-iron it was.

The shot came off exactly as I planned it, and finished thirty-five feet short of the hole. That felt good, that was what I was looking for. Then, standing over my putt, I realized that, if I hit it a bit too hard, the ball could catch a slight slope behind the hole, pick up speed, and roll over the green and down the hill. Was I being prudent or Hopewellian? I couldn't figure that one out, but I did know it would be stupid of me to putt off the green after hitting it on my tee shot. So I did what any golfer sloshing around in anxiety would do. I laid my putt up, as if I were laying up a second shot on a par-five short of a pond. I laid my putt up eight feet short of the hole and then I missed my putt, so I had made a bogey. Still, it was a decent start. Par-bogey. Greenberg had told me there was nothing wrong with a four-four start at Dornoch.

Note from my journal at Dornoch, May 1, 1977: "It is sensible not to be dismayed when things go wrong but to trust one's swing. After all, a two-handicap does not become a twenty in the space of a few holes."

I parred the third hole as well, although I didn't hit either my tee shot or my approach with any oomph. Still, I was just short of the green in two, and got down in two putts. Four-four-four. Greenberg had told me that that was a super start at Dornoch. He knew. I also knew. I was waiting for the Mannie to fall on my head. I was waiting for the highest tide ever seen at Dornoch, and I figured it would sweep over the course and take me with it. I was waiting for something really, really bad to happen on the course. I didn't know what would happen, but I was sure something would. If confidence exists in being sure of something, then I was full of confidence. Negative confidence.

My eyes glazed over on the fourth hole. I looked toward the Mannie, not a bad target. I'd lost all feeling for what I'd been working on following my sessions with David Thomson. Through a mental haze I visualized my ball flying down the center of the fairway, but then the weak image morphed into it bouncing along the ground and into one of the bunkers to the right. Nothing like any of this happened. Instead, I hit a low screamer of a shot that dove into the gorse bushes about one hundred yards ahead of the tee. The thick grass swallowed my ball rather like a shark would swallow its prey. The ball disappeared. Now I had to hit a provisional ball in case I couldn't find my first, and I wasn't even sure I wanted to find my first, it was so deep into the gorse. I launched my provisional ball fifty yards to the right of the fairway. It started to the right, and it continued in that direction. The angle was so extreme that the ball, which traveled about 250 yards in the air, was only about 150 yards ahead of the tee. After a cursory look for my first ball, in which I almost lost Andrew in the gorse, I traipsed across the fairway to my provisional ball, banged it up the fairway from high grass there, and finished with a triple-bogey on the hole. I could have used a not-so-wee dram at that point.

I did manage to par the fifth after hitting a laughably short drive to the right and then scuttling a three-iron between the bunkers short of the green and onto the green. The hole is usually a drive and a wedge, and had been just that during my Sunday round. Now I was in the Shield, where I hit a sickening drive to the right and a putrid three-iron along the ground. Two putts later, I had my par. It didn't make me feel any better. Neither did the twelve-foot putt I sank for bogey on the

sixth hole, which meant I was six over par after six holes. At this junc-
ture I removed my notebook from my golf bag, deciding I was here to
write a book, not lose my mind playing in a tournament. I didn't want
to miss any possible material from this first round at the Shield. Stories
were probably breaking out all around me. I needed the comfort of
my notebook.

Forty-two on the front nine. That was the cold number. Four con-
secutive bogeys to start the back nine. Eleven over par after thirteen
holes. But qualifying for the Shield takes place over thirty-six holes. I
wasn't going to give up. The idea was to give my best on each shot, and
then I could say what the pros say: "I tried on every shot. I gave it my
best on every shot, so I can look myself in the mirror and feel good.
I'll be able to sleep tonight." Spoken just like a tour pro.

But the round wasn't over. Not nearly. It was time to play the fourteenth, Foxy.

From the tees of the day, Foxy was playing at 440 yards. The double-
dogleg hole is named Foxy because it's smart enough to fool most
players: the shoulder that juts into its right side some 275 yards, the
green whose width is greater than its depth. Given the fact that
the green is raised some ten feet above the fairway, and the angle at
which it sits to the fairway, it's difficult to fly a ball onto the green
with anything more than a six-iron in hand. The long bombers who
played the Scottish Amateur were able to hit their drives so far down
the left side of the fairway that their short-iron second shots could
land and stay on the green. Most golfers find themselves trying to hit
a low second shot that will land short of the green and scamper up
the plateau to the green. That's from the left side of the fairway, from
which the green opens up. It's preferable from the right side of the
fairway to hit the second shot at the extreme left corner of the green,
leaving the ball below the green. Then a run-up shot can do the job
of getting near the hole for a one-putt par, or at least a bogey.

Nobody would build a hole like Foxy today, which is too bad. Modern golf would dictate that the shoulder be removed. No doubt most architects would turn the dogleg with a bunker or two. Yet Foxy is a baffling hole precisely because it's artless; it needs nothing. The firmer the green, the more difficult it is to keep a shot on it. A ball hit into the hill short of the green might run up and stop on the green. Then again it might not. The golfer has to be foxy to beat Foxy. Few players do beat Foxy, but to do so once is to remember the occasion always. I recall a long four-iron I hit into a strong wind from the left side of the fairway. My ball landed thirty yards short of the green, climbed the hill, which took most of the run off the ball, and then settled ten feet from the hole. "A classic Dornoch shot," my playing companion said. That was the only time all summer I succeeded in hitting this shot at Foxy.

Greenberg has played Foxy for fifteen years and it's confounded him for that long. He's developed a rap that he brings into play while caddying. Visitors enjoy his spiel, the first time anyway. Other caddies' eyes glaze over because they've heard it before. Greenberg delivers it with an unusual combination of malice aforethought and delicious anticipation in his voice. I could hear even a touch of sadism in his tone when he first made his customary speech in my presence, while we walked from the thirteenth green to the fourteenth tee. Greenberg: the Marquis de Golf.

"Okay boys, the course record is safe, your handicap is in flames, and we're coming to the most famous hole in Dornoch, number fourteen, Foxy. It's the toughest par-five on the course, and it's a par-four, four hundred and forty yards of double dogleg with no bunkers. Into the wind you can't get there, downwind you can't hold it, so today, boys, we're going to hit two solid shots and get there or thereabouts, and then we turn into Harrison Ford. Let the adventure begin," Greenberg recites with the delivery of an auctioneer.

I came to Foxy with my game in tatters and my confidence shattered. Still, I knew that I'd feel a surge of confidence if I could par Foxy. Then perhaps I could birdie the short par-four fifteenth and par in from there. That would give me a respectable eighty, a score from which I could still qualify for the Shield. Golf, not marriage, is the triumph of hope over experience. I don't know why I should feel hopeful after playing dreadfully for thirteen holes and now facing the most confounding hole on the course. That's golf. That's a golfer.

Drive: Left corner of the fairway, good shape. I just about ran off the tee, I was so happy to have hit a good drive.

Second: Trying a low, hard one to run up to the green. Instead I hit a high, soft one that collapses into a clump of ornery grass in the rough to the right. I'm beyond the sandhill, so I can see the green. At least I think I can see the green.

Third: My second shot finished on an upslope right in that clump of ornery grass. I couldn't see the green, but so what? Every shot in golf is a blind shot, because you're supposed to keep your head down. Well, it's a thought. Moreover, I was standing on a slope so severe that my left foot was well above my right. I could only see half the ball, too. My plan was to gouge the ball out of there, holding on to a square clubface through impact. The slope of the hill would send the ball high so that it would land softly on the green and stop. I had about forty yards to the green, so distance wasn't a problem. Unfortunately, I didn't hold on to a square clubface through impact. The clubface turned sharply to the left as soon as it met with the tangled mat of turf. The ball came out as far to the side as forward, and rolled up to finish left of the green and below it.

Fourth: I was twenty feet off the green, had a ten-foot slope in front of me and then forty feet of green to the hole. I picked a seven-iron to chip the ball up the hill and onto the green. Andrew pursed his lips, but didn't say a thing. Nonetheless I could see that he didn't agree with my choice of club. "Would you rather I putt from here?" I asked Andrew.

"As you wish, Lorne. But that would be my preference for the shot." Overly sensitive soul that I am, I didn't want to hurt Andrew's feelings by going against him. And so I handed the seven-iron to him and took my putter out of the bag. I knew this was the wrong play because, while I'm a decent putter, I don't like to putt from so far away and up a hill. Why not? Because I putt left-handed, and didn't feel I could gauge the speed on this unusual putt. I took to putting left-handed three years ago, because I'm naturally left-handed and feel more comfortable over the ball that way – except when I don't, that is. This was one of those times. Still, I figured that Andrew must be right and I must be wrong. I putted, my ball plodded up the hill, and then expired before coming back to my feet.

Fifth shot: I putted again, and this time barely got the ball on the green.

Sixth shot: I rammed the putt so hard after the last two that the ball rolled ten feet by the hole.

Seventh shot: I missed the ten-footer for triple-bogey.

Eighth shot: I holed out. The dreaded snowman. An eight.

Walking to the fifteenth green I realized that I was now fifteen over par and might not break ninety. That was a horrible thought. I felt woozy and finished bogey, bogey, double-bogey, double-bogey, to shoot 91.

The eight I made on the fourteenth hole did have its effect that first round, and not only on me. The Shield's evil scorekeepers kept the worst eclectic score for the day – the worst scores posted on each hole. My eight at Foxy counted toward the day's total of 146, seventy-six over par. I took no solace in this contribution.

• • • • • •

Nell and I went for cocktails that night at Bill Gifford's golf house, where various Dornoch members both local and from away showed up. Sandy Matheson had heard of my débâcle, and was sympathetic because he'd been there. "Put a card and a pencil in my pocket and my score goes up ten shots," Sandy said.

Nobody at the party played well in the first qualifying round. Sandy ribs us, but knows how we feel. Nell, meanwhile, is surprised when she learns that the wife of one dinner guest walked with him for all eighteen holes during his lousy round; doesn't she have anything better to do with her time? Another woman even caddied for her husband. Nell avoids watching my tournament play; she knows she'll hear about it anyway – and hear about it and hear about it. Instead, she had enjoyed a long, wine-saturated lunch with Jasmine Mackay, a new friend in town. To Nell, it had been much more pleasant lunching at the Royal Golf Hotel with the course as a backdrop than looping around it with a crestfallen spouse.

Andrew was also at the party. "How did he think he could play well?" Andrew asked, referring to me. "He was taking notes every hole."

Nell and I walked back to the flat through the peaceful streets of the village. I poured myself a whisky and read some Henry Longhurst. Longhurst was not only an elegant golf writer, whose essays have endured, but also a fine player. He was a sensitive man prone to attacks of nerves in competition, and a member of the Royal and Ancient Golf Club of St. Andrews. Longhurst liked to play in the club's big Medal tournament, but never did win it. I was comforted, perversely, when I read his description of one of his rounds in the Medal. "I myself have taken ninety – off a then handicap of five – which would have been unthinkable on any other occasion," Longhurst wrote in his autobiography, *My Life and Soft Times*.

I didn't sleep well after my unthinkable 91. What had happened to me? I had no answers. But I did have hope that I could redeem myself with a solid round of golf in the second round. Not so. I shot 86, and not only didn't I qualify for the scratch division of the Shield, but I missed out on the next section. For me the Shield was over. After I finished, I ran into Greenberg in the clubhouse; he had made the second division, although he shot 86 the first round. But he rebounded with a 79 the next day.

Still, something good happened that second day. A fellow was waiting for me to finish my round, and introduced himself to me in front of the clubhouse. "I'm John Louden," he said. "Does the name mean anything to you?" I'd heard the name before, but that's as far as any recognition went. "I played with you when you were here in Dornoch in 1977," John said. "My wife, Jenny, was with me. We had a super day and stayed over to have another round with you. We were doing a tour of the north and had to have a game at Dornoch. You were just crushing the ball."

Jenny had been working at the Royal and Ancient as a secretary then. She and John were living in Edinburgh when I met them in 1977, then moved to Perth, and now were in Inverness. They were members at Nairn, a first-rate links near Inverness, and also at Golspie. Their membership at Golspie for £100 a year allowed them three games at each of Royal Dornoch, Tain, and Brora. The only restriction was that they couldn't play in the busy months of July and August. Still, that was a superb arrangement.

Andrew was in the bar and joined Nell and me for a drink with the Loudens. Alan Grant also came through, like me a non-qualifier. Kind man that he is, Andrew said, "Don't worry. The older you get the harder it is to concentrate. But I do hope you will play in the Shield again. The sorts of rounds you've had here happen to all of us."

• • • • • •

Demoralized as I was after my futile golf, I didn't watch many of the
ensuing matches or even play. I did follow the final match, when Scott
Chisholm, a twenty-year-old roofer from Inverness, was playing
Andrew Biggadike, a twenty-one-year-old student at Guildford College
in New Jersey. Each was playing his first Shield. Andrew had a bad day
and was never in the match. Scott won nine and seven, about as thor-
ough a bashing as one golfer could give another, although it was the
first time Scott had played in front of a gallery. Andrew had a terrible
day and Scott had a wonderful day.

The Shield presentation ceremony took only ten minutes – the
Dornoch way, without pretension. That night Nell and I were invited
for dinner at Golf View, Curtis Behrent's home, where Dornoch's
club secretary in earlier times, John Sutherland, had once lived.
Curtis, an American, lives in Paris and makes frequent visits to
Dornoch. Bill Gifford was there, along with Willie and Mary Skinner.
There was some Shield talk, but the conversation soon turned to other
matters. Curtis showed us a crack in the glass on the front door of
the house. He's never had it repaired, because of the story attached
to it. The story is that Sutherland and his wife were in the kitchen
when they heard the glass crack. They received a telegram two
hours later informing them that their son had died in the war. A
photo of John Sutherland now greets visitors when they enter the gracious home.

Curtis also filled in an important detail on the twenty-three that
Adrian Bagott had made on the second hole during a Shield. Somebody
asked Adrian why he hadn't played out backwards from the bunker to
get the ball back on to grass.

"I never thought of that," Adrian said.

Golf can shatter our minds for the moment and strip us of our
dignity. It happened to Adrian on that one hole and it happened to me
during the qualifying rounds that week of the Shield. I was depressed

for more than a few hours after my experience. But, to quote Don Greenberg after he follows a series of bad shots with a good one, "I'm back." I'm back, that is, to knowing that sometimes there's no understanding golf, why we can play it well one day and miserably the next. Maybe the most intelligent strategy is to accept this. Maybe.

Chapter 17

My Heart's in the Highlands

On most days now, there was something distinctly different about the air. It was late August, and occasionally I was sheared by a cutting wind when I stepped onto the High Street from the windbreak in the narrow path between Cheadle House and the library. The winds off the sea hit harder, and the leaves that fell from the trees into the churchyard foretold the end of the summer, and my season in Dornoch. Nell had left to resume teaching in Toronto, so I was on my own as summer turned to autumn. Cheadle House seemed empty without her.

The end of summer seems to me the end of things in a way that the end of the calendar year has never represented. Summer was holiday time when I was in school, of course, so its end marked the start of a new academic year. It's also the end and the beginning of the Jewish year: a time for reflection. In Dornoch people were walking faster, and reflexively put their heads down in a wind that blew cold more frequently. They lingered longer in Luigi's over their coffees, as if readying themselves for a life that would be spent more indoors during the fall and winter. Angus Maclaren, who had pretty much run Skibo Castle until his recent retirement, and sensed subtle changes in the landscape, wrote in his journal about the coming of autumn. He left the journal out on a desk in Skibo's library, and I liked to consult it. He wrote of what he sensed and observed: "A keenness in the wind, perhaps, or a sharpness in the light and certainly the smallest of changes in the trees and the gardens, a loss of freshness in the blossoms."

The news was out: autumn was on its way. "The weather is lying down now," somebody at Luigi's says over his morning coffee. "We're on the downslope to autumn and winter. There's no getting around that."

* * * * * *

I'm visiting Jimmy and Liz Miller at their home in Brora. The big picture window in the home down near the sea looks out across dunes and unkempt ground to the firth. Here and there I spot a flagstick on a mound. We're looking at the Gleneagles Golf Course, a name meant to evoke the baronial resort in Perthshire that has three courses. But this Gleneagles is no resort. Its origins go back to 1891, when local people either too poor or unwilling to join Dornoch, Brora, or Golspie wanted to play rough-and-ready golf, just bat the ball around. This is a sort of paradise, basic golf behind Jimmy's home. Here's another man who, like Andrew Macleod, appears to know himself to the core.

"I have my own golf course out there," Jimmy says this morning, a few days before I'll leave Dornoch for Toronto. It's as if I've returned to the landscape where I first hit some golf balls, which I call the Highway Hideaway course. This rocky piece of ground in Toronto was being cut up and reshaped into a major highway across the top of the city. But for me it was a place to hit golf balls.

The name Gleneagles, applied here to this shaggy shore land, is
ironic. It's a statement in a way, because the theme of rough-and-ready
golf runs counter to the manicured and expensive Gleneagles. It's like
living in a hut compared to a mansion, skating on a bumpy natural
ice rink instead of in Madison Square Garden. At Gleneagles – Brora's
Gleneagles, that is – a boy comes around once a month to run a
mower through. Nobody is pretending that this is refined golf. It's still
golf, though.

Jimmy and I go out to his patio overlooking Gleneagles. He's proud
of the place, but not so proud of what led to its predecessor in 1891.
Back then the local fisherfolk were considered inferior and not allowed
on the Brora course. "Astonishing," Jimmy says. Any fisherfolk who did
manage to get onto the course couldn't go into the clubhouse. Finally
they had enough, and decided to carve out their own place to golf. That
first rough course eventually fell out of use, but a few locals recently
got together and started a course again here, then nicknamed it
Gleneagles. But it's really the anti-Gleneagles. No rules. Old-timers with
three clubs banging the ball around. Tiny greens on knobby hills. Jimmy
Miller attended the opening of the course in 1991, a century after the
locals did their first course here. Folks gathered for a barbecue, and
they were proud of what they had wrought here. What they had
wrought wasn't that far from what nature had wrought – linksland. "It's
a good practice ground for me," Jimmy Miller says. "I like to sneak out
and thrash around here."

Thrashing around. There's a description of golf as a true sport, one
where the participant doesn't think but just reacts to what's in front
of him – a ball and a target. We use the term nowadays to describe a
round in which we played poorly. "I thrashed it around today." But
thrashing it around could also suggest letting go of mechanics by just
swinging the club. That would be golf as a physical exercise, even a
physical release – and the release would be from self-consciousness.
That must have been what golf was like for most people in the early

days. Today teachers talk about how most good golfers play without conscious thought; they often advise a student to think about the swing while practicing, then to see and feel the shot on the course. They're asking us to return to thrash-around golf, aren't they? At least I consider this their subliminal message about playing, as opposed to practicing.

Jimmy advocates this sort of golf. "I don't really think of anything at all," he tells me, and I feel envious of his blank-mind, thrash-around golf state. "I just hit the ball. That's the way I've always played. I started when I was fifteen years old and back then a round of golf was two or two-and-a-half hours, even medal play. We just hit the ball, nothing more. We didn't have yardage books then, so we trusted the eye. Maybe that helped me stay away from mechanical thoughts. But I don't know another way. I've never played golf with all that thinking. It's not my way."

I figure Jimmy knows I shot that fat number in the Shield. If he doesn't, I'm not going to enlighten him. While listening to him describe the way he plays golf, I think I'd like to show him that I can see and feel and hit shots, too. Maybe we could thrash around for a few minutes here at Gleneagles. I'm glad I feel the urge. The Shield didn't kill my golfing spirit; it only froze it briefly. Still, I'd like to get out there and thwack and thrash around on this basic links. Maybe on my next visit.

"All the great players love links golf," Jimmy says. "Nicklaus, Trevino, Watson, Norman, Faldo, Tiger. They can play the shots. That's the original way to play golf at the end of the day, but people have forgotten this. Now they want to know the exact distance to the hole, because they play courses that are so soft they can land the ball on a sixpence and it will stop there. And they prefer full swings, because they know precisely how far they can hit the ball with every club. Peter Thomson put it best about links golf, though. He said that links golf is not about hitting greens, it's about staying on them." It's not about hitting greens all right, it's about hitting shots, one after the next.

Jimmy and I are soon talking about Stuart Shaw, the fiftyish caddy and Royal Dornoch member who has won the Carnegie Shield and many other northern tournaments with his homemade swing. Stuart is a short, feisty guy, who takes the club back around behind his back and in a whirlybird fashion brings it right round the other way. His shots fly low and true. Nobody hits the ball straighter than Stuart. "Quite extraordinary the way Stuart plays," Jimmy says. He uses a two-piece hard golf ball, knows his game, and doesn't fiddle with it. "I don't think he got the credit due him," Jimmy remarks. "When the selectors for Scottish teams looked at Stuart's swing, they didn't think he could play the game to a high standard."

They were wrong. Stuart, like Don Greenberg, demonstrates that there's nothing wrong with a swing that makes the ball fly right, as in the way the golfer wants it to fly. Johnny Miller has said that, if the golf ball flies as a player intends it to most of the time, then that player must be doing something right in his swing. Agreed.

Leaving Jimmy and Brora, I drive south on the A9. The Mannie ahead of me seems a live presence. Well, he is. It's been impossible to escape him here this summer, and I knew nothing about him when I arrived in Dornoch. For people who live here, it's not a matter of adjusting to his presence. He hurts by his presence. That's why memorials to counteract the monument to the Duke of Sutherland are being considered. The most significant, perhaps, is a monument seventeen miles north of the Mannie, on top of a six-hundred-foot-high hill. The plan is that this memorial will include statues of a cleared family. The father will be looking toward the sea while his wife will be looking back at the empty lands to the west; a wall will be inscribed with the names of people from around the world who are the descendants of Highlanders cleared by the first Duke of Sutherland. A center to educate people about the Clearances is also being planned.

I drive back to Dornoch from Brora slowly, taking the setting in. I'm listening to BBC Gaelic and a song from one Moira Anderson called "Dark Island," about these lands. Sheep graze on the north side of the A9, and now I hear some poems being read from a book called *Winds in the Heather*, published in 1931. The poems are set in the Highlands. As Alan Grant says, the Highlands inspire creativity.

I get off the A9 and drive east into Dornoch, where I stop by for a cup of tea at Jimmy and Jessie Bell's home. I've spent some time with this kindhearted couple during the summer. Jimmy is in his mid-eighties, while Jessie has a few years to go to reach that age. "He poached me when I was young," Jessie tells me. Their home looks south across meadows to the firth and Tain. Jimmy has been involved in the village's historical society for years, and he's a friend of Donnie Macdonald, the Birdman. Recently Jimmy has had to stop driving a car, which has meant he and Donnie can't explore as easily as they used to. But Jimmy retains his love of Dornoch and Sutherland. He and Jessie are Scottish-born and met in Inverness during the Second World War. He was raised in Fort Erie, Ontario, from the age of twelve, and taught public school from 1933 to 1940 before returning to Scotland. Dornoch is the Bells's true home – actual and spiritual.

Over a cup of tea and Jessie's shortbread, I mention that I had no idea when I first arrived in Dornoch that the Clearances were such a vital subject in the Highlands. Nor did I appreciate how much the people were attached to the land. I thought I was coming to Dornoch to write a book about golf, a village, and the people who lived here. I didn't realize there would be so much more.

We chat for a while, and, as I leave, Jessie points out a framed print in the conservatory at the front of the house. It's an old map of Dornoch, with an accompanying, curt description of the village. "Dornoch is the County Town of Sutherland. It is a place of no importance, having no Trade, or Manufacture, or Harbour."

It is a place of great importance, to Jimmy, to Jessie, to the thirteen hundred residents, to golfers from all over the world. To me. To Nell, who has told me she wants to return, and soon.

• • • • • •

John and Jenny Louden have invited me for a game at Golspie, which I happily accept. Here we are, twenty-three years later, in the Highlands. My friends. My rediscovered friends who met each other through golf, at the Elie Golf Club in the county of Fife, not far from St. Andrews. We didn't speak or exchange a word to one another in nearly a quarter-century, but it's as if we've been speaking all these years through our lives in golf. Parallel existences, maybe. We're the same age and have arrived at the same place at the same time, with our feelings for the game intact.

There's nobody on the course when we set out early in the morning, and our round, while leisurely, still takes only three hours. We trade stories of our high and low moments in the game, and our pursuit of the best in ourselves as golfers. Jenny has been having putting problems, and describes them so vividly that we can't help but laugh – and of course we know what she's feeling. Jenny putts cross-handed. John putts left-handed, though he hits the ball right-handed, a method I follow – if it can be called a method. He became a poor right-handed putter when he moved from North Berwick east of Edinburgh to Elie in Fife, and found the greens very different. We're all golf-goofy.

Should we care whether we believe we can make short putts? Do these things matter even now, when we are – can I bring myself to say it – fifty years old and a bit more? Jenny plays in a league for golfers of that certain age, but the women couldn't come up with a suitable name. "Vintage Vets" was suggested and quickly rejected, but I guess that's what we are: vintage vets. Baby-booming vintage vets who can't boom drives anymore. Jenny reminds me that I hit a driver and five-iron to the green at the par-five ninth hole when we played Royal Dornoch in 1977, and then holed a fifteen-foot putt for an eagle. Now I lay up with a five-iron most of the time on that hole, and then hit a short iron in. Where has my distance gone? Where have the years gone? Questions without answers.

"It's like you're in suspended animation sometimes in a tournament," John says. "You're watching yourself and you can't believe that you're hitting these shots." Tell me about it. I'm the guy who just shot that big number in the Shield. I can't bring myself to cite the number again.

"I knew a psychologist whose back garden was at the edge of the practice range at a course," Jenny remarks. "'I could do a roaring business from all the nutters on the practice ground,' he told me." Jenny thinks that all golf clubs should hire clinical psychologists.

Our round at Golspie ends. We have a drink in the clubhouse that overlooks the empty links and then say our goodbyes in the parking lot, promising that it won't be another twenty-three years before we see each other again. We hope we'll still be golfing. We know we'll still be friends.

• • • • • •

The days are going by too quickly. Friends have arrived from Canada and we've been playing golf most every day, all day. Howard Ganz is here with his father, Sam, who has never been to Scotland. Lee Abbott, another friend from Toronto, was also here. I've been telling them about Dornoch all summer via e-mail. We've had a splendid time playing at Dornoch, and also at The Carnegie Club, Tain, and Brora.

Now Sam and Lee have left, so it's just Howard and me. We're playing a match against Don Greenberg and Hamish Macrae, a local member, for the usual pound on game. Concurrently, I'm playing a match with Don. It's our final match of the season.

On the sixth hole, Don is already in for a three, and his partner, Hamish, has an eight-footer for a three. I'm also in for three, so our side has halved the hole. Howard has a short putt for a four, lines it up, and holes it. He can't figure out why Hamish didn't bother to try his putt, and so I tell him that there was no need, since he couldn't improve on Don's par. "I don't want to do that stuff," Howard says, meaning he wants to putt out on every green. He's been here for eight days, but he's not in Scottish golfing mode yet, not 100 percent anyway. He's still thinking score. Performance is everything. Numbers count. Totals count.

"The game has evolved," Howard says as we walk on. "There are lots of ways to play." He's kidding around and testing us. Fine. Later I read from the letters that Howard sent me when he first visited Scotland in the 1970s and chuckle. "WE ARE CONSTANTLY FIGHTING THAT BLANK STATE OF MIND BY THINKING SWING AND SCORE," he wrote from his room in Troon, capitalizing for emphasis, as much for him, I thought, as for me. "WE ARE FIGHTING OURSELVES." No kidding.

The talk turns to the changing of the season. Greenberg reminds us that Bobby Mackay and his greens staff will raise the mowers on Monday, when he'll close the course. That's three days before autumn starts. There's not as much growth in the grass as temperatures cool, days shorten, and nights lengthen. "Yes," Hamish says. "Winter is here."

Howard and I lose our match 3&2 to Don and Hamish, and I lose 3&1 to Don. Drinks in the clubhouse, toasts to a season ending – but not quite ended.

The next day Howard and I tee it up with John Duncan, the club secretary. John, a man in his mid-fifties, has the organizational abilities necessary to help conduct the affairs of a club that is on the map for keen golfers everywhere. I don't think I've ever asked him for something that he hasn't been able to find within five minutes. Earlier this summer I asked if the club still had its volumes of *Golf Illustrated* magazine from the early twentieth century. There they were, in a cabinet in a back office. John's an army man. He worked in the Royal Army's Pay Corps, where he achieved the rank of lieutenant-colonel prior to taking on his job at Royal Dornoch. He speaks crisply and walks briskly.

We've hit a golden day. It's seventy degrees, sunny, blue skies, the last Saturday of summer, and marked by the pipe band's final appearance of the season tonight in the square. There's been a concert every Saturday night all summer, but no more after tonight. I'm told everybody in Dornoch shows up in the square, accompanied by visitors from Brora, Golspie, Tain, and other villages. Howard and I had tickets to see Bob Dylan in Aberdeen tonight, and we were hoping he would sing "Highlands," a song he wrote that expresses his warm feelings for the area. But we decided to stay in the village for some golf and to hear tonight's concert.

It couldn't be possible to have a more pleasant last round together at Dornoch. Howard and I play well, telling each other from time to time what shots we're about to play. Maybe Howard is finally letting go. He's seeing shots and then playing them, although he's still wedded to yardages. He needs to know exactly how far it is from his ball to that bunker, or the front of the green. He should spend a whole season in Dornoch. Then he'd learn to trust his eye for distances.

Behind us the Caddies Cup is on. This annual tournament used to be for the caddies, but it's morphed over the years into the primary competition for juniors. The youngest kids are playing a nine-hole competition on the Struie as part of the Caddies Cup. I listen to these kids in the clubhouse after Howard and I have finished our rounds. They're done, too. Already the kids have the golf lingo down, and most of them have learned that golf is a tough game to master.

"What did you hit?" one kid asks another.

"Forty-nine."

"You're lucky. Do you usually hit forty-nine?"

"I hit forty-seven yesterday."

"I had sixty-one. I usually hit in the fifties." (The perils of the card and pencil, I think.)

"I missed a tiny putt like this." (Holds hands a foot and a half apart.)

"I missed one like this. (Holds hands a foot apart.)

"I had a seventeen on the fourth."

"And how did you manage that?"

"I was in the bunker a lot."

Golf talk. It begins at a young age. It can last a lifetime.

In the clubhouse I say goodbye to a few friends in case I don't see them the next few days. The club will close the course from Monday through Thursday for its annual repairs; courses, like people, need a rest from the game. "Haste ye back," somebody tells me. Outside, I run into John Macleod, who is standing alone on the grass near the beginning of the first fairway. John looks at the kids who are checking their prizes from the Caddies Cup, then gazes out across the links. I wonder what he's thinking in this year when the club history that he wrote has been published. (Months after my return from Dornoch, I learn that John has died after a heart attack. He helped me in Dornoch in many ways. John was a good man.)

I jog up the dozen steps from the side of the clubhouse to see Howard, who has been resting in the Royal Golf Hotel. I feel choked up after saying a few goodbyes, and also after watching these young-sters, who are only beginning their love affairs with golf. "May you always be courageous, stand upright, and be strong," Bob Dylan wrote in one of his songs. "May you stay forever young." These words are in my mind now. I know that I can't stay forever young, but perhaps I can retain a young man's exuberance for golf. I was twenty-four when I first came to Scotland. I'm middle-aged now. Dornoch has become a touchstone for me without my knowing it. I haven't been here for twenty-three years, but it's been with me all that time, in everything I've written, everything I've felt about golf.

• • • • • •

Shafts of early-morning light are streaming through tall ferns and pines as I begin my ascent to Ben Bhraggie. It's my last day in Dornoch. I've waited all summer to hike up to the top, where I'll see the Mannie up close. It's a pure morning, sunny and warm. The moon is still visible to the west, with the sun low over the sea. It's still, not a sound except for birdsong in the woods. I reach a gate, push it open, and emerge out of the woodland and into open moorland, high above the sea. Some purple heather remains, but not much, as autumn settles over Sutherland. There are empty lands all around. The Duke of Sutherland had his monument built where it could be seen most clearly, high on a mountain, in the lands that he cleared. But I'm not there yet. I still can't see the monument.

It's breezier up here, and the temperature has dropped. I continue walking up the path, with boulders on either side. Suddenly there it is, the monument, the duke's head, the whole thing rising like a spear out of the ground. A young woman jogs by me the other way with her cocker spaniel. The dog stops beside me. "He's not used to seeing anybody on his walk," the woman says.

From here I can see the golf course in Golspie and all the way down to Dornoch Point. The overwhelming impression is of space. I'm within fifty yards of the monument, and can see Brora, Golspie, Dornoch, and the bridge across the firth. It's only the Mannie and me, alone on a morning when nothing is stirring. Nothing now, but so much many years ago.

I read the monument's words, which seem cold and profoundly mendacious. "George Granville, First Duke of Sutherland, b. 1758, d. 1833, of

Loved, Revered and Cherished Memory. Erected by his Tenantry and Friends." The Mannie faces east in the direction of the villages by the sea, to where he sent people. Many eventually went west, clear out of the country.

Standing here, I feel it wouldn't take much to push the monument so that it would fall into the sea. Nothing is growing around the monument. There are only pebbles and stones. Mushrooms, ling, and some heather grow twenty-five feet away. But nothing grows next to the Mannie. I'm struck by the loneliness up here, the desolation I feel. I don't linger. I want to get out of here. A beautiful day? Elsewhere. Down there, where I'm going. Back to Dornoch.

I gallop down the path through the open moorland and the tree cover, past a fast-running brook. There's nothing behind me where once families lived. The land was difficult to work, but it was home for many people. Now I head home myself, to Dornoch.

Credits

Royal Dornoch Golf Course
Dornoch, Sutherland

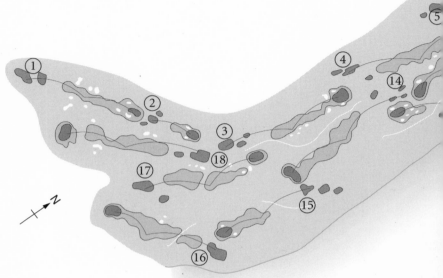

Dornoch and Surrounding Area

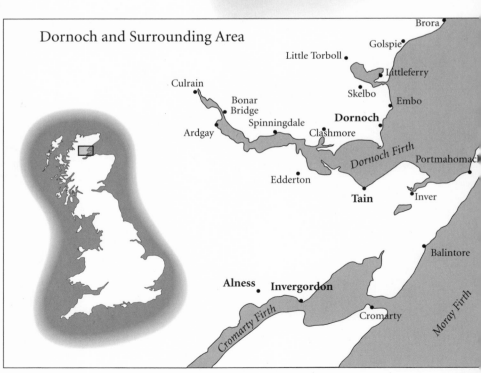